# A Special Message from the Globe Pequot Press

The Globe Pequot Press is proud to present the newest addition to our national parks series, *The Complete Guide to National Park Lodges*. This is the only book on the market dedicated solely to the wonderful array of lodging available inside the parks themselves, and it is written by our intrepid park experts, David and Kay Scott, who have been our park authors for more than twenty years.

But this book is special to us for another reason. Globe Pequot has been publishing books on the national parks and doing business with members of the Association of Partners for Public Lands, of whom we are a sponsor, for many years. We have helped thousands and thousands of people discover our nation's most sacred treasures. And while we are very proud of our part in this, we are also well aware that with park attendance at an all-time high, the parks themselves have suffered from excessive wear and tear. Even so, the National Parks Service receives less and less money each year for park preservation. We felt that if we were going to contribute to the damage of the parks by directing visitors to them, we also wanted to help offset that damage by directing funding to the parks.

The Globe Pequot Press will donate $1 from the sale of each copy of this book directly to the National Parks Foundation, the fundraising arm of the National Parks Service. This money will help repair trails; clean up streams, lakes, and rivers; preserve animal populations; conduct research; and protect historical and cultural sites.

If you would like to donate to the National Parks Foundation, please send a check or money order to:

Director of Development
The National Parks Foundation
1101 17th St., NW
Washington, D.C. 20036
(202) 785-4500

The Globe Pequot Press is committed to helping preserve our national parks and insuring that they will remain wonderful places to visit for generations to come.

The Staff of the Globe Pequot Press

Other Globe Pequot Press books by
David L. Scott and Kay Woelfel Scott

*Guide to the National Park Areas: Eastern States*

*Guide to the National Park Areas: Western States*

Other Globe Pequot Press books by David L. Scott

*The Guide to Buying Insurance*

*The Guide to Investing in Bonds*

*The Guide to Investing in Common Stocks*

*The Guide to Investing for Current Income*

*The Guide to Investing in Mutual Funds*

*The Guide to Managing Credit*

*The Guide to Personal Budgeting*

*The Guide to Saving Money*

*The Guide to Tax-Saving Investing*

# The Complete Guide to
# NATIONAL PARK
# LODGES

*by*

DAVID L. SCOTT

KAY WOELFEL SCOTT

A VOYAGER BOOK

The
Globe
Pequot
Press

OLD SAYBROOK, CONNECTICUT

*Cover and text design by Nancy Freeborn*
*Text illustrations by Carole Drong*

**Library of Congress Cataloging-in-Publication Data**

Scott, David Logan, 1942–
      The complete guide to national park lodges / by David L. Scott, Kay Woelfel Scott.
         p.  cm.
      ISBN 0-7627-0119-6
      1. Hotels—United States—Guidebooks.  2. National parks and reserves—United
States—Guidebooks.  I. Scott, Kay Woelfel.  II. Title.
TX907.2.S36  1997
647.9473'01—dc21                                 97-18476
                                                              CIP

Manufactured in the United States of America
First Edition/First Printing

# CONTENTS

Washington

1

2

Oregon

3

4

5

California

6

7

8

16

Nevada

Utah

13

12

14

17

18

Arizona

New Mexico

Colorado

15

Montana

North Dakota

South Dakota

19

Nebraska

Kansas

Okl

Idaho

9

Wyoming

10

11

Texas

20

Kauai

Nilhau

Oahu

Molokai

Maui

Hawaii

Hawaii

28

Alaska

29

30

Minnesota

21

22 Lake Superior

Wisconsin

Lake Michigan

Michigan

Lake Huron

Lake Erie

Lake Ontario

New York

Vermont

Maine

New Hampshire

Massachusetts

Rhode Island

Connecticut

New Jersey

Delaware

Maryland

Pennsylvania

Iowa

Illinois

Indiana

Ohio

West Virginia

25

Virginia

Missouri

23

Kentucky

24

26

North Carolina

Tennessee

Arkansas

South Carolina

Mississippi

Alabama

Georgia

Louisiana

Florida

27

Puerto Rico

Virgin Islands

31

# ALPHABETICAL LIST OF LODGES

# INTRODUCTION

We have spent a good part of our lives in America's national park areas. Most of our visits have occurred during the twenty-five summers we crisscrossed the United States in a series of four Volkswagen campers. We have driven several hundred thousand miles and visited nearly every one of the more than 365 areas managed by the National Park Service. During the trips we have spent nights in many of the lodges. Even on trips spent mostly in national park campgrounds, we often explored the wonderful buildings described in this book.

Most national park lodges are in the well-known and heavily visited parks, such as Grand Canyon, Death Valley, Everglades, Yosemite, Yellowstone, Olympic, and Glacier. However, some lesser-known park areas, including Oregon Caves National Monument, Isle Royale National Park, Big Bend National Park, and Lassen Volcanic National Park, each offer comfortable and interesting lodge facilities. Some of the biggest and busiest parks do not have lodges. For example, Great Smoky Mountains National Park, Rocky Mountain National Park, and Acadia National Park do not offer conventional lodging inside the park boundaries, although accommodations are available directly outside each of these parks.

Not all areas managed by the National Park Service are classified as national parks. In fact, only about 15 percent of the areas officially carry the title "national park." The Park Service also manages many national monuments, national lakeshores, national historic sites, national recreation areas, national memorials, and several other types of facilities. Each of these areas has something unique to offer or it wouldn't be included in the system. Some of them even have lodging. We mentioned Oregon Caves National Monument, in which a classic old lodge awaits you. Lodging is also available at Canyon de Chelly National Monument, Blue Ridge Parkway, Ozark National Scenic Riverways, and Glacier Bay National Monument.

Staying in a park lodge during your trip to a national park area will almost surely enhance your park experience. It certainly did ours. Spend some time talking to the employees and learning about the history of the building where you are staying. Most of all, travel and enjoy.

## Considerations in Planning a Stay at a National Park Lodge

National park lodges provide a different kind of vacation experience. Most of the lodges are in close proximity to the things you want to see, the places you want to visit, and the facilities you will want to use when you visit a park. At Crater Lake Lodge, you can sleep in a room with windows that overlook the crater rim. In Yellowstone's Old Faithful Inn, you can walk out the entrance and view an eruption of Old Faithful. At the Grand Canyon's El Tovar, you can walk a few steps outside the hotel and look down into the canyon. Many park lodges have large rustic lobby areas where you can relax with other guests in front of a blazing fireplace. The lodges are often near National Park Service visitor centers or campgrounds where guided walks originate and natural history programs are presented. Evening programs or other entertainment can be enjoyed in many of the lodges.

Most lodge facilities in national park areas are owned by the government but managed by private concerns subject to oversight by the park in which they are located. Managements of these lodges operate as concessionaires and are required to obtain the approval of the National Park Service for room rates, improvements, and the prices charged for everything from food to gasoline. Some lodges remain under private ownership on private property within a park. In general, lodges under private ownership were in operation prior to the establishment of a park or prior to an expansion of the park boundaries. Lodges on private property are subject to fewer restrictions regarding what they can offer and the prices they can charge.

Some basic information regarding reservations, facilities, and policies can be helpful if you have never stayed in a national park facility or have stayed in only one or two lodges. Most national park lodges experience large public demand for a limited number of rooms, especially during peak season, when you are most likely to want a room. Thus, you should make a reservation as early as possible, especially if your planned vacation coincides with the park's busiest period. Try to book rooms at a popular lodge at least six months before your expected arrival. Several lodges in very busy locations such as Yosemite Valley should, if possible, be booked nearly a year in advance. Choosing to vacation in off-peak periods, normally spring and fall, will make it much more likely that you are able to obtain a reservation on the dates you desire. Other important factors regarding national park lodges are discussed below.

**FACILITIES.** National park lodges range from luxurious and expensive facilities, such as Yosemite National Park's Ahwahnee and Death Valley National Park's Furnace Creek Inn, to very rustic cabins without bathrooms, such as those at Grant Grove in Kings Canyon National Park. Some facilities call themselves lodges but are not what most of us picture when we think of a lodge. For example, Old Faithful Lodge Cabins (not the more famous Old Faithful Inn, which sits nearby) offers only cabins as overnight accommodations. Likewise, Signal Mountain Lodge in Grand Teton National Park does not have a main lodge building with overnight accommodations; rather, it has several types of cabins that rent at a fairly wide range of prices. The variation in facilities between and within parks makes it important that you understand exactly what types of accommodations are being discussed when you are making a reservation.

Most national park lodging facilities don't have amenities such as spas, swimming pools, game rooms, and some of the other niceties you may expect to find at commercial facilities outside the parks. In fact, most park lodges don't have telephones or televisions in the rooms, although public telephones are nearly always available somewhere in the facility. Several older lodges, including Old Faithful Inn and Lake Crescent Lodge offer some rooms without a private bathroom. Community bathrooms and shower rooms are available for occupants of these rooms. Some cabins do not have private bathrooms.

**ROOMS.** Rooms in a lodge often vary considerably with regard to size, bedding, view, and rate. Likewise, a single lodging facility may offer rooms in the main lodge building, rooms in motel-type buildings, and a variety of cabin rooms. This is the case with Lake Crescent Lodge in Olympic National Park and with Big Meadows in Shenandoah National Park, for example. Potential differences in rooms mean that it is worthwhile to learn what options are available at a particular location where you plan to stay. If you wait to make a reservation near your planned arrival, you are likely to find a limited variety of accommodations. For example, you may find that all the rooms with private bathrooms are already taken. On the other hand, call early and you are likely to have a wide choice of rooms that are offered at a wide range of rates. Ask about a view room, for example. Sometimes rooms with an excellent view are more expensive and sometimes they are not. Some buildings do not have elevators, so the floor you are assigned may be important. Higher floors tend to offer better views but require more climbing. Rooms near the lobby may be noisy. Some lodges allow you to reserve a particular room, but most lodges guarantee only a particular type of room. Even when a particular room won't be guaranteed, a lodge will often make note of your preferences and attempt to satisfy the request when room assignments are made.

**RESERVATIONS.** Reservations can generally be made by either telephone or mail, and sometimes by fax. The disadvantage of using the mail is the uncertainty that a room will be available on the dates you request. If rooms are unavailable on the specified dates, you must wait for a reply and then start over again, but at a much later date, when even fewer rooms are available. This can sometimes be avoided by listing alternative dates that you find acceptable.

Choosing to make a reservation by telephone allows you to immediately determine room availability and, if necessary, choose alternative dates. Using the telephone will also allow you to discuss with the reservation agent the types of facilities that are available. The best bet is to write early for literature so that you have a basic understanding of the facilities and rates prior to calling. This will allow you to know which type of room and building to ask for and what to expect regarding rates. Be aware that it is often difficult to get through to a reservation agent via telephone, especially if you call late in the spring, when everyone else in the country seems to be trying the same number. Try calling at odd hours, such as weekend mornings.

Most lodges require a deposit of at least one night's lodging soon after making a reservation. Some lodges allow you to charge the deposit to a credit card, while other lodges will require that you send a check or money order. A few lodges permit you to guarantee the entire reservation with a credit card and to pay for the entire stay when you check out. When sending a deposit check or giving a credit card number, always ask for a deposit receipt to take on your vacation. In a couple of cases, our reservations have gotten lost. In the event your plans change, refund of a deposit requires advance notice, usually forty-eight hours, but this varies by lodge.

**RATES.** In general, accommodations in the national parks aren't cheap. You can expect to pay $80 and up for most double rooms, although some rustic cabins are much cheaper, while a room at one of the nicer facilities can run $125 and up. In addition, discounts for seniors, AAA members, and so on, that you expect at most commercial facilities are generally unavailable at national park lodges. Most lodges quote rates for two adults, which means that you must pay a double rate even if you travel alone. Additional adults pay extra, although children are generally free when staying with adults. Some lodges allow children twelve years and under to stay free, while other facilities limit free stays to children three and under. Lodges sometimes offer reduced rates during their off-seasons or have special packages that include meals or a lower rate for multiday stays. Ask about specials when you book a reservation, but don't get your hopes too high.

**PAYMENT, CHECK-IN, AND CHECKOUT.** Most lodges accept major credit cards, but you should determine acceptable methods of payment when a reservation is made. For example, you may end up at a lodge that will not accept any credit cards (unusual), will accept only a few major cards, or will not accept a personal check. A lodge that requires a personal check for a deposit may accept a credit card to satisfy the balance of your bill.

Most lodges specify an 11:00 A.M. checkout and a 4:00 P.M. check-in, but the times can be different depending on which lodge you will be using. For example, some lodges specify a 2:00 or 3:00 P.M. check-in, while some don't require a checkout until noon. The checkout time can generally be postponed by at least an hour with a request to the front desk the prior night or the morning of your planned departure. You may be able to check in prior to the specified time, but don't count on it. Arrive early in the morning and you are likely to roam around without a room until late afternoon. Lodges that assign a particular room to each guest are less flexible in getting guests into rooms before the scheduled check-in time.

**OBTAINING A ROOM WITHOUT A RESERVATION.** Some national park lodges have space available, especially during off-peak periods. Even busy lodges experience cancellations or early departures that free up rooms. Thus, you may be able to obtain a room without an advance reservation. For example, you may locate a room in a busy park like Yellowstone during peak summer months just by dropping in at one of the nine lodges and asking about a vacancy. If rooms are available, they are unlikely to be the exact configuration, location, or price category you would choose. For example, you may have to accept a room without a private bathroom or a room that is more expensive than you would ordinarily reserve. In a large park like Yellowstone or Glacier, the only available rooms may be in a different facility that is many miles from the lodge where you are making the request. Taking a chance on a vacancy is a risky strategy. Being unsuccessful may result in a long drive to a distant location where you are likely to overpay for an inferior room. Hedge your bets by calling ahead.

**REDUCING EXPENSES.** Most national park lodges are pricey. If you are on a limited budget but want to experience a stay at one or more of the lodges, it is possible to take steps to reduce your expenditures. Accepting a room without a private bathroom (if available) can often cost $20 per night less than comparable rooms with a private bath. These rooms also tend to be easier to reserve, because many individuals demand a private bath.

Another money-saving strategy is to spend every second or third night camping. Most parks with lodges also have campgrounds that charge $10 to $14 per night. Arrange the campground stays into your schedule when reservations are being made. For example, spend two nights in a lodge and then move to a campground for the third night. Keep in mind that some national park campgrounds operate under a reservation system.

Another strategy is to spend the night prior to arrival at an inexpensive commercial facility that is within an hour or two of the park. Staying in close proximity permits you to enjoy most of a full day in the park before checking in at the lodge. Likewise, obtain a reservation at a motel a couple of hours outside the park on your departure date so that you can spend most of an extra day finishing your park sightseeing.

Take along a cooler with some food and drink, including snacks such as pretzels, candy, soft drinks, and fruit. Most lodges have ice machines that can be used to resupply a cooler. Buy groceries outside the park, where they are likely to be cheaper. Eat a breakfast of fruit and cereal in your room, and have a picnic lunch or supper. If you take the trouble to visit a national park, you may as well enjoy nature. If you choose to eat in a lodge restaurant, keep in mind that lunch can be quite a bit less expensive than dinner. In parks that offer several restaurant facilities, examine the menus before choosing a place to eat, since prices can vary a great deal from one restaurant to another. In general, cafeterias are considerably less expensive places to eat than dining rooms.

Play it safe by establishing a budget for your trip before you leave. Estimate how much you are going to spend for lodging, food, transportation, and incidentals, and then make a real effort to stay within your budget. You might find that some things are more expensive than planned. You may be able to substitute a couple of picnic lunches for restaurant meals and save enough for a guided park tour. Using a budget may keep you from buying all the T-shirts during the first visit to a gift shop.

Take advantage of the many free things that are offered at virtually all the park areas. National Park Service personnel offer guided walks and programs, generally at no charge. These are fun and informative. Parks with campgrounds typically have evening history and nature programs that are offered without charge. Park visitor centers have exhibits and audio-visual programs to help you understand the park. Some of the lodges even offer free lodge tours. It is best to stop at the park visitor center and obtain a list of daily activities.

## Indicators for the Cost of Room and Food

Keep in mind that these categories represent our best judgment of the overall expense of staying and eating at a particular lodge. Prices change, and you may pay more or less than the indicated amounts, especially for food. In the food category, breakfast and lunch are generally less expensive than dinner, for which the rating applies.

**ROOM RATES** (based on a double room)

| | |
|---|---|
| $ | Inexpensive—up to $50 per night |
| $$ | Moderate—$50 to $75 per night |
| $$$ | Average—$75 to $100 per night |
| $$$$ | Expensive—$100 to $125 per night |
| $$$$$ | Quite expensive—more than $125 per night |

**FOOD** (based on the cost of one dinner)

| | |
|---|---|
| $ | Inexpensive—up to $7.50 |
| $$ | Moderate—$7.50 to $10.00 |
| $$$ | Average—$10.00 to $15.00 |
| $$$$ | Expensive—$15.00 to $20.00 |
| $$$$$ | Quite expensive—more than $20.00 |

# ALASKA

## DENALI NATIONAL PARK AND PRESERVE

P.O. Box 9
Denali National Park, AK 99755
(907) 683–2294

Denali National Park and Preserve comprises six million acres of mountains, glaciers, and rolling lowlands with wide rivers. The central focus of the park is 20,320-foot Mt. McKinley, the highest mountain on the North American continent. Most of the park is covered with alpine tundra, rock, and ice. The interior of Denali (native Athabascan, meaning "the High One") is accessed via an 87-mile road that connects the park entrance with Wonder Lake. The park lies beside State Highway 3, which connects Alaska's two main cities of Anchorage (238 miles) and Fairbanks (122 miles). Service to Denali National Park is provided by several transportation companies, including the Alaska Railroad.

## Lodging in Denali National Park and Preserve

The Denali National Park Hotel, with 103 rooms, is the main lodging facility inside Denali National Park. The hotel is a little more than a mile inside the park entrance, across from the railroad depot. Other lodging facilities, including McKinley Chalet Resort and McKinley Village Lodge operated by the same company, are a short distance outside the park entrance. Several other lodging facilities are near the entrance. Lodging inside the park on private land near Wonder Lake is provided by Kantishna Roadhouse (800–942–7429), Denali Backcountry Lodge (907–683–2594 summer; 907–783–1342 other), and Denali National Park Wilderness Centers (907–683–2290).

# DENALI NATIONAL PARK AND PRESERVE

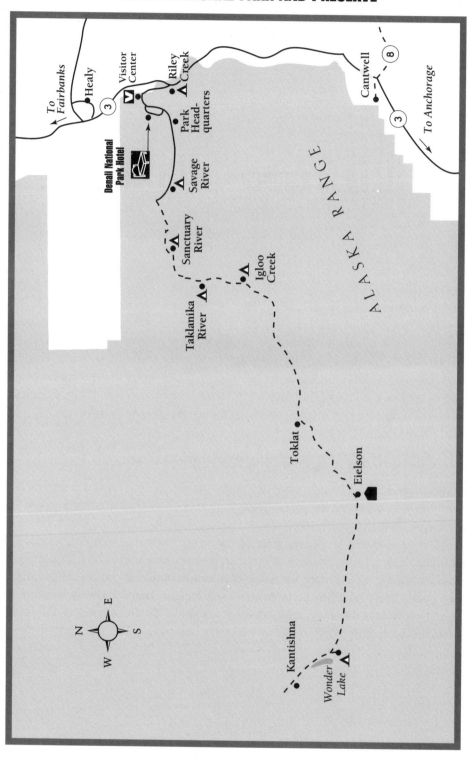

To Fairbanks

Healy

Visitor Center

Riley Creek

Park Head-quarters

Denali National Park Hotel

Savage River

Sanctuary River

Igloo Creek

Taklanika River

ALASKA RANGE

Cantwell

To Anchorage

Toklat

Eielson

Kantishma

Wonder Lake

N E S W

# DENALI NATIONAL PARK HOTEL

241 West Ship Creek Avenue • Anchorage, AK 99501 • (907) 683–2215

*Denali Park Lodge*

Denali National Park Hotel is a one- and two-story wooden hotel constructed in 1973 to replace the original hotel, which burned in 1972. The current structure, which was built as a temporary replacement for its predecessor, has undergone interior upgrading of both the lobby and the rooms. The hotel is constructed with the rooms in two parallel arms connected by a central dining and lobby section. The parquet-floored lobby houses the registration desk, a tour desk, and chairs for relaxing. Just off the lobby are the dining room, a cafe, a gift shop, and a saloon fashioned from two old railcars. A covered walkway outside the lobby leads to a 300-seat auditorium in which National Park Service personnel regularly present visitor programs.

The hotel has 103 nearly identical rooms, most with two double beds. Five slightly smaller rooms have either one double bed or two twin beds. When available on a walk-in basis, the smaller rooms can be rented for somewhat less than regular rooms. All rooms are carpeted and have heat and a private bathroom containing a combination shower-tub. None of the rooms have air conditioning, telephone, or television. Public telephones are in the hotel lobby and on the outside porch. Seventy-five rooms are on the first floor, and the remaining rooms are on the second floor and reached via a stairway from the lobby. All rooms in the hotel are entered from inside corridors. One handicap-accessible room with a double bed is available.

The Denali National Park Hotel is not one of the classic national park lodges. Still, it has the sort of rustic atmosphere that you probably seek in a national park stay, and the hotel is conveniently located for a visit to this large and unique park. The hotel is a short distance inside the park entrance, which places it at the center of park activity. Courtesy transportation is provided to the nearby National Park Service visitor center, where you can view exhibits and obtain information from Park Service rangers. The auditorium connected to the hotel is used for nightly programs, and videos are presented regularly during the day. A dining room serves three meals a day at reasonable prices, and a cafe opens early and closes late to offer a less expensive alternative. Staying near the park entrance allows you to explore shops and eating facilities outside the park. A variety of hiking trails that range from a half-mile to 7 miles are easily accessible from the hotel.

■ **ROOMS:** Singles, doubles, triples, and quads. All rooms have private baths with a combination tub-shower.

■ **RESERVATIONS:** Denali Park Resorts, 241 West Ship Creek Avenue, Anchorage, AK 99501. Phone (800) 276–7234, or (907) 683–2215 for last-minute summer bookings; fax (907) 258–3668. One-night deposit required. Advance notice of seven days required for refund. Five to six months' advance reservation is advised for visits during the peak season of early June to late August.

Denali National Park and Preserve was initially named Mt. McKinley National Park when it was established in 1917. Not until 1980, when the park's size more than tripled, was the name changed to its current designation. Somewhat surprisingly, the park was established to protect the large mammals, including caribou, moose, and grizzly bears, rather than because of the well-known mountain.

■ **RATES:** All rooms ($$$$$). Rates are quoted for one adult. Each additional person is $10. Children eleven years and under are free with an adult. A few rooms, if available, are offered to walk-ins at a reduced rate. Specials are offered during spring and fall.

■ **LOCATION:** A mile and a half inside the park entrance.

■ **SEASON:** Late May through the second week in September. The hotel tends to be full from early June to late August.

■ **FOOD:** A full-service restaurant ($$) serves three meals a day. A cafe offers continuous food service from 5:00 A.M. to 11:00 P.M. Limited groceries are sold at a nearby store.

■ **TRANSPORTATION:** The nearest scheduled airline service is at Anchorage and Fairbanks, where rental vehicles are available. Private firms in both cities offer regular transportation to the park. The Alaska Railroad serves Denali National Park from both cities. The hotel offers courtesy transportation from the Denali train depot to the hotel.

■ **FACILITIES:** Restaurant, cafe, gift shop, saloon.

■ **ACTIVITIES:** Hiking, fishing, wildlife tours, sightseeing airplane flights, dinner theater (at a sister hotel just outside the park), raft trips, evening natural history programs, videos.

# GLACIER BAY NATIONAL PARK

Glacier Bay National Park
Gustavus, AK 99826
(907) 697-2230

Glacier Bay National Park is comprised of 3.3 million acres, including some of the world's most impressive examples of tidewater glaciers, twelve of which calve icebergs into Glacier Bay. Park headquarters is at Bartlett cove, 7 miles north of the mouth of Glacier Bay. The park is located in southeastern Alaska, approximately 65 miles northwest of Juneau. No roads lead to the park, and entrance is obtained via either plane or boat.

##  Lodging in Glacier Bay National Park

Glacier Bay Lodge offers the only overnight accommodations in Glacier Bay National Park. The rustic 56-room lodge is located in the southeastern section of the park near the mouth of Glacier Bay, about 9 miles from the small town of Gustavus. A bed and breakfast is in Gustavus.

## GLACIER BAY LODGE

199 Barlett Cove Road • Gustavus, AK 99826 • (907) 697-2225

Glacier Bay Lodge is a wilderness resort situated among Sitka spruce in a rainforest. The complex includes a two-story wooden chalet-type lodge building that houses a lobby, registration desk, restaurant, theater, gift shop, and cocktail lounge, connected by boardwalk to sixteen nearby one-story wooden buildings that provide guest accommodations. The lodge is located on Bartlett Cove, 9 miles from the town of Gustavus in the southeastern corner of the park. Although a gravel road connects the lodge with the town of Gustavus and its small airport, no roads lead from the mainland into the park. Access is only via boat or airplane.

The lodge provides a total of 56 rooms in sixteen one-story wooden buildings that are close to but separate from the main lodge building. These buildings each contain from two to six rooms that sit side-by-side. The rooms each have electric heat, telephone, and a private bathroom with either a shower or a combination tub/shower. All the rooms are the same size and most have two double beds or two twin beds, although two rooms have a queen bed. The rooms have wood paneling and a vaulted ceiling. The lodge also offers two less-expensive dormitories, each with three bunk beds. The dorms have a community shower and bathroom and appeal primarily to hikers and kayakers.

# GLACIER BAY NATIONAL PARK

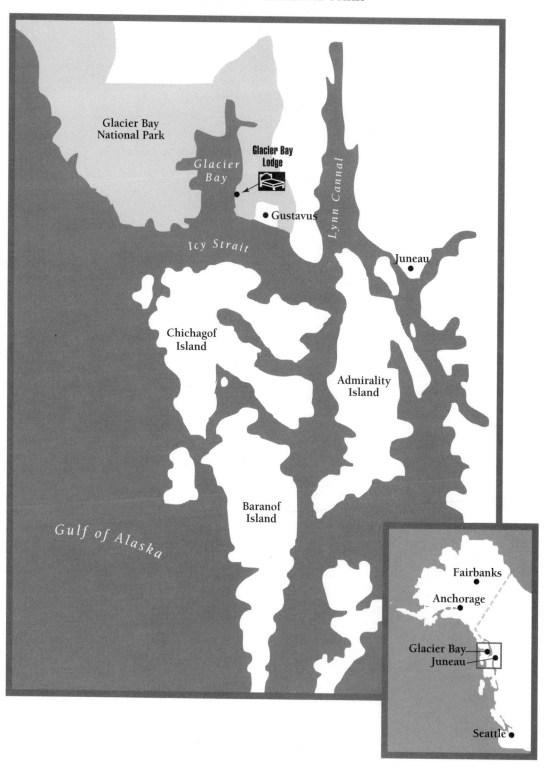

Glacier Bay
National Park

Glacier Bay
Lodge

*Glacier Bay*

*Lynn Canal*

● Gustavus

*Icy Strait*

● Juneau

Chichagof
Island

Admirality
Island

Baranof
Island

*Gulf of Alaska*

Fairbanks ●

Anchorage ●

Glacier Bay
Juneau

Seattle ●

*Glacier Bay Lodge*

Glacier Bay Lodge is certainly a place to get away from it all. It is in a very remote location that offers spectacular scenery, unusual wildlife, and a wild and unique environment. A deck attached to the main lodge allows guests to sit and watch the sun set over Bartlett Cove. A variety of activities are available including guided nature walks, kayaking, hiking, and whale watching. Whale watching excursions, overnight wilderness cruises, and sportfishing charters depart from a nearby dock. Films about Glacier Bay are presented by National Park Service rangers each evening in the lodge theater.

- **ROOMS:** Singles, doubles, triples, and quads. All rooms in the lodge have private baths. Dormitories have community shower and restroom facilities.

- **RESERVATIONS:** Glacier Bay Lodge, Inc., 520 Pike Street, Suite 1400, Seattle, WA 98101. Phone (800) 451-5952; fax (206) 623-7809. Cancellation is required 91 days prior to first day of arrival.

- **RATES:** Lodge rooms ($$$$$); dormitory rooms ($). Rates for lodge rooms are quoted per person, double occupancy. The rate for dormitory rooms is quoted per person. Children under 2 stay free with adults.

- **LOCATION:** Approximately 9 miles northwest of Gustavus, on the shore of Bartlett Cove.

- **SEASON:** Early May through mid- to late-September.

- **FOOD:** A dining room ($$$$) specializing in fresh Alaskan seafood serves three meals daily. Lighter meals including sandwiches, nachos, and halibut tacos are served in the cocktail lounge. A small grocery is in the town of Gustavus.

- **TRANSPORTATION:** Daily passenger ferry service operates between Juneau and the community of Gustavus. A small airport is nearby Gustavus. A lodge shuttle that operates between the lodge and Gustavus is available for a fee.

- **FACILITIES:** Restaurant, cocktail lounge, theater, gift shop. A ranger station and boat dock are nearby.

- **ACTIVITIES:** Hiking, fishing, guided walks, fishing charters, wildlife and whale watching cruises, and day cruises to the glaciers.

The glaciers here remain from the Little Ice Age that began about 4,000 years ago. Glaciers form when mountain snowfall exceeds snow melt. Accumulating weight of the snow presses lower layers into solid ice that eventually flows slowly downslope. Glacier Bay National Park includes sixteen glaciers that terminate at the sea's edge. The most spectacular are the twelve glaciers that actively calve icebergs into the bay.

# ARIZONA

## CANYON DE CHELLY NATIONAL MONUMENT

P.O. Box 588
Chinle, AZ 86503
(520) 674–5436

anyon de Chelly (pronounced "d' Shay") National Monument comprises nearly 84,000 acres that include ruins of Indian villages built between A.D. 350 and 1300 in steep-walled canyons. Twenty-two-mile Rim Drive, along the south rim of Canyon de Chelly, provides access to scenic overlooks and the trailhead to White House Ruins. All other trails require a park ranger or authorized guide. The monument is in northeastern Arizona, approximately 85 miles northwest of Gallup, New Mexico, near the town of Chinle, Arizona.

###  Lodging in Canyon de Chelly National Monument

Thunderbird Lodge, near the monument entrance, is the only lodging facility in Canyon de Chelly National Monument. The lodge includes a cafeteria and gift shop. Guided tours leave from the lodge. Motels are in the town of Chinle and a short distance outside the monument entrance.

# CANYON DE CHELLY NATIONAL MONUMENT

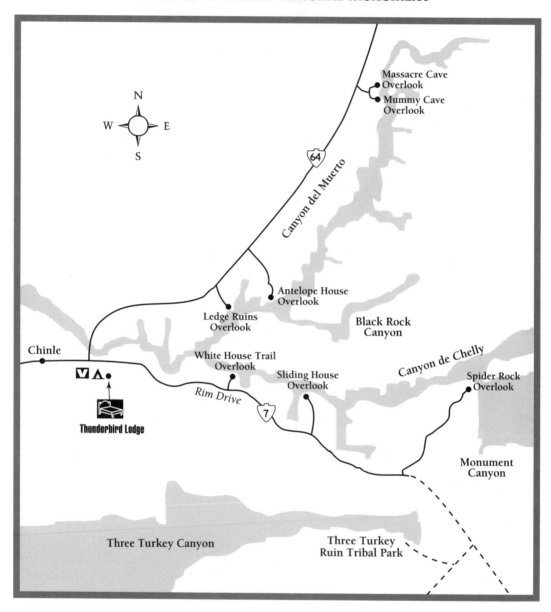

# THUNDERBIRD LODGE

P.O. Box 548 • Chinle, AZ 86503 • (520) 674–5841

*De Chelly Units at Thunderbird Lodge*

Thunderbird Lodge is an attractive and well-maintained motor lodge, offering seventy-two rooms just inside the entrance to Canyon de Chelly National Monument. The lodge, situated in a grove of cottonwood trees, comprises a complex of several adobe and stone buildings, including three adobe units that contain most of the lodging rooms. The adobe registration building is separate but adjacent to the buildings containing the rooms. Separate stone buildings house a small number of rooms, a gift shop, and a cafeteria. Thunderbird Lodge is on Navajo Route 7, 3 miles east of the intersection with Highway 191 in the town of Chinle.

The lodge offers several types of rooms, although the majority are very similar. All rooms have televisions and telephones, and several ice machines are in the lodge complex. The interiors are newly redone in an attractive Southwest style. Forty-one "Adobe" motel-type rooms have two queen beds and a full bath. These rooms are housed in a single long building built into the back of a hill. Adequate parking in front of the building obstructs the view these rooms offer from the front window. Twenty-two "De Chelly" rooms each contain two double beds and a full bath and are in two buildings constructed around a grassy courtyard with cottonwood trees. Rooms in these buildings back up to one another, with half facing the courtyard and half facing the parking lot. Four of the De Chelly rooms are fully handicap accessible. One suite in a separate stone building in the center of the complex has one king bed, a queen sofa sleeper, and a refrigerator. Eight smaller rooms in stone buildings each have two double beds and are rented only on-site. We recommend you choose from De Chelly rooms 14 through 18 or 24 through 29, which face the courtyard. These offer quiet and a nice grassy front yard.

Thunderbird Lodge is a handy accommodation for visitors who wish to tour Canyon de Chelly National Monument. The lodge is a half-mile walk from the National Park Service visitor center, which contains a variety of exhibits including a Navajo home called a hogan. Interpretive programs at the visitor center include talks by rangers and guided walks. Evening campfire programs are offered at the monument's campground, a short walk from the lodge. Half- and full-day guided tours into the canyon in four- and six-wheel drive vehicles begin at the lodge, where tickets may be purchased at the gift shop. Half-day tours only are offered in winter months. All-day and overnight horseback trail rides are also available. The lodge cafeteria offers food service from early morning to evening, and fast-food restaurants are a short distance away in the town of Chinle. The lodge gift shop contains a Navajo rug room with a large selection of handwoven Navajo rugs.

- **ROOMS:** Doubles, triples, and quads. All rooms offer a full private bath.

- **RESERVATIONS:** Thunderbird Lodge, P.O. Box 548, Chinle, AZ 86503. Phone (800) 679-2473; fax (520) 674-5844. Reservations may be made up to a year in advance. Cancellation must be made twenty-four hours in advance for a full refund.

- **RATES:** Summer rates from April 1 to November 15 ($$$); winter rates from November 16 to March 31 ($$). Special weekend packages are offered during winter months. A combination of state sales tax and Navajo tribal tax will add nearly 15 percent to your lodging expense.

- **LOCATION:** The lodge is a short distance inside the park entrance.

- **SEASON:** The lodge is open year-round. Heaviest season is from April through October, when reservations are advised.

- **FOOD:** A lodge cafeteria ($) offers basic food at reasonable prices from 6:30 A.M. to 9:00 P.M. daily. Several types of steaks are added to the dinner menu. Alternative eating facilities are in two nearby motels and in the town of Chinle.

- **TRANSPORTATION:** No public transportation serves Canyon de Chelly National Monument or the town of Chinle.

- **FACILITIES:** Cafeteria, gift shop, stable, National Park Service visitor center. Three miles west the town of Chinle has fast-food outlets, service stations, grocery stores, Laundromats, and a bank.

- **ACTIVITIES:** Hiking, guided tours into the canyon, National Park Service interpretive programs, horseback riding.

Thunderbird Lodge was originally constructed in 1902 as a trading post on the Navajo Reservation. The post served as a store, bank, post office, community meeting place, and courtroom. The owner began offering rooms and food service to accommodate an increasing number of tourists, who came to view the cliff dwellings and spectacular scenery. The present-day cafeteria is in the original trading post, while the building housing the gift shop originally served as home for the trading post's owner.

# GLEN CANYON NATIONAL RECREATION AREA

P.O. Box 1507

Page, AZ 86040

(520) 608–6200

Glen Canyon National Recreation Area comprises 1.25 million acres of high desert surrounding and including Lake Powell and its nearly 2,000 miles of shoreline. Lake Powell is formed by the Glen Canyon Dam near Page, Arizona, which backs up the Colorado River for nearly 200 miles. Most of the activities here, including boating, fishing, and waterskiing, are water-related. Houseboat rental is available at several locations on Lake Powell. Although nearly all of the recreation area is in southern Utah, the most accessible part is along U.S. Highway 89 near Page, Arizona, where the Glen Canyon Dam is located.

##  Lodging in Glen Canyon National Recreation Area

Four locations in Glen Canyon Recreation Area offer overnight lodging facilities. The largest and nicest facility by far is at Wahweap, 6 miles north of Page, Arizona, on Highway 89. Wahweap also has the largest marina on the lake. Smaller and less elaborate facilities are at Bullfrog and Halls Crossing, in the central section of Lake Powell, and Hite, in the northern section. Houseboat rentals are available at all four locations.

## WAHWEAP LODGE

Box 1597 • Page, AZ 86040 • (520) 645–2433

Wahweap Lodge offers 350 rooms as part of a marina resort complex on Lake Powell, just north of Page, Arizona. Wahweap (an Indian term for "bitter water") also offers twenty-five less expensive rooms at Lake Powell Motel, which sits on a bluff overlooking Lake Powell, 2.5 miles west of the lodge. The lodge comprises a separate registration building and eight identical two-story lodging buildings laid out in a V formation along a peninsula on Lake Powell. The landscaped stucco buildings are finished and decorated in a Southwest design. The complex also contains two swimming pools, a fitness center, a gas station, a store, and several restaurants. An RV park and campground are a short distance away. A very large marina complex sits beside the lodge, which is situated directly on Lake Powell.

All 350 spacious rooms (other than the two suites) in Wahweap Lodge are identical except for bedding and vistas. The large majority have two queen beds, while forty-three rooms have one king bed. Rooms with a king bed rent for slightly more. All of the rooms have heat, air conditioning, a television, a telephone, a full bath, a desk, a table, and three chairs. Each room has a private balcony or patio with chairs. Each building is constructed with rooms on both sides and access through an interior corridor that runs the length of the building. Four rooms are fully handicap accessible. Half the rooms face Lake Powell, and the other half face the large cen-

# GLEN CANYON NATIONAL RECREATION AREA

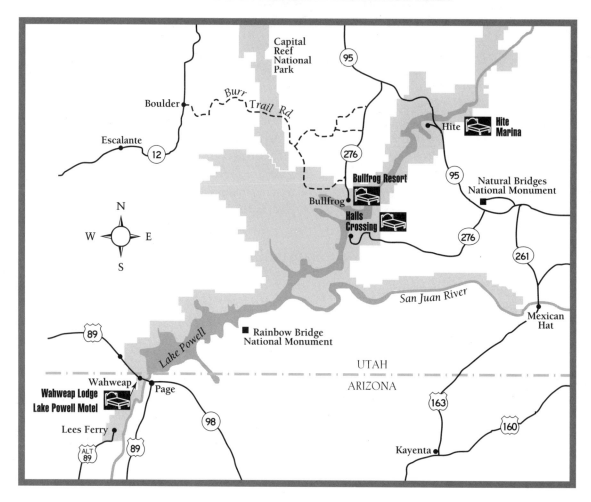

*Wahweap Lodge*

tral parking area. Although the lakeside rooms cost about $10 per night extra, you may feel that the lake view is well worth the additional expense. The two suites each have a bedroom with one king bed and a living room with a wet bar. An extra-large balcony wraps around the room. Each room in the suites has a television.

The Lake Powell Motel sits by itself, 2.5 miles west of the lodge complex. The two-story stucco building faces the lake but is some distance from both the lake and any facilities. Twenty-four basic rooms each contain two queen beds, a television, a telephone, a small table, two chairs, and a full bath. A front sliding glass door provides access to each room. One suite on the first floor has a bedroom with two queen beds and a separate living room. It also has a full bathroom, kitchen (with utensils), telephone, television, refrigerator, and microwave. The suite has a private backyard with a grill. No restaurant is at the motel.

Wahweap Lodge offers most of the amenities one expects at a lakeside resort, including conference facilities with meeting and banquet rooms. Two swimming pools, a pool bar, an outdoor spa, and an exercise room are part of the lodge complex. The registration building contains a large gift shop, a tour desk, an attractive full-service restaurant, a lounge, and a special Navajo Room that during summer serves an evening buffet accompanied by Native American entertainment. The Navajo Room is used as a meeting room during the off-season. The lobby area has a stone fireplace and chairs and sofas for relaxing. The main restaurant is a tiered circular dining room with a wall of windows that present a panoramic view of the lake. Various types of boats, from canoes to 59-foot houseboats, can be rented at the marina. A variety of half- and full-day boat tours can be arranged in the lobby of the registration building. Air tours are available at the Page Airport. Special packages that include a boat tour and room at the lodge are available. A gas station and general store are nearby.

- **ROOMS:** Doubles, triples, and quads. All rooms have private baths with a combination tub-shower.

- **RESERVATIONS:** Lake Powell Resorts & Marinas, P.O. Box 56909, Phoenix, AZ 85079. Phone (800) 528-6154 or, from the greater Phoenix area, (602) 278-8888; fax (602) 331-5258.

- **RATES:** Lodge ($$$$$/$$$$) from April 1 through October 31, ($$$$) the remainder of the year; motel ($$$). Rates are quoted for two adults. Children under eighteen years are free.

- **LOCATION:** Wahweap Lodge is on Highway 89, 6 miles north of Page, Arizona. Lake Powell Motel is 2.5 miles west of the lodge.

- **SEASON:** The lodge is open all year. The heaviest season is during the summer months. The motel is open from April 1 to October 31.

- **FOOD:** A full-service restaurant ($$$$) offers three meals a day and overlooks the lake. Room service is available. Each evening during the summer season, a dinner buffet is served along with traditional Native American dance entertainment, in the Navajo Room. Itza Pizza provides indoor/outdoor dining or delivery service to your room during the summer season. From April through October the Canyon King paddlewheeler provides breakfast, lunch, and dinner cruises. Advance reservations are required. No food service is available at Lake Powell Motel.

- **TRANSPORTATION:** Regularly scheduled flights to Page, Arizona, operate from Phoenix. Charter flights are available to other cities within the region. Rental cars are available at the airport. From mid-May through mid-October, Wahweap operates scheduled bus service between the lodge and the airport, as well as other destinations in the town of Page. A courtesy shuttle service to various locations around the Wahweap area is offered year-round to lodge guests.

- **FACILITIES:** A general store with limited groceries, cocktail lounge, gift shop, gas station, two restaurants, pizza parlor, and marina. Two swimming pools, an outdoor spa, and an exercise room are at the lodge. A coin-operated laundry is at the nearby RV park. Postal services and stamps are available at the marina. Fax service is available for a fee.

- **ACTIVITIES:** Swimming (two pools and a beach); various outdoor games, including volleyball, badminton, croquet, shuffleboard, and horseshoes; walking and hiking; boat rentals (all sizes); waterskiing; fishing; float trips, half-day and all-day; many water tours of from one hour to all-day; evening campfire programs at Wahweap campground are presented by the National Park Service.

Additional Lodging Facilities at Glen Canyon National Recreation Area

Although Wahweap Lodge is the major lodging facility at Glen Canyon National Recreation Area, overnight accommodations are offered by the same concessionaire at three other locations. The three facilities are on a much smaller scale than Wahweap and at relatively remote locations in southern Utah. Reservations are made using the same address and phone number listed for Wahweap. All of the locations permit pets.

## BULLFROG RESORT

Box 4055 • Lake Powell, UT 84533 • (801) 684–3000

Bullfrog Resort offers forty-eight lodge rooms at Defiance House Lodge plus eight housekeeping units. The lodge rooms ([$$$/$$$$], April 1 to October 31; [$$$] November 1 to March 31) are in a single stucco building that sits atop a high bluff overlooking Bullfrog Bay. Both the building, constructed in the early 1980s, and the rooms within are identical to those in Wahweap Lodge. Eight freestanding prefabricated housekeeping units ([$$$ to $$$$$] depending on season for up to six persons per unit) each contain three bedrooms, two full baths, a living room, a stove, an oven, dishes, a refrigerator, linens, and a television but no telephone. Pay phones are available. All of the units have heat and air conditioning. The interiors are attractive and nicely furnished. One housekeeping unit has a ramp for handicapped access.

The resort is located at Bullfrog Basin on Utah Highway 276 on the west side of Lake Powell. A toll ferry at Bullfrog crosses the lake and provides for a continuation of the highway. Bullfrog Resort offers a restaurant, liquor store, cocktail lounge, gift shop, and marina. Like the resort, the restaurant is open year-round. It offers cocktails and three meals a day. A fast-food restaurant at the marina is open from Memorial Day through Labor Day. A marina store sells basic food supplies and beverages. A gas station is located at Bullfrog. Ranger programs and a medical clinic operate during summer months. A National Park Service visitor center adjacent to the resort contains exhibits concerning the Colorado Plateau and the evolution of Glen Canyon plant and animal life. A concessionaire offers half- and full-day boat tours during the summer. Boat rental is available.

## HALLS CROSSING

Box 5101 • Lake Powell, UT 84533 • (801) 684–7000

Halls Crossing is located on Utah Highway 276 between Blanding and Hanksville. It offers twenty freestanding housekeeping units identical to those at Bullfrog Resort. One unit has handicap access. Halls Crossing has auto service, a marina, and a store with limited supplies. Boat rentals and tours are offered. A toll ferry provides continuation of Highway 276. Transportation is available from a small airport 10 miles from Halls Crossing. Rates are the same as at Bullfrog Resort.

## HITE MARINA

Box 501 • Lake Powell, UT 84533 • (801) 684–2278

Hite Marina is off Utah State Highway 95 on the north end of Lake Powell between Blanding and Hanksville. This is the smallest of the four lodging complexes at Lake Powell, offering only five housekeeping units that are identical with those at Bullfrog and Halls Crossing. One housekeeping unit is totally handicap accessible. Hite offers a gas station, a ranger station, a supply store, and a marina where boats can be rented. Rates for housekeeping units are the same as at Bullfrog Resort.

*Lake Powell was created by the Glen Canyon Dam, which lies just south of Wahweap. The dam backs up the Colorado River for 200 miles and supplies water and electricity to California, Arizona, and Nevada. Concrete for the dam and power plant was poured around the clock for more than three years. The visitor center, 2 miles north of Page, with exhibits on the the dam and power plant, is open daily from 8:00 A.M. to 5:00 P.M. Hours are extended during summer months. Guided tours of the structure are available year-round.*

# GRAND CANYON NATIONAL PARK

P.O. Box 129
Grand Canyon, AZ 86023
(520) 638–7888

Grand Canyon National Park, with 1,904 square miles of area, is one of the most popular parks operated by the National Park Service, especially the South Rim section. The Grand Canyon itself is so massive and so spectacular that first-time visitors are likely to think they are viewing a painting. The canyon has been created by the cutting effect of the Colorado River, which originates in the Rocky Mountains. The river now flows nearly a mile below the South Rim and even farther below the higher North Rim. Although the developed areas of the North Rim and the South Rim are separated by only about 10 miles, the distance by road is 214 miles. An alternative is the 21-mile Kaibab Trail, which leads from Yaki Point on the South Rim to within 2 miles of Grand Canyon Lodge on the North Rim. A daily shuttle service (fee charged) is offered between the South Rim and the North Rim.

 ## Lodging in Grand Canyon National Park

Grand Canyon National Park has seven lodges, six at the popular South Rim and one at the North Rim. We have also included Moqui Lodge, which is immediately outside the south entrance to the South Rim. Lodging alternatives range from small lodge rooms without a private bath, to rustic cabins, to rooms in a classic historical hotel building. Rates also vary a great deal depending on where you decide to stay (or are able to locate a room). The wide variation in accommodations means that you should have a basic understanding of the alternatives when you call or write for reservations. All the lodges are operated by one firm, and reservations are made using the same address and telephone number. The lodges are all very popular, and reservations should, if possible, be made many months in advance. Keep in mind that several motels are a short distance outside the south entrance, which is only 6 miles from Grand Canyon Village and the South Rim.

# SOUTH RIM (SEVEN LODGES)

Most visitors reach the South Rim of the Grand Canyon via Highway 64 from Flagstaff, Arizona. An alternative route via Highway 89 to Highway 64 and the east entrance is longer and slower but offers numerous views of the canyon. The center of activity for the South Rim is Grand Canyon Village, where you will find the lodges, cabins, gift shops, restaurants, a large National Park Service visitor center, and the start of numerous tours. Grand Canyon Village is very busy and generally very crowded. Parking is often difficult to locate unless you are willing to park away from the rim and walk or ride the free village shuttle that connects all the lodges with the visitor center, restaurants, and Yavapai Observation

# GRAND CANYON NATIONAL PARK

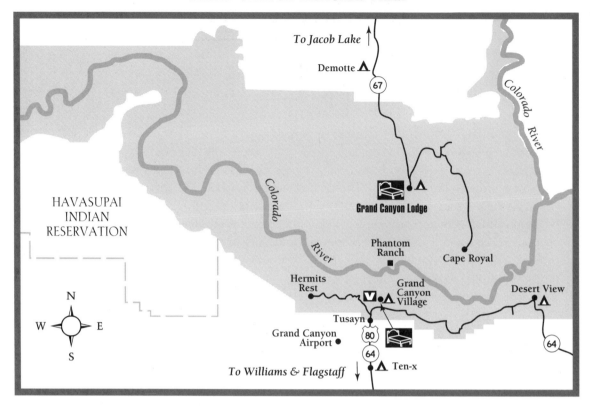

# GRAND CANYON VILLAGE

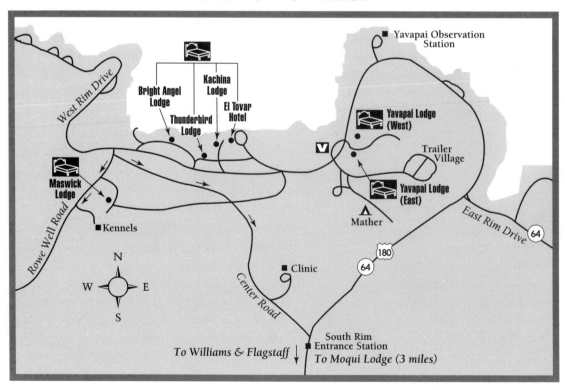

Station. A second free shuttle operates from the western edge of Grand Canyon Village to observation points along the road to Hermit's Rest. The shuttles operate every fifteen minutes from mid-May through mid-October.

The seven lodges at the South Rim offer very different accommodations. Some are quite rustic, while others are more luxurious. All have their individual charm and prices. Because the lodges are in close proximity, most of the facilities, activities, and reservation information are described in the following section. All of the restaurants, gift shops, and guided walks are equally accessible no matter where you choose to stay, especially in view of the free shuttle.

- **RESERVATIONS:** Grand Canyon National Park Lodges, AmFac Parks and Resorts, 14001 East Iliff Avenue, Suite 300, Aurora, CO 80014. Phone (303) 297–2757; fax (303) 297–3175. Reservations may be made up to twenty-three months in advance. Try to make reservations six or more months in advance for the busy summer months.

- **FOOD:** A variety of restaurants and snack bars are scattered around Grand Canyon Village. Inexpensive cafeterias are at Maswik and Yavapai, while an elegant and expensive restaurant is at El Tovar. Excellent steaks are served at the Arizona Steak House just outside the rim entrance to Bright Angel Lodge. Make reservations early at El Tovar. The Arizona Steak House does not take reservations but does maintain a wait list. A full-service grocery store is at Mather Business Center.

- **TRANSPORTATION:** Commuter air service from Phoenix, Los Angeles, and Las Vegas is available to Grand Canyon Airport at Tusayan, 6 miles south of the park visitor center. Rental cars are at the airport, and hourly shuttles operate between the airport and Grand Canyon Village. Air service from Phoenix is also available on America West or Delta to Flagstaff, where several rental car agencies operate. Train service on Amtrak is available to Flagstaff.

- **FACILITIES:** Grand Canyon Village *is* truly a village. It includes a full-service grocery store, a post office, a full-service bank, a unisex hair salon, a Laundromat, gift shops, a gas station with propane and diesel fuel, an auto service garage, emergency medical and dental services, a newsstand, a bookstore, film processing, an ice cream shop, and an array of restaurants.

- **ACTIVITIES:** A variety of activities begin in the village, including all-day tours of Monument Valley and Native American heritage sites. Shorter tours of various sites along the South Rim are also offered. Additional activities, some of which begin outside the village, include river raft excursions, hiking, mule rides to the canyon floor, horseback riding, and helicopter and airplane trips over the canyon. The National Park·Service offers programs on the history and geology of the park throughout the day and evening. A fall chamber music festival is offered annually. Make the visitor center an early stop so you can obtain a full list of activities.

# BRIGHT ANGEL LODGE

*Historic Cabin at Bright Angel Lodge*

Bright Angel Lodge is a complex consisting of a main registration building plus eighteen cabins and dormitory-style buildings that provide a total of eighty-nine rooms. The buildings with lodging are separate from but adjacent to the main registration building, which also houses a tour desk, gift shop, unisex hair salon, lounge, steak house, and coffee shop. The complex is at the center of South Rim activity and handy to the other hotels, eating facilities, and gift shops. This area of Grand Canyon Village is very busy with people and vehicle traffic, which makes it a hectic setting for individuals and families intent on discovering nature. On the plus side, Bright Angel provides some of the least expensive rooms on the South Rim and the cabins retain a flavor of the South Rim's historic nature.

Bright Angel Lodge provides three types of rooms. All have heat but no air conditioning, which typically isn't needed. The least expensive "standard," or "lodge," rooms are in Powell Lodge and Bucky Lodge, two dormitory-style buildings. Thirty-eight basic rooms each contain one double bed and a telephone. Some also have a television. Some of the rooms have a full bath, some have a sink and a toilet, and some have only a sink. Common bath and shower facilities are in the hallway for sharing with other residents. These rooms are particularly popular with hikers who want a relatively inexpensive place to crash after returning from the bottom of the canyon to the rim.

The oldest surviving structure on the South Rim is Bucky O'Neill's cabin, which was constructed in the early 1890s. O'Neill, a prospector-turned-tourism-promoter, was killed in Cuba while serving as a member of Theodore Roosevelt's Rough Riders. The cabin was preserved by Mary Colter, architect of Bright Angel Lodge, who incorporated the structure into her design for one of the lodge buildings. Today the cabin is rented to guests as the "Bucky Suite."

One step up are thirty-eight rooms in sixteen wooden or wood and stucco buildings called historic cabins. Some of these buildings have a single cabin, while others have two, three, or four cabin-style rooms. Although the exteriors are very rustic, the interiors are nicely furnished and comfortable. Each of the historic cabins has a full bath, television, and telephone. The most expensive rooms in Bright Angel are fifteen rim cabins that provide a view of the Grand Canyon. These rooms are situated in several buildings that sit beside a paved walking trail along the rim. Rim cabins each have one queen bed, a full bath, a telephone, and a television. Some also have a fireplace and a refrigerator. A single "Bucky Suite" has two rooms with a king bed, a queen sleeper, a refrigerator, a wet bar, a television, and a telephone. The suite rents for three to four times the cost of other lodging at Bright Angel.

*Bright Angel Hotel was constructed in 1895 to serve stagecoach passengers passing through this area. In 1905 the hotel became Bright Angel Camp, which eventually included cabins and an adjoining tent village to serve tourists who were attracted by the canyon's spectacular scenery. In 1935 the Fred Harvey Company replaced the camp with today's Bright Angel Lodge.*

Bright Angel Lodge is a handy location for all the activities and facilities the South Rim offers. The main registration building, which is a short walk from all of the Bright Angel lodging buildings, contains a gift shop, lounge, ice cream shop, and moderate-priced coffee shop. A wooden thunderbird hangs above a giant stone fireplace in the lobby. Although none of the rooms are directly on the rim and most don't offer a view of it, spectacular vistas of the canyon are only a few steps from any of the buildings. Other dining facilities, including a cafeteria, a steak house, and the most elegant dining room on the South Rim, are a reasonable walk from any of the rooms at Bright Angel. Parking can be a problem in the busy season, when a relatively large parking lot directly in front of the lodge is generally packed. Parking spaces scattered among the cabins can generally be counted on to yield a few empty slots, although they may not be directly outside your room.

- **ROOMS:** Singles and doubles. Rollaways are available. All but rooms in the two lodge buildings have full private baths. The two lodge buildings with standard cabins have common baths and showers.

- **RATES:** Standard cabins ($); historic cabins ($$); rim cabins ($$$/$$$$); suite ($$$$$).

- **LOCATION:** On the South Rim at the center of activity in Grand Canyon Village.

- **SEASON:** Rooms at Bright Angel Lodge are open year-round.

- **FOOD:** A full-service restaurant ($$$) is inside the main registration building and convenient to all the rooms. The restaurant is open daily from 6:30 A.M. to 10:00 P.M., and alcoholic beverages are served. The Bright Angel Fountain ($), open May through September, directly outside the registration building, offers hot dogs, soft drinks, and ice cream. A fine steak house ($$$$) offering steaks, poultry, and seafood is attached to the east end of the Bright Angel registration building. Open only for dinner, this restaurant serves great steaks.

# EL TOVAR HOTEL ✓

*El Tovar Hotel*

El Tovar is the regal hotel of the Grand Canyon's South Rim. Constructed in 1905 by the Santa Fe Railroad to promote the firm's transportation services, the hotel was named after Spanish explorer Pedro de Tovar, who led a 1540 expedition to this area. El Tovar is the type of hotel most people envision when they think about a national park lodge. It is a single large wood and stone four-story structure that commands a hilltop vista on the canyon rim. The two-story lobby area is complete with log beams, a large stone fireplace, and comfortable sofas and chairs for chatting with other guests. Several verandas and a large covered front porch have rocking chairs for relaxing in the early morning or after dinner or an evening walk. A nice mezzanine with an overlook of the lobby area contains tables, stuffed chairs, a television, and a fireplace. Complimentary coffee and tea are served here each morning.

El Tovar offers four classes of accommodations in a total of seventy-eight rooms, all of which are more expensive than any of the other lodging facilities at the South Rim. All the rooms have a full bath, heat, a telephone, and a television. This is the only hotel in Grand Canyon Village that has cooling units in each room. Although a number of rooms provide good window views, the siting of the hotel results in only a few rooms having an excellent view of the Grand Canyon. The least expensive lodging at El Tovar is a standard double that contains one double bed in a relatively small room. Deluxe rooms offer either a king or two queen beds with a larger living area. Eight nonview suites each have one king or two queen beds in one room, plus a separate living room with a couch (some make into a bed), chairs, a refrigerator, and a second television. Some of these suites have a balcony. Four view suites, two on the second floor and two on the third floor, each offer the same accommodations as the nonview suites. The view suites, which should be reserved at least a year in advance, each have a balcony that faces the canyon.

El Tovar provides most of the things you will want or need during a trip to the Grand Canyon. The ground floor has a gift shop, a newsstand, a lounge, and the elegant El Tovar dining room (reservations recommended), which offers an extensive menu in a formal setting. The dining room looks like it belongs in a national park. Murals on the walls reflect customs of different Indian tribes, and a number of tables offer diners a view of the rim. A small private dining room that holds up to ten persons is available at no charge with a forty-eight-hour advance reservation. The lounge has a bar and windows that overlook the canyon. Travel information is available, and tours can be booked at a small tour desk in the lobby across from the registration desk. Service at El Tovar is a cut above that found at other lodging facilities at the Grand Canyon. For example, room service is available from El Tovar dining room, and mints and a flower are placed on your bed each evening. No elevators are in the building, but bellhops are stationed near the registration desk to assist with baggage. A circular drive in front of the hotel is available for registration and baggage drop-off, but parking near the hotel is very limited.

- **ROOMS:** Singles, doubles, triples, and quads. Some suites can sleep up to six, and roll-aways are available. All rooms have full baths.

- **RATES:** Standard queen ($$$$); deluxe ($$$$$); suites ($$$$$+). Rates are quoted for two adults. Additional persons are charged $11 per night.

- **LOCATION:** Center of Grand Canyon Village, directly east of Kachina Lodge and just up the hill from the historic train depot.

- **SEASON:** El Tovar Hotel is open year-round.

- **FOOD:** A first-class dining room ($$$$$) off the lobby serves three gourmet meals daily. Alcoholic beverages are available, and reservations are recommended. A lounge is in the lobby area. Other, less expensive food service is within easy walking distance.

*El Tovar Hotel was built to be a first-rate lodging facility, and at its completion, in 1905, many considered it to be the most elegant hotel west of the Mississippi. Designed as a cross between a Swiss chalet and a Norwegian villa, the hotel was constructed of stone and Oregon pine. The building was equipped with a coal-fired steam generator to provide electric lighting, and Santa Fe railroad tank cars brought fresh water from a distance of 120 miles. Hens raised here supplied fresh eggs, and a dairy herd provided milk. Fresh fruit and vegetables were grown in greenhouses on the premises.*

# KACHINA LODGE/THUNDERBIRD LODGE

*Kachina Lodge*

**K**achina Lodge and Thunderbird Lodge are two virtually identical facilities that sit side by side on the South Rim of Grand Canyon Village between El Tovar Hotel and Bright Angel Lodge. The two-story stone buildings house a total of 104 rooms that, other than the view they provide, are identical. Approximately half the rooms, on the north side, face the rim, while the remainder, on the south side, face the road and parking lot. No registration facilities are in either of the lodges. Registration for Kachina Lodge is at the registration desk of El Tovar Hotel, and registration for Thunderbird Lodge is at the registration desk in the main building of Bright Angel Lodge.

Of all the lodging on the South Rim, Thunderbird and Kachina most resemble what one expects in a standard hotel. All rooms in both lodges are identical, with two double beds and a sofa that can be converted into a single bed. Rollaways are available but result in a crowded room. All rooms have a full bath with a combination tub-shower. Thunderbird has only a single row of rooms on the second floor, and all have a window that faces the canyon. Kachina has two rows of rooms on the second floor, and only half face the canyon. Rim-view rooms in both buildings rent for about $10 per day extra. Two medium-size conference rooms in Thunderbird can be reserved. Some rooms on the first floor of both buildings are handicap accessible.

Thunderbird and Kachina Lodges are in a convenient location at the center of South Rim activity. On the other hand, the rooms don't have much

*The Colorado River carved the Grand Canyon over a period of 4 to 6 million years to expose nearly half of the earth's 4.6-billion-year history. The Glen Canyon Dam, constructed in 1964, reduced much of the river's erosive power. Although the Grand Canyon area is now a high-desert plateau, this region once contained numerous seas and mountains as high as the Himalayas. The geologic history of this region lies exposed in the walls of the canyon.*

of the ambience that some people may desire in a national park visit. Once inside a room, you may as well be in Flagstaff or Phoenix. Also, the central location results in insufficient parking during the busy summer season. No information desk or commercial facilities are in either building, but food service, gift shops, and anything else offered at the South Rim is just a short walk from any of the rooms at these two lodges.

- **ROOMS:** Singles, doubles, triples, and quads. A fifth person can be accommodated on the sofa. All rooms have full baths.
- **RATES:** ($$$$) An extra charge of $9.00 per person for more than two persons.
- **LOCATION:** On the Rim between El Tovar Hotel and Bright Angel Lodge.
- **SEASON:** All rooms are available year-round.
- **FOOD:** No eating facilities are available in either building. Restaurants and cafeterias are within walking distance.

## MASWIK LODGE

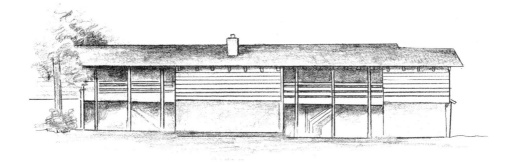

*Maswik North at Maswick Lodge*

Maswik Lodge (named for a Hopi kachina who guards the Grand Canyon) is a complex of modern apartment-type buildings and older cabins that provide 278 rooms in two large areas on each side of a centrally located registration building. All of the buildings with rooms are separate from the main lodge building, which houses registration and eating facilities. All of the rooms other than the cabins have two double beds, a full bath, heat, a telephone, and a television but no air conditioning. The cabins have one double bed, a telephone, a television, and a bath with shower but no tub. Some rooms in the North Unit are handicap accessible.

The North Unit, nearest the canyon rim, offers the newer and more expensive rooms in a cluster of twelve buildings. Most of the structures in this section are ten- and twelve-unit two-story buildings that resemble small apartments or college married-student housing. Each room runs the length of the building, with a front window and either a window or a sliding glass door in back. Two one-story buildings in the North Unit each have six rooms. Some of the buildings have rooms with balconies and patios, while others do not. The South Unit comprises six two-story motel-type buildings with smaller rooms that back up to one another. These rooms have no balcony or rear window and rent for about $30 per night less than rooms in the North Unit. Seven rustic quad-style cabin buildings house a total of twenty-eight rooms. These basic rooms rent for about half the price of rooms in the North Unit.

The lodge's location on the west side of the village, across the main road from the rim, is relatively peaceful. Staying in Maswik allows you to avoid the hustle and bustle of vehicles and crowds that roam over the rim area and yet remain within easy walking distance of the rim and most facilities in Grand Canyon Village, including hotels, gift shops, and restaurants. Of course, you are unable to view the Grand Canyon from the window of your room, but the same disadvantage exists with many rooms in other complexes closer to the rim. Maswik offers plentiful parking, a considerable advantage if you are driving, because other areas of the village are often very crowded.

The only eating facility at Maswik is a cafeteria in the main lodge building. It offers an extensive menu, and you can also purchase sandwiches, fruit, and snacks when the facility is open, from 6:00 A.M. to 10:00 P.M. Seating is plentiful, and customers move through the food and checkout lines rapidly. The food is typical cafeteria fare and relatively inexpensive, so this is a good place to eat when you are in a hurry. Maswik also offers a full-service sports lounge with a big-screen TV. Other services and food establishments are within easy walking distance of any of the rooms at Maswik.

Grand Canyon Railway operates a vintage train that offers daily service between Williams, Arizona, and Grand Canyon Village from Memorial Day weekend through September. The 65-mile trip from Williams to the canyon leaves on the two-and-a-quarter-hour trip each morning and returns to Williams each afternoon. Live entertainment is provided on board. Tours from Grand Canyon Village allow visitors to travel one way in a motor-coach and return on the train. Three classes of service, from coach to a parlor car, are available. The railway offers package plans that include overnight accommodations and meals. For information or reservations call (800) 843–8724.

- **ROOMS:** Singles, doubles, triples, and quads. All rooms have private baths, most with a combination tub-shower.

- **RATES:** Rustic cabins ($$); South Unit ($$); North Unit ($$$$)

- **LOCATION:** West side of Grand Canyon Village, approximately a quarter-mile from the canyon rim.

- **SEASON:** All rooms except for cabins (closed in winter) are open year-round.

- **FOOD:** A full-service cafeteria ($) within walking distance of all the rooms offers full meals and snacks from 6:00 A.M. to 10:00 P.M. Additional dining facilities of all types are within walking distance.

# MOQUI LODGE

*Moqui Lodge*

**M**oqui Lodge (Moqui is an Indian term for *vanishing* that was applied to a group of Hopi who fled the tribe and settled this area) provides 136 rooms in a motel-type setting a half-mile outside the south entrance to Grand Canyon National Park. The lodge is 3 miles from Grand Canyon Village. We have included Moqui because the facility is managed by the same firm that administers other Grand Canyon lodges and it will be offered as one of the housing options when you make reservations.

This lodge comprises two large motel-type buildings, one of which is connected to the main A-frame lodge building that faces the highway and houses the registration desk, lobby area, and dining room. The second building contains only rooms and is perpendicular to and slightly north of the main lodge building. The two-story wooden buildings that house the rooms in Moqui were built in the 1960s. The main lodge building includes part of the original lodge that was constructed here in the 1920s. The A-frame registration building includes an impressive lobby, highlighted by a massive stone fireplace and huge log ceiling beams. Just off the entrance a nice sitting area is filled with chairs and sofas for relaxing after a day at the canyon. The main lodge building also contains a lounge, a small gift shop, and a unisex hair salon. A gas station is next to the lodge.

Of 136 rooms at Moqui Lodge, 105 have two double beds. The other thirty-one rooms are slightly smaller and contain one double bed. All rooms are decorated in a Southwest motif, with a table, two chairs, a large television, a telephone, and a full bath. All have heat and a large ceiling fan but no air conditioning. The rooms have an outside entrance with a front window but no back window. There are no balconies or patios. Two rooms on the first floor are fully handicap accessible, including a roll-in shower. Each of the handicap-accessible rooms has a connecting door to an adjoining room. Lodging at Moqui includes a complimentary full breakfast in the lodge dining room. Dinner but not lunch is also served in the dining room. The attractive dining room specializes in Southwestern dishes for dinner, although popular American entrees are also offered. A separate lounge off the lobby area serves beer, wine, and cocktails, beginning at 5:00 P.M.; cocktails are also served in the dining room during dinner. A tour desk in the lobby can provide travel information and book tours.

Moqui Lodge suffers the disadvantage of being 3 miles from the main activity area of the South Rim. Guests with a vehicle must drive to Grand Canyon Village, where parking is at a premium. Alternative transportation is available on a private shuttle (fee charged) that operates between the town of Tusayan (and Grand Canyon Airport) and the South Rim. The shuttle makes stops at Moqui on request. If you consider the location to be a problem, you should attempt to obtain a room at one of the other lodges. On the other hand, the remote location proves to be relatively quiet, especially during the daytime, when most guests are at the canyon. Moqui is also close to the town of Tusayan, which offers restaurants, fast food, a grocery, and a gas station.

*Many visitors to Grand Canyon National Park decide to take an air tour of the canyon. Nearly a dozen airline and helicopter companies in the town of Tusayan and at the Grand Canyon Airport offer scenic flights over the canyon. The helicopter tours are generally shorter and somewhat more expensive than flights in fixed-wing aircraft but add extra excitement to the trip. Most firms offer several types of tours of various lengths. Any of the tours presents a very different perspective of the Grand Canyon. Prices begin at $50.*

- **ROOMS:** Singles, doubles, triples, and quads. All rooms have a private bath.

- **RATES:** All rooms ($$$).

- **LOCATION:** Moqui Lodge is on Highway 64, a half-mile south of the south entrance to Grand Canyon National Park.

- **SEASON:** The lodge is open from Presidents' Day through the end of November.

- **FOOD:** A dining room in the main lodge building specializes in Southwestern food but offers a full supper menu ($$/$$$) from 6:00 to 10:00 P.M. A complimentary full American breakfast is offered each morning for lodge guests. The dining room is closed from 10:00 A.M. to 6:00 P.M.

# YAVAPAI LODGE

*Yavapai West at Yavapai Lodge*

Yavapai Lodge is a complex of sixteen buildings a short distance from a separate registration building that houses a gift shop and large cafeteria. The sixteen buildings with lodging are in two separate clusters about equidistant from the registration building. Yavapai Lodge is located on the east side of Grand Canyon Village near the Mather Business Center, between Yavapai Point and El Tovar. It is a moderate walk from the rim of the Grand Canyon. Although the lodge is not in the center of Grand Canyon Village activity, free shuttle transportation to various points in the village is available.

Yavapai Lodge, with 358 rooms, is the largest lodging area in Grand Canyon National Park. The facility is divided into two separate complexes composed of very different styles of buildings. The newest (constructed in the mid-1970s) and more expensive rooms are in Yavapai East. Six two-story wooden buildings each contain thirty-two spacious rooms that have two double beds, a telephone, a television, a full bath, heat, and a fan but no air conditioning. The buildings have an outside staircase that leads to an inside corridor with access to the rooms. A large window in each room provides a nice view of the pine and juniper woodlands in which the buildings sit. None of the rooms have balconies or patios. The buildings, which sit well back from large parking areas, have the appearance of a nice apartment complex. Handicap-accessible rooms are available both here and in the Yavapai West complex.

Ten buildings in the slightly less expensive Yavapai West were constructed in the late 1960s and have the appearance of a motel. These one-story brick buildings each contain sixteen rooms with two double beds, a telephone, a television, a daybed, and a full bath. The rooms are quite small compared with rooms in Yavapai East. Plenty of parking is immediately in front of each structure, and the buildings are widely spaced in two large circles.

Rooms are accessed via a front door that faces the parking lot. None of the rooms have a balcony or window in the rear.

Yavapai Lodge provides a relatively quiet setting and plenty of parking, two items that are in short supply in most other lodging units in the park. With the free shuttle service throughout the village area, Yavapai's location outside the main activity area isn't a significant disadvantage. Also, Yavapai is convenient to the park's main visitor center and to Mather Business Center, which contains a post office, a general store with a relatively large grocery selection, and a large cafeteria with reasonable prices. The larger rooms in Yavapai East are worth the extra $15 per day compared with the older rooms in Yavapai West. If you don't mind climbing a few stairs, ask for a second-floor room for more privacy and a better view.

*At the bottom of Grand Canyon, Phantom Ranch provides food and overnight accommodations for hikers, rafters, and mule riders. Cabin accommodations are included with two-day mule tours, while dormitory-style lodging and a limited number of cabins are available to backpackers. The ranch was originally constructed in 1922, and dormitories were added in 1976. Space is limited, so plan to make reservations (phone 303–297–2757; fax 303–297–3175) well in advance for both lodging and food service.*

- **ROOMS:** Doubles, triples, and quads. All rooms have a full bath.

- **RATES:** All rooms ($$$). Rates are quoted for two adults. An extra $9.00 per person is charged for each additional person.

- **LOCATION:** On the east side of Grand Canyon Village, across from Mather Business Center.

- **SEASON:** Yavapai Lodge is open from mid-March through November. Rooms are also available seasonally at Thanksgiving and Christmas.

- **FOOD:** A nice large cafeteria is a moderate walk from both Yavapai East and Yavapai West. A general merchandise store at Mather Business Center offers a full line of grocery items, including beer, wine, and other alcoholic beverages.

# NORTH RIM

**V**isiting the North Rim of Grand Canyon National Park makes you feel you are in an entirely different park compared with a visit to the South Rim, except, of course, for the Grand Canyon itself, which is the common thread dividing these two areas. With fewer visitors, the North Rim provides fewer facilities and is much more relaxing to visit than the South Rim. Also, the North Rim offers only a single lodge in which to stay. The address, phone number, activities, and facilities for Grand Canyon Lodge are different from those for the seven lodges on the South Rim discussed above.

## GRAND CANYON LODGE

North Rim, AZ 86023 • (520) 638–2611

*Western Cabin at Grand Canyon Lodge (North Rim)*

**G**rand Canyon Lodge is the only lodging facility at Grand Canyon National Park's North Rim. The lodge consists of a classic main lodge building that houses the registration desk, lobby, and dining room, and more than 200 cabin units scattered along a peninsula of the Kaibab Plateau. The peninsula is surrounded by two spectacular canyons that snake off the Grand Canyon, which can be viewed at the tip of the peninsula. All of the rooms are in buildings that are separate from but within walking distance of the main lodge, which itself has no overnight rooms. The lodge is at the end of Highway 67, which leads into the park from the town of Jacob Lake.

The main lodge building at the North Rim was constructed in 1936, after the original lodge burned. It is what every national park lodge should look like. Designed by Gilbert Stanley Underwood, the same individual who was the architect for the Ahwahnee Hotel at Yosemite National Park and the lodge at Bryce Canyon National Park, the U-shaped building is constructed of massive limestone walls and timber beams. The spectacular high-ceilinged dining room provides wonderful vistas of the canyon. A large sunroom filled with stuffed chairs that is just off the registration area has canyon views through three huge windows. A veranda off the sunroom provides an area where guests can enjoy equally spectacular views from wooden rocking chairs. The building has two huge stone fireplaces, one in the sunroom and the other outside on the veranda. The lodge also houses a snack shop, gift shop, post office, and saloon.

More than a hundred rustic log cabins constructed in the 1920s provide just over 200 rooms for visitors. Four basic types of rooms are offered. Fifty-six Western Cabins are constructed either two or four to a building. These are log cabins with finished interiors. All have a fireplace and private front porch, two double beds, a full bath, a desk, a table, chairs, heat, and a telephone. These are the largest and most modern units at the North Rim. Two Western Cabins are handicap accessible. Eighty-two small Frontier Cabins are constructed two units to a building. Each unit has one double and one single bed, a private bath with shower, a telephone, heat, and a desk and chair. Two Frontier Cabins with one double bed are handicap accessible. Twenty-three Pioneer Cabins each have two bedrooms, one on each side of a shared small bath. The Pioneer Cabins have a telephone, heat, and a private bath with a shower but no tub. One bedroom in each cabin has two single beds, and the other bedroom has a double and a single bed. Relatively steep cement walks lead to some of the Pioneer Cabins. Two motel-type wooden buildings provide a total of forty rooms, some with one double bed and others with two double beds. All the motel rooms have desk, chair, telephone, heat, and private bath with shower but no tub.

We recommend the Western Cabins, which are slightly more expensive but offer more room and a nicer interior. Some units are near the rim and provide impressive views from the windows and a private front porch. Cabins 301, 305, 306, and 309 are rim-view units that rent for about $10 extra per day. Cabins 310 and 320 also offer a nice view and rent for the regular rate. The Pioneer Cabins farthest from the road (and parking) offer the best views.

**N**orth Rim or South Rim? The two sides of the Grand Canyon are so different that they share little other than the same canyon and river. The more popular South Rim has easier canyon access, more facilities, and many more visitors. The South Rim offers more eating facilities, more stores, more places to walk, and more people to bump into. Vehicles and people are in constant motion. Things seem to move much more slowly at the North Rim, where services and visitors are limited. The higher elevation of the North Rim results in cooler temperatures and more trees. Vistas from the North Rim seem more intimate, and fewer people will be standing next to you straining for the same view. If you are lucky, you will be able to sample both rims, perhaps on the same trip.

Choose units 98, 103, 107, 111, 123, 131, 135, 139, 142, or 145 if this is what you are seeking. Motel units 415, 416, 432, and 433 are larger than other motel units in the same building but rent for the same price. If you choose the motel, try to obtain a room on the back side, which provides better views. Be aware that few rooms at the Grand Canyon Lodge have nearby parking. You should first register and determine where your room is located. You will probably want to unload your luggage before driving back to the parking area. Bellhops are available to assist with luggage.

Grand Canyon Lodge offers everything you will need for an enjoyable vacation. The main lodge building houses a large gift shop, a wonderful restaurant, a saloon, a post office, and a snack shop. A gas station and a Laundromat are near the campground, 1 mile north of the lodge. The campground also has a store that sells groceries, camping supplies, and fast food. Several hiking trails originate near the lodge, and guests can enjoy mule rides and evening programs. Guided hikes are provided by the National Park Service.

- **ROOMS:** Doubles, triples, and quads in the Western Cabins and the motel units. Doubles and triples in the Frontier Cabins. Pioneer Cabins are priced for four or five occupants. All rooms have private baths, although only the Western Cabins offer bathtubs.

- **RESERVATIONS:** TW Recreational Services, Inc., AmFac Parks and Resorts, 14001 East Iliff Avenue, Suite 300, Aurora, CO 80014. Phone (303) 297–2757; fax (303) 297–3175. Reservations may be made up to twenty-three months in advance.

- **RATES:** Western Cabins ($$$); Frontier Cabins ($$); Pioneer Cabins ($$$); motel units ($$). Children under twelve years are free.

- **LOCATION:** Forty miles south on Highway 67 from the town of Jacob Lake, Arizona.

- **SEASON:** The lodge is open from mid-May to mid-October.

- **FOOD:** A spectacular restaurant ($$$) in the main lodge building offers three full meals a day. Breakfast is from 6:30 to 10:00 A.M., lunch from 11:30 A.M. to 2:30 P.M., and dinner from 5:00 to 9:30 P.M. Reservations are required for dinner. A snack bar ($) serving sandwiches and beverages is open from 7:00 A.M. to 9:00 P.M. Limited groceries and a snack bar are available 1 mile away at the campground.

- **TRANSPORTATION:** Scheduled air service is available to Kanab, Utah, and Page, Arizona, where rental cars are available. A daily shuttle (fee required) is offered between the North Rim and the South Rim.

- **FACILITIES:** A gift shop, post office, full-service restaurant, lounge, and snack bar are at the main lodge. A snack bar, grocery, Laundromat, and gas station are 1 mile north at the campground.

- **ACTIVITIES:** Hiking, mule rides, horse rides, van tours, evening interpretive program, and guided nature walks. Several short- and intermediate-length trails originate near the lodge.

# CALIFORNIA

## DEATH VALLEY NATIONAL PARK

Death Valley, CA 92328
(619) 786–2331

Death Valley National Park comprises 3.3 million acres of harsh desert environment that includes the lowest point in the Western Hemisphere. The park contains a desert mansion, ruins of old mining towns, abandoned borax works, mountain peaks, volcanic craters, and some of the highest summer temperatures you have ever encountered. The visitor center is at Furnace Creek. The major part of Death Valley National Park is in southeastern California. The main road is California Highway 190, which provides access to many of the major features and activity areas.

### Lodging in Death Valley National Park

Four lodging facilities in Death Valley National Park range from exquisite and expensive to quaint and moderately priced. Furnace Creek Inn, Furnace Creek Ranch, and Stovepipe Wells Village are each operated by Fred Harvey Company, a division of AmFac Parks and Resorts. The first two are near one another and remain under private ownership. Stovepipe Wells Village is owned by the National Park Service and operated as a concesssion. Stovepipe Wells Village is quite isolated, which may make it more or less desirable than the Furnace Creek facilities, depending on your taste. Privately owned Panamint Springs Resort, a small facility near the park's western boundary, only recently became the fourth lodging facility, when Death Valley National Park was expanded. High season for all four lodging facilities is from early July to late August, when temperatures in the valley area regularly reach 120 degrees Farenheit and above. Europeans, especially Germans, comprise the majority of visitors during this period.

# DEATH VALLEY NATIONAL PARK

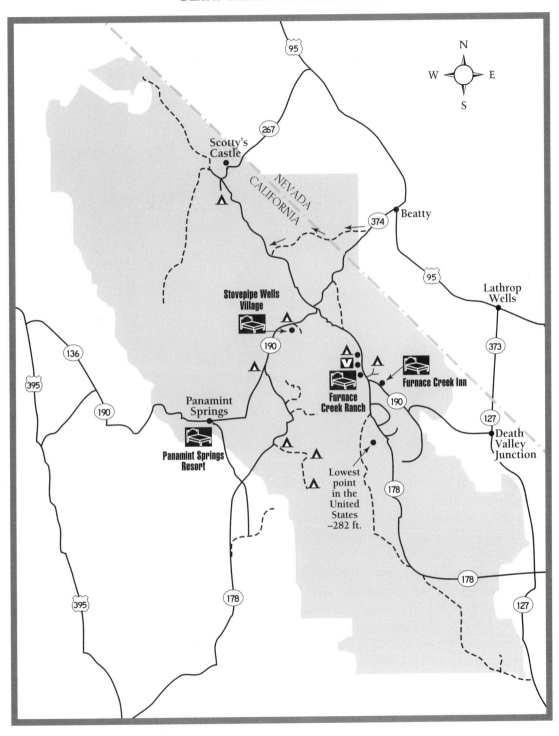

# FURNACE CREEK INN

P.O. Box 1 • Death Valley, CA 92328 • (619) 786–2361

*Furnace Creek Inn Resort*

Furnace Creek Inn may be the most elegant hotel located in a National Park Service–administered area, and it is certainly one of the most unique lodging facilities in the United States. Located in the middle of one of the country's most inhospitable environments, the hotel has retained its original grandeur. Pacific Coast Borax Company commenced construction of the hotel in the early 1920s to accommodate the increasing number of visitors to Death Valley. Improvements and additions continued into the mid-1930s. Furnace Creek Inn was purchased by Fred Harvey in 1969. The inn is built of stone and adobe in a Mission-style architecture. It sits on a hill overlooking a desolate but starkly beautiful desert that encompasses both the lowest point in the Western Hemisphere (282 feet below sea level) and the Panamint Mountain Range, which soars to more than 11,000 feet. Furnace Creek Inn sits on the back side of an oasis of green grass and palm trees. Services include room service, shuttle service to Furnace Creek Ranch or the nearby airstrip, and massage therapy. A large conference room with stone walls, beamed ceiling, and large windows that face the swimming pool has stone fireplaces at each end. A bar at the end of the pool serves beverages and snacks. The library can be utilized for smaller meetings.

Furnace Creek Inn offers a total of sixty-six rooms in three separate buildings. All of the rooms have heat, air conditioning, a refrigerator, a telephone, and a television. Most standard rooms have a king bed (several have two doubles or two twins), full bath, ceiling fan, dresser, chair, and nightstand. A second category of rooms, called spa rooms, are similar to standard rooms but have a spa tub and rent for approximately $40 extra per night. Second-floor rooms in one wing have balconies. Rooms in the main building and in one wing are accessed from interior back hallways, so most of the rooms have a view out the front (toward the west) of the building. An elevator for guests is in the main building. Handicap access is available to the hotel and some rooms. We recommend room 199, which is isolated from other rooms and requires decending several staircases but is worth the effort. It is located on the second floor of a separate building with a private outside staircase to the swimming pool. The room has stone walls and a beamed ceiling.

Furnace Creek Inn has about anything you will need for a first-class (and expensive) vacation. The attractive, spring-fed swimming pool offers a respite from the summer heat. Four lighted tennis courts, a nearby eighteen-hole golf course, horseback riding (October through May), and hiking are available for sports-minded visitors. A first-class hotel dining room serves three meals a day, and two other restaurants at nearby Furnace Creek Ranch can be reached by hotel shuttle. A unique stone-walled lounge is at the inn. A variety of guided tours (October through May) to surrounding sites in the valley and nearby areas are offered by Fred Harvey Company. The Death Valley National Park Service visitor center, with exhibits and naturalist talks, is about 2 miles from the inn.

*The rumor is that room 199 at Furnace Creek Inn is haunted by a ghost, most probably the former chef for which the room is named. The inn's maids claim to have made up the room, closed the curtains, and turned off the lights, only to find the curtains open and the lights on again soon after they had left. Despite the rumor, this room remains much in demand so you will need to make an early reservation in order to check if the rumor is really fact.*

- **ROOMS:** Doubles, plus a limited number of triples and quads. All rooms have a private bath, many with a combination tub-shower.

- **RESERVATIONS:** Furnace Creek Inn & Ranch Resort, P.O. Box 1, Death Valley, CA 92328. Phone (800) 236–7916 or (619) 786–2345; fax (619) 786–2514. Cost of the first night's lodging is required as a deposit. Cancellation of forty-eight hours required for full refund.

- **RATES:** All rooms ($$$$$). Rates are quoted for two adults. Children five and under are free. Additional persons are $14 each.

- **LOCATION:** Furnace Creek Inn is 130 miles northwest of Las Vegas, Nevada, and 300 miles northeast of Los Angeles, California.

- **SEASON:** The inn is open all year. The busiest season is mid-July to August, when the hotel is frequently full.

- **FOOD:** Diners are treated to a scenic view of the Panamint Mountains from the elegant Inn Dining Room ($$$$$), which offers a complete menu for breakfast, lunch, and dinner. Two less expensive restaurants at nearby Furnace Creek Ranch are described in the write-up of that facility.

- **TRANSPORTATION:** The nearest major airport is in Las Vegas, Nevada, where rental cars are available. The resort has a concrete airstrip with lights for private or chartered planes. Transportation from the airstrip is available when the inn is contacted in advance.

- **FACILITIES:** The inn has a large, spring-fed swimming pool (constant eighty-two degrees Farenheit), a sauna, massage therapy (October through May), four lighted tennis courts, a restaurant, a lounge, and large and small banquet or meeting rooms. A gas station and general store are at Furnace Creek Ranch.

- **ACTIVITIES:** Swimming, tennis, and golf; horseback riding, group hay rides, and carriage rides (mid-October to mid-May). Guided tours of Death Valley and surrounding areas are offered by Fred Harvey Company. The National Park Service offers interpretive programs throughout the park.

## FURNACE CREEK RANCH

P.O. Box 1 • Death Valley, CA 92328 • (619) 786–2345

*Deluxe Units at Furnace Creek Ranch Resort*

Furnace Creek Ranch is the family alternative to the more expensive and elegant Furnace Creek Inn. Located in an oasis area of Furnace Creek, about 1.5 miles from the inn, Furnace Creek Ranch offers a total of 224 rooms in three classifications of accommodations. The buildings sit amid tall palm and tamarisk trees, with an eighteen-hole golf course at one end. The ranch offers more activities and eating places than the more famous inn. A small building just to the right of the stone entrance gate houses the registration desk. Inside the gate and to the left in a Western-style wooden building are a general store, a saloon, an ice cream shop, and two restaurants. Lodging rooms are in six one- and two-story motel-type buildings that sit behind the restaurant building, plus eight freestanding wood cabins beside the registration building. All the buildings with overnight rooms are within easy walking distance of the registration building and restaurants. Plentiful parking is available near each of the buildings.

All of the rooms at Furnace Creek Ranch have heat, air conditioning, television, and telephone. A hundred and sixty Deluxe rooms are in four two-story wooden buildings constructed in the 1960s. These buildings have an entrance at each end, with access to the rooms through an interior corridor. Second-floor rooms each have a balcony, and rooms on the bottom floor have a patio. Each Deluxe room has two double beds, a refrigerator, a desk, two chairs, a dresser, and a nightstand. Half the 160 rooms face either the golf course or a grassy area surrounding the swimming pool. Rooms on the opposite side of each building face one another. All these rooms rent for the same price, so try for one with a view toward the golf course.

Two one-story wood buildings contain forty-eight Parkside rooms, which each have a sliding glass patio door on the back side that opens to a large grassy area near the swimming pool. These rooms rent for about $20 per night above the rate for rooms in the two-story units. Parkside rooms may be a little bigger but are priced higher because they are somewhat newer and offer closer access to the swimming area. Parking is immediately outside the front door of these units, which are furnished in an identical manner to that of the Deluxe units described above.

Sixteen newly remodeled Cabin units are constructed two to a building, and each has two double beds and a bath with a shower but no bathtub. The Cabin units are nicely done but quite a bit smaller than the Deluxe or Parkside rooms.

Furnace Creek Ranch provides all the facilities you will need for a comfortable stay in Death Valley National Park. Best of all, the facilities are near the rooms. The golf course, the Borax Museum with interesting displays, and the National Park Service visitor center are a walk from any of the rooms. If you desire a special dinner, take the free shuttle or drive a little more than a mile to the Furnace Creek Inn. If one of the many unique places in Death Valley interests you, it is likely that a guided tour will be offered. Tours are available to Scotty's Castle, Titus Canyon, Amargosa Opera, and the Lower Valley. You can play golf in the morning, swim in the afternoon, have a beer in the saloon, take a nap, and walk to a restaurant without ever getting in your vehicle. Keep in mind that some of these things are easier to handle in the spring, winter, and fall than in the heat of the summer. In fact, the guided tours are suspended in the hot summer months. On the other hand, this is a great place to spend a spring weekend, when daytime temperatures are more reasonable.

*Large groves of date palms growing at Furnace Creek Ranch and at Furnace Creek Inn were planted during the 1920s by the Pacific Borax Company. The date palms require the high-heat and low-humidity environment found at Death Valley. A healthy palm carries up to fifteen bunches that each contain from 600 to 750 dates. The dates are harvested beginning in October of each year by pickers who climb long extension ladders. The palms produce a good crop of fruit that is sold at a small store at the entrance to Furnace Creek Ranch.*

- **ROOMS:** Doubles, triples, and quads. All rooms have a private bath with a combination tub-shower except the cabins, which have only a shower.

- **RESERVATIONS:** Furnace Creek Inn & Ranch Resort, P.O. Box 1, Death Valley, CA 92328. Phone (800) 236–7916 or (619) 786–2345; fax (619) 786–2514. Cost of the first night's lodging is required as a deposit. Cancellation of forty-eight hours required for full refund.

- **RATES:** Cabins ($$$), Deluxe ($$$$), and Parkside ($$$$). Rates are quoted for two adults. Children eighteen and under are free when accompanied by an adult. Additional persons are $14 each.

- **LOCATION:** Furnace Creek Ranch is 130 miles northwest of Las Vegas, Nevada, and 300 miles northeast of Los Angeles, California. The ranch is approximately 1.5 miles north of Furnace Creek Inn.

- **SEASON:** The ranch is open all year. The busiest season is mid-July through August, when the hotel is frequently full.

- **FOOD:** The Wrangler Steakhouse ($$$/$$$$) offers a buffet for breakfast and lunch. Dinner is ordered from a menu that includes steaks, seafood, and poultry. The 49er Cafe ($$/$$$) offers breakfast, lunch, and dinner. The Ice Cream Shop ($) has ice cream and some fast foods. The Saloon ($$) offers hot dogs and sub sandwiches. Beer, wine, other beverages, and limited groceries are sold in the general store.

- **TRANSPORTATION:** The nearest major airport is in Las Vegas, Nevada, where rental cars are available. The resort has a concrete airstrip with lights for private or chartered planes. Transportation from the airstrip is available when the ranch is contacted in advance.

- **FACILITIES:** The ranch has a large, spring-fed swimming pool (constant eighty-two degrees Farenheit), two lighted tennis courts, a basketball court, a horseshoe area, a volleyball court, an eighteen-hole golf course, the Borax Museum, two restaurants, an ice cream shop, a saloon, a gas station, and a general store.

- **ACTIVITIES:** Swimming, tennis, golf, basketball, volleyball, horseshoes, and hiking. Horseback riding, group hay rides, and carriage rides are offered from mid-October to mid-May. Guided tours of Death Valley and surrounding areas are offered by Fred Harvey Company. The National Park Service offers interpretive programs throughout the park except during summer.

# PANAMINT SPRINGS RESORT

P.O. Box 395 • Ridgecrest, CA 93556 • (702) 482–7680

*Panamint Springs Resort*

Panamint Springs Resort is a small facility that, if not for the surrounding landscape, causes you to wonder if you are in Key West, Florida. In fact, walk in the front door of the main building that houses the registration area and dining room and you might expect to see Ernest Hemingway sitting on one of the stools at a bar made from a large slab of walnut supported by redwood roots. Most likely, he would be listening to the imitation Wurlitzer jukebox. A large porch wraps around the building, with one side serving as an outside dining area. A small grassy area on one side has chairs for relaxing. Three wooden buildings directly behind the main building house fourteen motel rooms. All of the buildings are wood shingled.

Panamint Springs offers fourteen rooms of varying size, but all are relatively small. Some rooms have one double bed, while others have either two or three double beds. Each room has heat, air conditioning, and a private bath with shower but no tub. No television is available, and the only telephone is a cellular unit in the registration building.

The best-known man-made structure in Death Valley National Park is Scotty's Castle, which lies just inside the park's north entrance. This unique rock building, which cost nearly $2 million, was constructed in the 1920s as a vacation retreat for Albert Johnson, a partner and lifelong friend of Walter Scott, alias Death Valley Scotty, for whom the castle is named. Today you can take a fifty-minute tour conducted by Park Service rangers in period clothing. The tours are offered daily from 9:00 A.M. to 5:00 P.M., and waits of an hour or two can be expected during busy times of the year. The castle also includes a bookstore, gift shop, exhibit room, and snack bar.

Panamint Springs Resort is a small, quaint motel-type facility in the middle of the desert. The resort generates its own electricity, and water is piped from 5 miles away. Panamint Springs certainly isn't fancy, but it is a fun and unique place that you will remember. It is unlikely that you will be interested in staying more than one night, since the rooms are small and there isn't much to do other than hike. The dining room on one side of the main building holds about twenty-five persons and is much nicer than you might expect. The bar is terrific, and the atmosphere of the whole place can't be beat. Stay here and you will think you are a thousand miles from civilization.

- **ROOMS:** Two people in one double bed to six people in three double beds. All rooms have private baths with a shower but no tub.

- **RESERVATIONS:** Panamint Springs Resort, P.O. Box 395, Ridgecrest, CA 93556. Phone (702) 482–7680; fax (702) 482–7682. A check or credit card is required to guarantee a room.

- **RATES:** All rooms ($$). Rates quoted for two adults. Charge for extra person varies from $4.00 to $10.00, depending on bedding requirements.

- **LOCATION:** The resort is on the western edge of Death Valley on Highway 190, 48 miles east of Lone Pine, California.

- **SEASON:** The resort is open all year. The busiest season is mid-July through August.

- **FOOD:** The attractive dining room ($$) serves breakfast, lunch, and dinner from 6:30 A.M. to 10:00 P.M. Beer, wine, and soft drinks are available from coolers just off the registration area. The bar remains open until the registration desk closes at midnight.

- **TRANSPORTATION:** The nearest airport is in Bakersfield, California, where rental cars are available.

- **FACILITIES:** Dining room, bar, and gift shop area. Unleaded regular gasoline and propane are available.

- **ACTIVITIES:** Hiking.

## STOVEPIPE WELLS VILLAGE

Death Valley, CA 92328 • (619) 786–2387

Stovepipe Wells Village is a complex of eleven wooden buildings that provide overnight rooms and supporting services. A general store, a small gas station, and a National Park Service ranger station are directly across the road. The village has the appearance of a small western town, which in some respects it is. Six separate one-story buildings each contain from eight to twenty-three rooms. The guest registration area is at the center of the complex in a building that also houses an auditorium, gift shop, and small lobby area. Employee housing is scattered around the back of the complex. Stovepipe Wells Village is situated in about the middle of Death Valley National Park, on Highway 190, approximately 25 miles northwest of Furnace Creek. It is about 33 miles southwest of Beatty, Nevada.

*Cottonwood Units at Stovepipe Wells Village*

Stovepipe Wells offers three categories of rooms that range from a limited number of small, inexpensive Patio rooms to Deluxe rooms similar to those at Furnace Creek Ranch. All the rooms have heat, air conditioning, and a private bath but no telephone or television. Be aware that only two of the buildings have potable water in the rooms. Guests in other rooms will find drinkable water in several locations outside the buildings. Water at Stovepipe Wells has a high mineral content and is treated for drinking purposes. Forty-nine recently renovated Deluxe rooms in three separate buildings each have either two double beds or one king bed, a full bath, a refrigerator, a table, and a desk. Rooms 212 through 223 in the Roadrunner building face the East and provide the best view. Less expensive and smaller Standard rooms in two buildings each have two single beds (one has a double bed) and a bath with shower but no bathtub. Standard rooms rent for about $25 less per night than Deluxe rooms. Eight even smaller Patio rooms, constructed in 1927 as part of the original building, each have one double bed and a bath with shower but no tub. These rooms are attached to the front of the registration building near the highway. All of the buildings with rooms are a short walk from the registration building.

Stovepipe Wells is particularly appealing for someone seeking the solitude of the desert. Being located on Highway 190, which passes through Death Valley, makes it a convenient stop for travelers crossing the park. Stovepipe Wells Village offers an attractive restaurant and saloon with a real western atmosphere. The dining room and saloon have vaulted ceilings and were built with timbers from an old Death Valley mining operation. In fact, staying at Stovepipe Wells is itself a bit of the Old West, even though many of the rooms are quite comfortable and modern. A general store across the road offers supplies, beverages, and limited groceries. A pool with heated mineral water is available for guests.

- ■ **ROOMS:** Doubles, triples, and quads. All rooms have private baths, although the Patio and Standard rooms have showers but no tubs.

- ■ **RESERVATIONS:** Stovepipe Wells Village, Death Valley, CA 92328. Phone (619) 786–2387; fax (619) 786–2307. The first night's lodging is required as a deposit. Cancellation of forty-eight hours required for full refund.

- **RATES:** Patio ($), Standard ($$), and Deluxe ($$$). Rates are quoted for two adults. Children eighteen and under are free when accompanied by an adult.

- **LOCATION:** Stovepipe Wells Village is on Highway 190, near the middle of Death Valley National Park. It is approximately 25 miles northwest of the Furnace Creek Ranch and about 33 miles southwest of Beatty, Nevada.

- **SEASON:** The facility is open all year. The busiest season is mid-July through August, when it is frequently full.

- **FOOD:** The Toll Road Restaurant ($$/$$$) offers a buffet for breakfast, lunch, and dinner during summer. From mid-October to mid-May, all three meals are ordered from a complete menu. The Badwater Saloon just off the restaurant offers draft beer, cocktails, and appetizers. Beer, wine, other beverages, and limited groceries are sold in the general store.

- **TRANSPORTATION:** The nearest major airport is in Las Vegas, Nevada, where rental cars are available. A concrete airstrip with lights for private or chartered planes is near Furnace Creek Ranch. Another airstrip is beside Stovepipe Wells.

- **FACILITIES:** Stovepipe has a mineral springs swimming pool, restaurant, saloon, gift shop, gas station, and general store.

- **ACTIVITIES:** Swimming, walking, and hiking. The National Park Service offers interpretive programs throughout the park except during summer.

*Although not covered with sand, Death Valley does have a few areas where large amounts of sand have collected to form dunes. The best known and easiest to visit are near Stovepipe Wells. These can be accessed from Highway 190 or from the unpaved Sand Dunes Road. Dunes can also be viewed north of Highway 190 on the west side of the park at Panamint Dunes. Other dunes are in both the extreme north and south ends of the park. Dunes require a source of sand, a wind to move the sand, and a place for the sand to collect. Death Valley has an abundance of the first two but only a few of the latter.*

# LASSEN VOLCANIC NATIONAL PARK

Mineral, CA 96063
(916) 595–4444

Lassen Volcanic National Park comprises 106,000 acres of a beautiful and relatively uncrowded mountainous area centered on Lassen Peak, a 10,457-foot plug-dome volcano that last erupted during a seven-year period beginning in 1914. The park contains other evidence of geothermal activity, including hot springs, mud pots, fumaroles, and sulfurous vents. Lassen Volcanic National Park is located in north-central California, 42 miles east of Redding on State Highway 44.

##  Lodging in Lassen Volcanic National Park

Lassen Volcanic contains only a single lodging facility, and it is an out-of-the-way location for most visitors who will drive along the single paved road through the park. Drakesbad Guest Ranch is in the southern part of the park, 17 miles north of the small town of Chester. Private accommodations are available in Chester.

### DRAKESBAD GUEST RANCH

End of Warner Valley Road • Lassen Volcanic National Park
Chester, CA 96020 • (See below for phone information)

Drakesbad Guest Ranch provides a total of nineteen rooms in a relatively isolated complex of cabins, bungalows, and a two-story lodge. The ranch also has a central dining hall, a swimming pool, and several service buildings. The complex lies beside a meadow in the southeast portion of Lassen Volcanic National Park. It is surrounded by trees, hills, and mountains. Drakesbad Guest Ranch is reached via a 17-mile road from the town of Chester, California. The first 14 miles are a winding but well-maintained paved road. The last 3 miles, through national park land, are on a relatively rough gravel road. Drakesbad can be called directly by asking the long-distance operator for the Susanville, California, operator in area code 916. Tell the Susanville operator to connect you with Drakesbad Toll Station No. 2.

Drakesbad offers four types of room accommodations, all of which are fairly expensive because they include three meals a day. The rooms all have heat but no air conditioning, telephones, television, or electrical outlets. The two-story wooden lodge building has six rooms, all on the second floor. The three even-numbered rooms have one double bed and one single bed. Odd-numbered rooms are a little smaller and have one double bed. All the lodge rooms have electric lights and a private bath with a sink and toilet but no tub or shower. Four freestanding rustic cabins each have a double and a single bed and the same type of bath as in the lodge. The cabins are paneled and relatively small. No electricity is avail-

# LASSEN VOLCANIC NATIONAL PARK

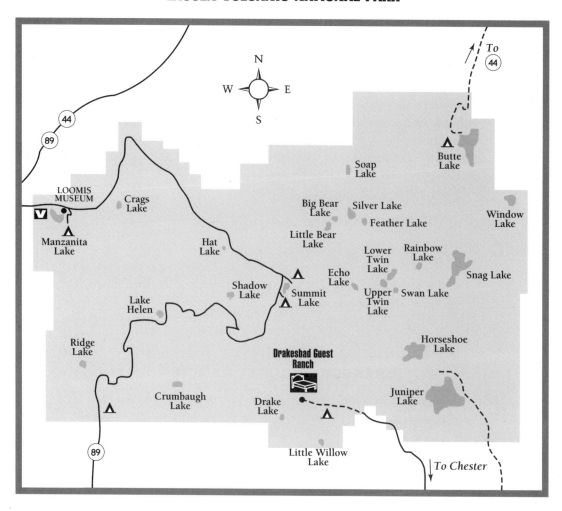

*Lodge Building at Drakesbad Guest Ranch*

able in these units, and light is by means of kerosene lanterns. A bathhouse at the swimming pool has showers and bathtubs for lodge and cabin guests. Eight bungalows, constructed two to a building, each have two double beds, a full bath, and a back porch that overlooks the meadow. A single wooden duplex has two rooms on each side of a central full bath. One room has two double beds, and the other room has one double and one single bed. The duplex is rented as a single unit to large families.

For most travelers, even frequent visitors to national parks, staying at Drakesbad will be a very different experience. Drakesbad is not for people who expect a fancy lodge with room service; it is a place for individuals who want to get away from it all and experience nature, but without giving up good food and friendship. The facilities at Drakesbad are comfortable but basic. A dinner bell rings three times a day to announce that food is being served in a rustic paneled dining room. The entire bottom floor of the lodge building, filled with chairs, tables, and sofas, serves as a meeting place to read and chat with other guests. A wood stove is near the middle of the room, and a large stone fireplace occupies one end wall. Chairs and sofas are also on the outside porch, which wraps around the lodge. Riding horses are at the nearby stable, and the swimming pool has naturally heated spring water. Equipment is provided for a variety of activities, including table tennis, volleyball, badminton, croquet, and horseshoes. Fly-fishing for trout is excellent for experienced anglers. Several trails, both short and lengthy ones, lead from the lodge to some of Lassen's best spots; trails also connect with some of the park's other trails. Campfires are held each evening, and programs are presented for both adults and children. Best of all, both employees and guests seem to be family members that have found a good thing few other people have even heard about.

■ **ROOMS:** Singles, doubles, triples, and quads. A single duplex holds up to seven individuals. Cabins and lodge rooms have half-baths. Other rooms have a full bath.

- **RESERVATIONS:** California Guest Services, 2150 North Main Street, Suite 5, Red Bluffs, CA 96080. Phone (916) 529–1512 or 529–9860; fax 529–4511. Reservations should be made by mid-February to ensure a choice of rooms and dates. Reservations can be made up to a year in advance. Two nights' deposit is required, and a thirty-day cancellation is required for a full refund.

- **RATES:** ($$$$$) includes room and three meals per day. Rates are quoted per person and reduced for weekly stays.

- **LOCATION:** Seventeen miles north of Chester, California, on Warner Valley Road.

- **SEASON:** Open from the first Friday in June to the second Sunday in October.

- **FOOD:** An attractive dining room serves three meals a day. Breakfast and lunch are served buffet-style, while dinner is served at the table. Sack lunches can be requested by guests who will be hiking or horseback riding during lunch.

- **TRANSPORTATION:** Scheduled airline service is available to Redding and Chico, California, and Reno, Nevada, where rental cars are available. Private planes may land at a small lighted airport at Chester, where rental cars are available. The lodge will pick up guests at Chester if prior arrangements are made. Amtrak serves Redding and Chico.

- **FACILITIES:** Hot-spring-fed swimming pool, dining hall, and stables.

- **ACTIVITIES:** Horseback riding, fishing, swimming, hiking, canoeing, and a variety of games, including volleyball, croquet, Ping-Pong, horseshoes, and badminton.

*Drakesbad Guest Ranch is more than one hundred years old and predates Lassen Volcanic National Park, which did not achieve national park status until 1916. The ranch was founded and operated by E. R. Drake, who sold it in 1900 to the Sifford family. The ranch's name is a combination of the original owner's name and the German term for warm-water baths, which at Drakesbad are fed by hot springs. The water is cooled and used in the swimming pool, which sits just below a spring. Several of the park's many geothermal areas are a modest hike from the ranch.*

# SEQUOIA NATIONAL PARK/KINGS CANYON NATIONAL PARK

Three Rivers, CA 93271

(209) 565–3341

Kings Canyon and Sequoia are separate parks that adjoin one another. The parks are administered jointly and nearly always visited together, so they are discussed here as one unit. The two parks have a combined area of 1,300 square miles, including groves of giant sequoias in canyons surrounded by the scenic High Sierra. The parks are located in central California, between Yosemite National Park and Death Valley National Park. Access from the west is via State Highway 180 from Fresno, which leads through the Grant Grove section of Kings Canyon to Cedar Grove. From the south State Highway 198 leads to the Giant Forest area of Sequoia National Park and then connects with Highway 180 at Grant Grove.

##  Lodging in Kings Canyon and Sequoia National Parks

Three facilities in Kings Canyon National Park and Sequoia National Park offer overnight accommodations that range from very rustic cabins to a modern two-story lodge. Giant Forest Lodge is in Sequoia, near the park's south entrance at Three Rivers. Two lodging facilities are in Kings Canyon, rustic cabins at Grant Grove and a nice motel unit at Cedar Grove. Stony Creek Lodge in Sequoia National Forest between Giant Forest and Grant Grove is included as a fourth lodging alternative, even though it is just outside the northern boundary of Sequoia National Park on Highway 198. Although not included in this book, another private facility is on the road to Cedar Grove, just outside the park boundary in Sequoia National Forest.

All three park lodges as well as Stony Creek Lodge in Sequoia National Forest are managed by one concessionaire, Kings Canyon Park Services, that took over the operation in November 1996. The same address, phone number, and deposit and cancellation regulations apply to reservations at each of the four facilities. One management company is advantageous because a single letter or phone call provides access to many accommodations. If Giant Forest accomodations are full, you may have a shot at the lodges at Grant Grove, Stony Creek, or Cedar Grove.

Although lodging facilities in most national parks exhibit few changes from year to year, Kings Canyon and Sequoia may undergo major transformation in the next several years. New accommodations for the Grant Grove area of Kings Canyon National Park are being planned as this book is written. In addition, consideration is being given to eventually closing the current lodging and commercial operation at Giant Forest in Sequoia National Park. Be certain to obtain current information about both of these areas when making reservations.

■ **RESERVATIONS:** Kings Canyon Park Services, P.O. Box 909, Kings Canyon National Park, CA 93633. Phone (209) 335–5500; fax (209) 335–5502. First night's lodging is required as a deposit.

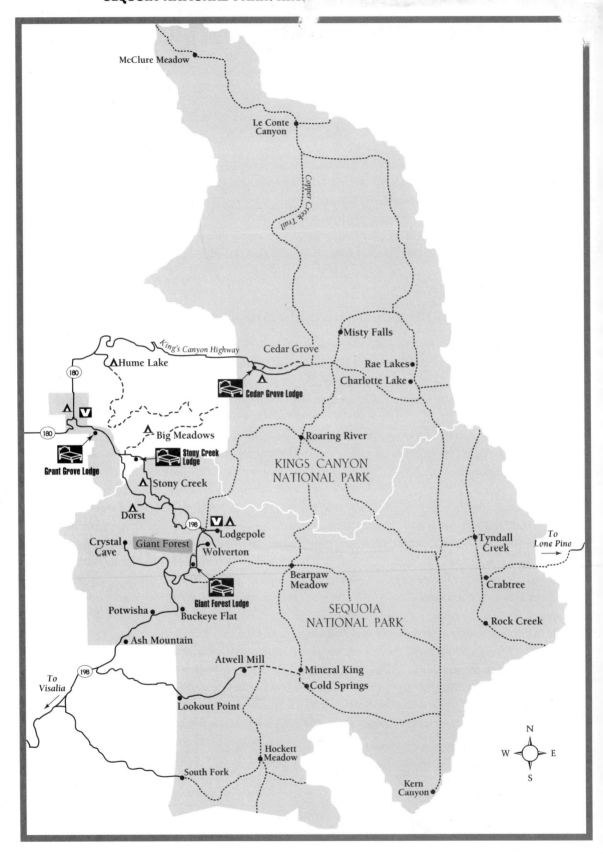

McClure Meadow

Le Conte Canyon

Copper Creek Trail

Misty Falls

King's Canyon Highway

Cedar Grove

Rae Lakes

Hume Lake

Charlotte Lake

Cedar Grove Lodge

Big Meadows

Roaring River

KINGS CANYON NATIONAL PARK

Stony Creek Lodge

Grant Grove Lodge

Stony Creek

Dorst

Lodgepole

Crystal Cave

Giant Forest

Wolverton

Tyndall Creek

To Lone Pine

Bearpaw Meadow

Crabtree

SEQUOIA NATIONAL PARK

Giant Forest Lodge

Potwisha

Buckeye Flat

Rock Creek

Ash Mountain

Atwell Mill

Mineral King

Cold Springs

To Visalia

Lookout Point

Hockett Meadow

N
W E
S

South Fork

Kern Canyon

*Also John Muir Lodge (KC), Wuksachi (Seq)*

# CEDAR GROVE LODGE

P.O. Box 909 • Kings Canyon National Park, CA 93633 • (209) 335–5500

*in the ? of KC*

*Cedar Grove Lodge*

Cedar Grove Lodge is a modern (1979) two-story wooden building in the isolated Cedar Grove area of Kings Canyon National Park. The lodge has the appearance of a ski chalet, with all eighteen rooms on the second floor. The bottom floor houses a combination market/gift shop, a cafe, and a small guest registration desk just inside the entrance to the market. The lodge sits among giant cedar and pine trees beside the South Fork of the Kings River. Picnic tables are scattered about the grounds, many near the river. A large, covered second-floor balcony provides a restful place to read and relax while viewing the surrounding tree-covered mountains and listening to the river roar. Another large deck area, one floor below on the same side of the building, has tables and chairs just outside the snack bar. Cedar Grove Lodge is 31 miles east of Grant Grove Village, 6 miles from the terminus of Kings Canyon Highway. The drive to Cedar Grove is probably the most scenic in either Sequoia or Kings Canyon and worth the time and effort even if you don't plan to stay at the lodge.

All of the modern, motel-type rooms at the lodge are identical in size and furnishings, with two queen beds and a private bath that includes a shower but no tub. One handicap-accessible room contains a bathtub. All of the rooms have heat and air conditioning but no telephone or television. Each room has a modest back window but no balcony. The rooms have plenty of space for two people and adequate room for a family of four. The rooms are all on the second floor and entered through a relatively narrow inside corridor that runs the length of the building between a ramp at one end and a wide stairway at the opposite end. Plentiful parking is in front and beside the lodge. Rooms 2 and 4 provide the best river views.

Cedar Grove is a very pleasant place to spend several days. The lodge is 2,000 feet lower and about twenty degrees warmer than Giant Forest and Grant Grove. It's also somewhat out of the way, near the end of a 30-mile road that leads into Cedar Grove. The remoteness reduces visitation to this area of the park so that Cedar Grove is not nearly as crowded as other, more popular locations. The cafe serves the usual sandwiches, fries, and soft drinks. It also offers other items including breakfasts, fried chicken, steak, and some Mexican dishes at fairly inexpensive prices. The market has a modest selection of essentials, such as milk, ice cream treats, beer, wine, fresh vegetables and fruits, and drugstore items. A small National Park Service visitor center is a short walk down the road and across the bridge. Park rangers conduct evening programs at the campground amphitheater.

- **ROOMS:** Doubles, triples, and quads. All rooms have private baths with showers. One handicap-accessible room has a bathtub.

- **RATES:** Doubles ($$$). Rates are quoted for two adults. Children under twelve are free unless an extra bed is requested.

- **LOCATION:** Cedar Grove Lodge is located 6 miles from the end of Highway 180, Kings Canyon Highway. It is 31 miles east of Grant Grove Village.

- **SEASON:** The lodge is open from mid-May through mid-October, depending on the weather.

- **FOOD:** The cafe ($) with fast food, beverages, and ice cream, is open from 7:00 A.M. to 9:00 P.M. Limited food items can be purchased in the market.

- **TRANSPORTATION:** Scheduled air service is available to Fresno, California, where cars may be rented.

- **FACILITIES:** Laundromat. Gift items are available in the market. A small National Park Service visitor center is a quarter-mile away.

- **ACTIVITIES:** Hiking, fishing, evening campfire programs, horseback riding.

*part of* →

## ~~GIANT FOREST LODGE~~ *the one torn down, Historic District in Sequoia*

P.O. Box 909 • Kings Canyon National Park, CA 93633 • (209) 565–3550

*AKA "Camp Sierra"*

Giant Forest Lodge is a complex of ten rustic wooden structures that provide a total of eighty-three rooms in a setting of giant trees, including sequoias, cedar, and white pine. The lodging buildings sit on a hill opposite Generals Highway from the registration office, market, and restaurant. The lodge offers older one-story motel buildings and a newer two-story lodge structure. Parking is down a hill from the buildings. Giant Forest offered cabins until the end of the 1996 season, when the old structures were closed due to a combination of safety, health, and environmental reasons. Giant Forest Village, located 16 miles north of the south park entrance, is the only lodging facility in Sequoia National Park.

Two types of accommodations are offered at Giant Forest Lodge. All rooms have heat and a full bath but no air conditioning, telephone, or television. One type of lodging is thirty-six Standard rooms with two queen beds, a sofabed, and a balcony. The second type of lodging, Kaweah rooms, are newer but rent for the same price. Many of these rooms require climbing numerous stairs.

*Kaweah Motel Units at Giant Forest Lodge*

Giant Forest Lodge is in an attractive setting for a vacation to view the big trees of Sequoia National Park. At an altitude of 6,500 feet, summer days are normally pleasant and nights are cool. The village offers everything you will require for a stay of several days, including a restaurant, two gift shops, a pizza pub, and a market with groceries. A small National Park Service information kiosk is located next to the registration building. A large visitor center is at Lodgepole, 4 miles north. Also at Lodgepole are a large market, a Laundromat, a mountain shop, a deli, a post office, and the Walter Fry Nature Center, which offers hands-on experience for children of all ages. A shuttle service (nominal fee charged) operates between Giant Forest and Lodgepole from early July to early September. The area around Giant Forest boasts many trails, including a paved self-guided trail of Round Meadow, where you can view a beautiful meadow area surrounded by giant sequoia trees. Two miles north of Giant Forest Village is the General Sherman Tree, the world's largest living thing. Near the village a short hike to Moro Rock presents a grand view of the sequoia landscape.

- **ROOMS:** Doubles, triples, and quads. All rooms have a private bath with a shower but no tub.

- **RATES:** All rooms ($$$). Rates are quoted for two adults. Children under twelve years are free unless an extra bed is required.

- **LOCATION:** Sixteen miles north of the south entrance to Sequoia National Park. Giant Forest Village is 4 miles south of the Lodgepole visitor center.

- **SEASON:** Giant Forest is open from mid-May through October.

- **FOOD:** A restaurant ($) across the road from the lodge offers a good selection of entrees, salads, and desserts. The restaurant is open for breakfast, lunch, and dinner. A market in the same building offers a limited selection of grocery items. A larger market and deli with similar merchandise are 4 miles north at Lodgepole.

- **TRANSPORTATION:** The nearest major air service is at Visalia, California, where rental cars are available.

- **FACILITIES:** A restaurant, gift shop, market, pizza pub, and National Park Service information kiosk are directly across the road from Giant Forest Lodge. Lodgepole, 4 miles north, has a post office, a deli, a mountain shop, a Laundromat, and a large National Park Service visitor center.

- **ACTIVITIES:** Hiking and fishing are the principal activities here. Guided mule and horse rides are offered 1 mile north of the General Sherman Tree. Tours are available into the Kings Canyon River Valley.

## Cabins
## GRANT GROVE LODGE

P.O. Box 909 • Kings Canyon National Park, CA 93633 • (209) 335–5500

*Rustic Cabin with Bath at Grant Grove Lodge*

Grant Grove Lodge encompasses fifty-two wood cabins grouped behind a small commercial center that houses the registration area, together with a restaurant, market, cocktail lounge, and gift shop. No guest rooms are in the registration building, although all the cabins are nearby. Most of the cabins sit on a hillside overlooking the road. A nice National Park Service visitor center is across the road. The Grant Grove area is busy, especially in summer, so expect heavy traffic from both vehicles and people. Most parking is close but not directly beside the cabins. Grant Grove Lodge is located 30 miles north of Giant Forest on a small peninsula of Kings Canyon that juts northwest from the northwest corner of Sequoia National Park. It is 3 miles from the Kings Canyon entrance on Highway 180 from Fresno, California.

Grant Grove offers three types of cabin accommodations, all quite rustic, with electricity and propane heat. The least expensive option is nineteen rustic sleeping cabins without bath. These older cabins have one double bed and one single bed in a stark bare interior. Guests must use a nearby central bathhouse; sheets, towels, and maid service are provided. One step up are twenty-four somewhat larger, rustic semi-housekeeping cabins without bath. These units have a double bed and a single bed, and an inside wood stove provides heat. Each cabin has a covered patio area with a picnic table and an outside wood stove for cooking. Again, guests must use a central bathhouse. Both the sleeping cabins and the semi-housekeeping cabins have very small windows and dark interiors.

The top accommodations at Grant Grove are nine cabins with bath that are much nicer and larger than cabins in the previous categories. These cabins have two double beds plus a single bed, nice furniture, a finished interior, and a private bathroom with a bathtub but no shower. These are constructed two to a building except for one freestanding unit (cabin 9). Although these cabins cost approximately twice as much as other cabins at Grant Grove, they are worth the difference.

Grant Grove is the main center of activity in Kings Canyon National Park. If you are looking for lots of people and rustic accommodations, this is the place. If you are looking for nice accommodations and quiet, then choose to stay down the road at Stony Creek Lodge or in Cedar Grove. These two alternatives are close enough that you can spend time browsing through the groves near Grant Grove and still enjoy a nice room at Stony Creek or Cedar Grove. On the other hand, Grant Grove does offer more facilities and activities. It is in the midst of an outstanding grove of giant trees. You will also find horseback riding, guided hikes, and evening programs. Winter activities, including cross-country skiing and snowshoeing, are also available. Equipment is available for rental at the market.

- **ROOMS:** Doubles and triples. Only the nine cabins in the top category have a private bath. Other guests must use a central bathhouse.

- **RATES:** Rustic sleeping cabins ($); rustic semi-housekeeping cabins ($); cabins with baths ($$). Rates quoted for two adults. Children under twelve are free unless an extra bed is requested.

- **LOCATION:** Three miles inside the entrance to Kings Canyon National Park on Highway 180.

- **SEASON:** Grant Grove Lodge is open year-round.

- **FOOD:** An attractive restaurant/coffee shop ($) is open daily from 7:00 A.M. to 9:00 P.M. (8:00 A.M. to 7:00 P.M. in winter) and within easy walking distance of all the cabins. Groceries are sold in a market.

- **TRANSPORTATION:** Scheduled air service is available to Fresno, California, where cars can be rented.

- **FACILITIES:** Restaurant/coffee shop, cocktail lounge (summer only), market, gift shop, post office, and National Park Service visitor center.

- **ACTIVITIES:** Horseback riding, hiking, and interpretive programs. During winter months snowshoeing and cross-country skiing are popular.

# STONY CREEK LODGE

HC 38, P.O. Box 500 • Sequoia National Park, CA 93262 • (209) 335–5500

*Three Rivers*

*Stony Creek Lodge*

Stony Creek Lodge is a cozy two-story river rock and wood building that offers only eleven guest rooms, all on the second floor. The first floor contains a registration desk, market and gift shop, restaurant, and attractive lobby area with a huge stone fireplace. The lodge is likely to remind world travelers of an intimate European hotel. Stony Creek Lodge is located just off Generals Highway, 15 miles north of Giant Forest Village. It is in Sequoia National Forest between Sequoia National Park and Kings Canyon National Park. Even though Stony Creek Lodge isn't within the park boundary, it is certainly a viable option for visitors to the parks. The lodge doesn't always fill, so you may be able to obtain a room without a reservation.

The eleven rooms in Stony Creek Lodge are of different sizes and different bedding. Some rooms have one queen bed or one double bed. Other rooms have either a queen or a double bed and a single bed. Two rooms have two single beds. All of the rooms have heat and a private bath but no air conditioning, telephone, or television. All but one of the rooms have a shower but no tub, while room 11 has two single beds and a tub. The second floor is accessed via either of two stairways, one in the lobby and the other at the opposite end of the building. Rooms are at both the front and the back of the building, with entrance through an interior hallway. No handicap access is available to the second floor, where all the rooms are located. Rooms on the parking side of the building can be noisy, so it is best to choose a room on the highway side. Plentiful parking is directly outside the building.

Surrounded by big pine, fir, and cedar trees, Stony Creek Lodge is a pleasant place to get away from the hustle and bustle common at other busy locations in Sequoia and Kings Canyon National Parks. You can spend the day driving through the park or roaming through the busy areas and then spend a quiet, restful night at this secluded spot. The location is especially convenient if you plan to spend one day in Sequoia and the next day in Kings Canyon. An attractive restaurant with two walls of windows and a vaulted ceiling serves three meals a day. A small market offers supplies, including a large selection of beer and wine, and some groceries. Nearby Stony Creek (the stream after which the lodge is named), a short downhill walk from the lodge, offers several small swimming holes to beat the summer heat. Many trailheads are near the lodge, including one that provides access to the Jenny Lake Wilderness Area.

- **ROOMS:** Doubles, triples, and one quad. All rooms have a private bath with a shower, but only one room has a bathtub.

- **RATES:** All rooms ($$$). Rates are quoted for two adults. Children under twelve are free unless an extra bed is required. Extra adults and children over twelve are charged $7.50 each.

- **LOCATION:** In Sequoia National Forest, 15 miles north of Giant Forest on Generals Highway. The lodge is just outside the northern boundary of Sequoia National Park.

- **SEASON:** Stony Creek Lodge is open May through Labor Day, depending on weather.

- **FOOD:** An attractive restaurant ($$/$$$) serves breakfast from 7:00 to 10:00 A.M., lunch from 11:00 A.M. to 4:00 P.M., and dinner from 5:00 to 9:00 P.M. Limited groceries, beer, and wine are available in the market.

- **TRANSPORTATION:** Scheduled airlines serve Fresno, California, where rental cars are available.

- **FACILITIES:** Restaurant, Laundromat, and a market with gifts, supplies, and groceries.

- **ACTIVITIES:** Fishing and hiking.

# YOSEMITE NATIONAL PARK

P.O. Box 577

Yosemite National Park, CA 95389

(209) 372–0200

Yosemite National Park is one of America's most beautiful and popular national parks. The park comprises 761,000 acres of scenic valleys, high country meadows, and granite peaks and domes. The scenery here is absolutely spectacular. The park is also very busy, especially during summer. The main activity area and most of the crowds are in Yosemite Valley. Yosemite is in east-central California, approximately 190 miles due east of San Francisco.

##  Lodging in Yosemite National Park

Yosemite has seven lodging facilities, four of which are in busy Yosemite Valley. These include The Ahwahnee, Yosemite Lodge, Curry Village, and Housekeeping Camp. Accommodations in the valley range from the upscale and expensive Ahwahnee to downscale and relatively inexpensive tent cabins. Outside the valley the Wawona Hotel is a wonderful old hotel near the park's south entrance. Two separate facilities, Tuolumne Meadows Lodge and White Wolf Lodge, offer canvas tent cabins and a few wood cabins on Tioga Pass. Yosemite is packed during summer months, so make reservations at the earliest possible date. Accommodations with private bath are often booked ten to twelve months in advance.

- **RESERVATIONS:** A central reservation office services all the lodging facilities in Yosemite National Park. For reservations write or call Yosemite Reservations, 5410 East Home Avenue, Fresno, CA 93727. Phone (209) 252–4848. Reservations may be made up to a year and a day in advance. Cancellation with a full refund requires a seventy-two-hour notice.

- **TRANSPORTATION:** Scheduled air service is available to Fresno, where cars can be rented. Amtrak serves Yosemite Valley through a combination train-bus service. A free shuttle bus system within Yosemite Valley serves all the lodges and other popular points of interest.

*Reservations for all Yosemite lodging can be made up to 366 days prior to your intended arrival date. For a summer stay in The Ahwahnee, Yosemite Lodge, and Wawona Hotel, it is not a bad idea to make reservations on the first possible day—that is, a year and a day before your stay will begin. If this isn't possible and the hotels are fully booked when you call, call again 30, 15, or 7 days prior to your arrival, when previous reservations by others are most likely to be canceled. Another possibility is to take a chance and stop by the front desk at any of the seven hotels and place your name on a waiting list for canceled rooms. Keep in mind that the tent cabins at Curry Village can often be reserved with only a couple of weeks' notice.*

# YOSEMITE NATIONAL PARK

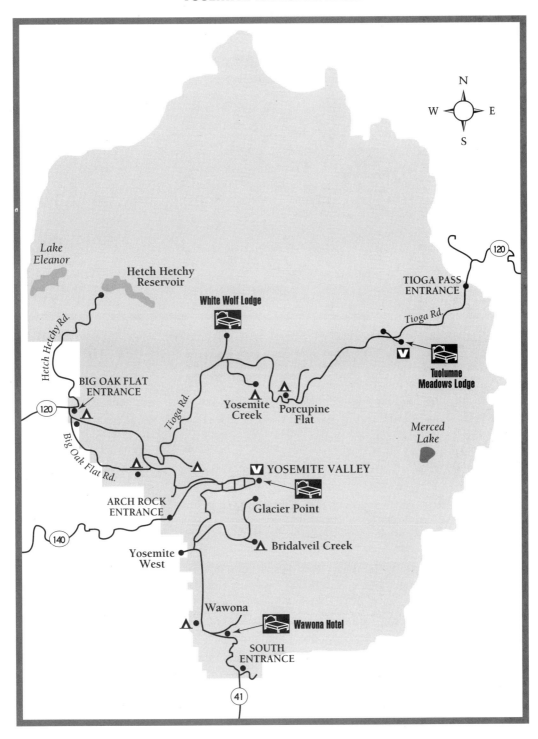

Lake Eleanor

Hetch Hetchy Reservoir

White Wolf Lodge

Hetch Hetchy Rd.

BIG OAK FLAT ENTRANCE

120

Big Oak Flat Rd.

Tioga Rd.

Yosemite Creek

Porcupine Flat

TIOGA PASS ENTRANCE

Tioga Rd.

Tuolumne Meadows Lodge

Merced Lake

ARCH ROCK ENTRANCE

140

YOSEMITE VALLEY

Glacier Point

Bridalveil Creek

Yosemite West

Wawona

Wawona Hotel

SOUTH ENTRANCE

41

N
W E
S

# YOSEMITE NATIONAL PARK—YOSEMITE VALLEY

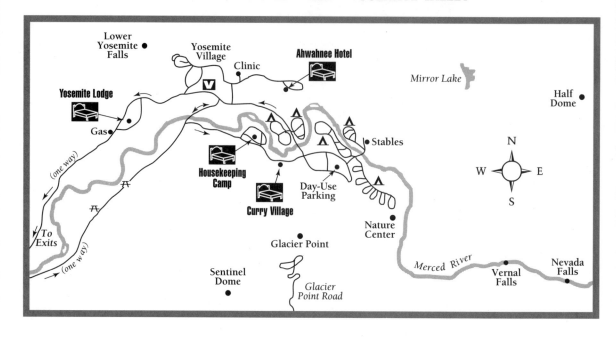

## YOSEMITE VALLEY LODGING

Yosemite Valley has four very different lodging facilities that range from tents to what is probably the most elegant hotel in any national park. A free shuttle stops at each facility as well as other major points of interest in the valley. The valley is congested, so plan on parking your vehicle and using the shuttle.

### THE AHWAHNEE

Yosemite National Park, CA 95389 • (209) 372–1407

Many travelers argue that The Ahwahnee in Yosemite Valley is the finest lodging facility at any national park. It is difficult to dispute the claim. The Ahwahnee, built in the late 1920s with a name that Native Americans gave to what is now Yosemite Valley, is both a National Historic Landmark and a world-class facility. Best of all, it has a personality that makes you comfortable at the same time as you look around in wonderment. Everything about this granite and wood six-story hotel makes you want to stay, except perhaps the cost, which is rivaled only by Death Valley's Furnace Creek Inn. The Great Lounge, with a beamed ceiling, stained glass windows, and two of the largest stone fireplaces you will ever see, is a jewel. The spectacular dining room, with its 34-foot-tall vaulted beamed ceiling and floor-to-ceiling windows, is one of the most beautiful you will ever enter. Native American baskets, paintings, and rugs are placed throughout the public rooms. The Ahwahnee offers a total of 123 rooms in both the main hotel building and several nearby

*The Ahwahnee Hotel*

secluded cottages. The Ahwahnee is located in the northeast section of Yosemite Valley, at the base of the Royal Arches. The location is remote enough to avoid most of the congestion that typifies much of the valley. Adequate parking is nearby, and valet parking is available. Bellhops will assist with luggage.

The Ahwahnee offers two types of lodging. The main hotel has ninety-nine rooms on six floors. Most rooms have one king bed, while a few have two double beds. The rooms are nicely furnished, with matching chair and love seat, television, telephone, refrigerator, and full bath. Four elegant parlor rooms are available for guests who wish to convert their regular room into a suite. A large window in each room offers different views depending on the room location; the best views are from corner rooms that have windows on two sides. The Ahwahnee has eight separate but nearby buildings that house a total of twenty-four recently redecorated cottages. Most cottages have one king bed, while five have two double beds. The single-story cottages are in a secluded and quiet wooded area near the hotel but away from the hotel traffic. The interi-

The Ahwahnee is famous for The Bracebridge Dinner, a three-hour Christmas pageant and feast that is presented five times each season, on December 22, Christmas Eve, and Christmas Day. The pageant, which is adapted from Washington Irving's "Sketch Book" of a Christmas Day in 1718 at Squire Bracebridge's Old English Manor, is held in The Ahwahnee's main dining room. The event is so popular—60,000 requests are made for a total of 1,675 seats—that seats are allocated by lottery. Applications for the lottery can be obtained by writing Yosemite Concession Services Corporation, 5410 East Home Avenue, Fresno, CA 93727. Applications are accepted from December 1 through January 15 for the following year's dinner.

ors, which are larger than the hotel rooms, are beautifully decorated to highlight Yosemite's Native American heritage. While many frequent Ahwahnee guests request the cottages, first-time visitors should choose a room in the main hotel in order to fully appreciate the delight of staying overnight in this outstanding facility.

The Ahwahnee offers fine lodging in a beautiful setting. If you can afford it, it is a wonderful place to spend a week while exploring the beauty and enjoying the many activities offered by Yosemite National Park. If you can't, try to schedule at least one night's lodging in this unique hotel. Walk through the lobby into the Great Lounge, where afternoon tea accompanied by background piano music is an Ahwahnee tradition. On through the lounge past the second fireplace provides entry to the Solarium, whose massive windows furnish a sweeping view of a grassy area surrounded by trees with a background of granite cliffs. The hotel also offers a cocktail lounge, a sweetshop, a swimming pool, tennis courts, and a very nice gift shop. A free bus shuttle operates throughout Yosemite Valley, so that activities and facilities in other locations are only a few minutes away.

- **ROOMS:** Singles, doubles, triples, and quads. All rooms have a full bath.

- **RATES:** Hotel rooms ($$$$$); parlor ($$$$$); cottages ($$$$$). Children twelve and under stay free in the same room with an adult. A variety of packages are offered.

- **LOCATION:** North section of Yosemite Valley, at the end of a dead-end road.

- **SEASON:** The Ahwahnee is open year-round. It is often fully booked a year ahead for busy periods such as holidays and summer months.

- **FOOD:** An elegant dining room ($$$$$) serves breakfast, lunch (light lunch from 2:30 to 3:30 P.M.), and dinner until 10:00 P.M. Dinner requires reservations and appropriate attire; athletic clothing is not allowed. A Sunday buffet is served from 7:00 A.M. to 3:00 P.M. The cocktail lounge ($$$$) serves sandwiches and salads daily from 3:30 to 10:00 P.M. Room service is available.

- **FACILITIES:** Swimming pool, tennis courts, gift shop, tour desk, cocktail lounge, sweet-shop, and concierge service.

- **ACTIVITIES:** Hiking, swimming, tennis, evening programs, guided hotel tours.

# CURRY VILLAGE

Yosemite National Park, CA 45389 • (209) 372–8333

*Cabins without Baths at Curry Village*

Curry Village is the largest lodging complex in Yosemite Valley, with a total of 628 rooms, mostly in canvas tents. The term *village* is certainly appropriate for this facility, because Curry is much like a small town, with tents, cabins, cafeteria, fast-food restaurants, camp store, sitting lodge building, post office (summer only), shower building, restrooms, and big crowds of people. People are everywhere. The location, in the southeast section of Yosemite Valley, is near several campgrounds and a convenient place for campers to roam and eat.

Curry Village offers four types of accommodations. The least expensive lodging is 427 canvas tent cabins with a wooden platform and canvas walls and roof. These units are available in different sizes, with a variety of bedding options that range from two singles to a double and three singles. The bedding consists of metal cots, with linens, towels, soap, and maid service provided. A padlock is available for the front door. A light is in each tent, although there are no electrical outlets, heat, or plumbing. Restroom and shower facilities are centrally located.

Curry Village also has 183 wooden cabins, 103 of which have private baths, mostly with showers but no tubs. The remaining cabins have no bath or running water. Cabins with a bath are older and have electric heat and a porch. Some units have one double bed, while others have a double and single or two doubles. Units 61A and 61B are the nicest of these units, and both are handicap accessible. Cabins without a bath all have propane heat and two double beds. These cabins have interior paneling and are nicer than the more expensive cabins with a bath. Curry Village also has three deluxe cabins, which contain a living room, a bathroom, and one or two bedrooms. These deluxe cabins sleep from two to four persons; they are by far the nicest lodging facilities at Curry Village. A single motel-type building provides a total of eighteen standard rooms with a private bath that has a shower but no tub. These units have heat and a ceiling fan. Bedding ranges from one double to three doubles; the three double beds are in units with a loft.

Lodging facilities at Curry Village are tightly packed. Basically, this is a low-cost alternative to The Ahwahnee and Yosemite Lodge. The many tent cabins are the cheapest of Yosemite's overnight offerings outside the campgrounds. That Curry includes a variety of eating facilities makes it a handy center of operations. Food options include a cafeteria, a sandwich shop, a pizza patio, and an ice cream shop. Evening programs are presented at an outside amphitheater. Curry is served by the free shuttle service that will transport you to other areas of the valley. The decision on whether to stay here depends on how much you are willing to spend, how well you tolerate noise and crowds, and what lodging facilities are available when your reservation is made.

Yosemite National Park is open all year, and many people prefer to visit in winter. Yosemite Valley generally experiences moderate winter weather while the park's Badger Pass Ski Area receives an average snowfall of 180 inches. Winter activities include ice skating (outdoor rink at Curry Village) and cross-country skiing (ski rental at Curry Village). A sightseeing tour of Yosemite Valley is also available in winter months. Badger Pass, located 23 miles from Yosemite Valley, has four chair lifts and one cable tow to serve nine ski runs. Ninety miles of marked cross-country ski trails begin here.

- **ROOMS:** Doubles, triples, and quads; a few units will hold five or six persons. Most rooms, including all the tent cabins, do not have private baths.

- **RATES:** Canvas tent cabins ($); cabins without bath ($$); cabins with bath ($$$); deluxe cabins ($$$$/$$$$$); standard motel-type rooms ($$$).

- **LOCATION:** Southeast side of Yosemite Valley.

- **SEASON:** All of the lodging facilities in Curry Village are open spring through fall. Some of them are also open during the winter.

- **FOOD:** A cafeteria ($) serves three meals a day from spring through fall. Pizza, hamburgers, and ice cream are available from 8:00 A.M. to 8:00 P.M. at small fast-food stands. A bar is open from noon to 9:00 P.M.

- **FACILITIES:** Gift shop, mountain shop, bicycle rental and river raft rental stands, camp store, outdoor swimming pool, and post office (summer only). In winter an outside ice-skating rink is available and equipment for cross-country skiing can be rented.

- **ACTIVITIES:** River rafting, hiking, bicycling, swimming, and evening programs. Cross-country skiing and ice skating in winter.

# HOUSEKEEPING CAMP

Yosemite National Park, CA 95389 • (209) 372–8338

*Housekeeping Camp*

ousekeeping Camp is a complex of 266 concrete and canvas guest rooms surrounding several larger wooden structures that provide support facilities, such as a registration desk, a Laundromat, and common bathrooms and showers. Rooms are built two to a unit, with the back of each room sharing a concrete wall with another identical room. The rooms are constructed of cement on three sides (each two-room unit has concrete walls constructed in an H pattern), with a canvas entry and a canvas roof that extends over a concrete floor and a front concrete patio area that has a food storage locker, a picnic table, and a cooking shelf. A metal grill for charbroiling is on the ground outside each patio area. A privacy fence constructed of branches surrounds the front of each room. The canvas entry door cannot be secured, which means that you must leave valuables locked in your vehicle.

Each room contains one double bed and two fold-down bunk beds. The interior also has a mirror, an electric light, and electrical outlets. None of the rooms have a private bathroom, so guests are required to use centrally located bathhouses. Guests must supply their own sheets, blankets, and pillows, although the latter two items can be rented at the registration building. Soap and towels for bathing are supplied without charge in the common bathhouses. The dozen or so housekeeping units on the bank of the Merced River are the best choice. Other units have little in the way of privacy or a view.

Housekeeping Camp rooms represent national park lodging at its most basic. These relatively inexpensive rooms are preferable in Yosemite Valley only to the tightly packed tent cabins in Curry Village. No eating facilities are available here, although a camp store is near the registration building. Housekeeping Camp does have showers and a Laundromat. This is a stop on the free shuttle so that guests can ride to other valley locations for food and frolic.

- **ROOMS:** The rooms are identical, with beds for four persons. Two additional cots can be rented. None of the rooms have a private bath.

- **RATES:** One to four persons pay the same price ($); each additional person is $4.00.

- **LOCATION:** On the bank of the Merced River in the southeast section of Yosemite Valley, a short distance west of Curry Village.

- **SEASON:** Spring to mid-October.

- **FOOD:** No restaurant or snack bar is at Housekeeping Camp. A small market has limited groceries. A variety of restaurants and snack facilities can be reached via the free valley shuttle.

- **FACILITIES:** Small market, shower, and Laundromat.

- **ACTIVITIES:** River rafting, swimming, and hiking.

## YOSEMITE LODGE

Yosemite National Park, CA 95389 • (209) 372–1274

*Lodge Rooms at Yosemite Lodge*

Yosemite Lodge is a large complex of wooden buildings that provide five very different categories of overnight guest facilities, including two types of cabins, two types of one- and two-story motel units, and several one- and two-story lodge units. Some of these units have private bathrooms, and some do not. In all, Yosemite Lodge provides a total of 249 rooms. The units are scattered about a service area that includes the registration building, located just north of the main road. A variety of other stores and restaurants are near the registration building and within easy walking distance of any of the guest rooms. Registration parking is directly in front of the registration building, but overnight guest parking is a distance from some of the rooms. Bellhops are available to assist with luggage. Yosemite Lodge is located in the northwest section of Yosemite Valley, near the foot of Yosemite Falls.

None of the rooms at Yosemite Lodge have television or air conditioning, and the cabins do not have telephones. Other amenities vary.

Standard rooms constructed in the late 1950s all have a private bath, most with a tub-shower combination. Bedding in these rooms varies from one double bed to two queen beds. These motel-type rooms each have heat and telephones but no balconies or patios. Although the buildings are situated in a nice shady area, the views are minimal. This group includes eight extra-large "family" rooms that each contain one double bed and four single beds and rent for the same price as other standard rooms.

Fourteen newer one- and two-story buildings constructed in the middle to late 1960s contain 226 lodge rooms that each have a dressing area, a balcony or patio, a telephone, and additional furniture including a desk, a table, three chairs, and a nightstand. Two chairs and a table are on the patio. These units each have a full bath. The three newest of the lodge buildings in a nice shaded area are Aspen, Dogwood, and Tamarack. Rooms 621–624 offer a fairly good view of Upper Yosemite Falls; most of the other rooms have views obstructed by trees and bushes. Two of the fourteen buildings are scheduled for removal.

> A variety of tours are offered to Yosemite visitors. These include the two-hour Valley Floor Tour, the four-hour Glacier Point Tour, the Mariposa Grove Tour, the Big Trees Tram Tour, the Tuolumne Meadows Hikers' Bus, and the full-day Grand Tour, which combines the Glacier Point and Mariposa Grove Tours with a lunch at the Wawona Hotel. Most tours depart from Yosemite Lodge. Tickets can be purchased at several locations in the valley. Call (209) 372–1240 for information.

Yosemite Lodge is a busy location that serves as a center of facilities and activities. The complex sits in front of scenic Yosemite Falls. Food service, with a cafeteria and two restaurants, is more varied than other locations in Yosemite Valley. You will also find an ice cream stand, an Environmental shop, a gift shop, and a cocktail lounge. A tour desk is inside the registration building. The free shuttle stops across the street from the registration building and provides access to all the facilities and activities in the valley.

- **ROOMS:** Doubles, triples, and quads, with six persons in a limited number of rooms. About half the cabins and most rooms have private baths.

- **RATES:** Rooms without baths ($$); standard rooms ($$$); lodge rooms ($$$$).

- **LOCATION:** In the northwest section of Yosemite Valley, near the double waterfall.

- **SEASON:** Yosemite Lodge is open year-round.

- **FOOD:** A cafeteria ($) is open for breakfast, lunch, and dinner. The Garden Terrace ($$) offers a moderately priced buffet. The Mountain Room Restaurant ($$$$) serves upscale dinners with an excellent view of Yosemite Falls. The ice cream stand ($) is open from noon until 5:00 P.M. Limited food service is offered in the Mountain Room Lounge during afternoons.

- ■ **FACILITIES:** Gift shops, cafeteria, restaurants, cocktail lounge, branch post office, service station, bicycle rental, tour desk, swimming pool, outdoor amphitheater.

- ■ **ACTIVITIES:** Evening programs, swimming, biking, hiking.

# LODGING OUTSIDE YOSEMITE VALLEY

Three lodging facilities in Yosemite National Park are outside the busy valley. The Wawona Hotel sits alone near the south entrance from Fresno. Tuolumne Meadows Lodge and White Wolf Lodge are on Tioga Pass, which crosses the Sierra.

## WAWONA HOTEL

P.O. Box 2005 • Wawona, CA 95389 • (209) 375–6556

The Wawona (an Indian term meaning "big tree") Hotel is the grande dame of the national parks. While some would argue that Death Valley's Furnace Creek Inn and Yosemite's own Ahwahnee are more elegant, the Wawona is without doubt one of the grandest, and it is probably the oldest lodging facility in any national park. The Wawona Hotel is a complex of six white frame buildings, the oldest of which was constructed in 1876. The newest of the buildings was built in 1918. The complex is similar in appearance to a late-1800s western military post. The Wawona Hotel is 4 miles inside the south entrance to Yosemite National Park and 25 miles south of popular Yosemite Valley. No public transportation operates between the hotel and Yosemite Valley.

The six buildings at Wawona offer a total of 104 rooms. Each of the buildings contains overnight lodging rooms, although the size of the buildings and the rooms within them vary considerably. The main building, which houses registration, a large dining room, and an attractive lounge area, has twenty-eight rooms, all on the second floor. Both floors of this large, two-story, white frame building have an impressive wraparound veranda with white railings and posts. Wicker benches, chairs, and tables on the lower veranda offer a place for guests to relax while viewing the grassy front lawn that surrounds a stone fountain. Beverages are served here during the afternoon and early evening. The other five buildings are smaller but have a similar architectural style.

Although rooms vary by size, view, and building, only two price categories are used: with or without private bath. Fifty of the 104 rooms have a private bath and rent for about $30 per night more than rooms without a private bath. Guests in rooms without private bath must use community shower and bathroom facilities located in three of the buildings. Community bathrooms, accessed from the outside porches, are a distance from some of the rooms. Nearly all the rooms in the main building are relatively small and without a private bathroom.

*Main Hotel Building at Wawona*

Views vary, with some rooms providing a scenic view toward the front lawn and others in an inside hallway having no view at all. Since the view is not considered in the rate, request a room in the front with a view of the lawn.

If staying in the main building isn't important, request a room in one-story Clark Cottage. This building sits directly beside the main building, and its rooms are the nicest at Wawona. All the rooms in Clark Cottage have a ceiling fan and private bath. Two-story Washburn Cottage has a total of sixteen rooms, all with queen beds. The upstairs rooms have an interior hallway that causes them to be somewhat smaller than downstairs rooms, and these rooms do not have a veranda. Moore Cottage, with nine rooms, sits on a hill directly behind the main hotel building, with private parking next to the building. Two of these rooms have private baths. The upstairs rooms are smaller and do not have a veranda. This is the only building in which children are not allowed. White Cottage has only three rooms, two with private baths. The third room, room 51, must use bathrooms in the Annex. The two-story Annex has thirty-nine rooms, all of which enjoy a veranda. Two handicap-accessible rooms are in this building. All of the buildings are clustered closely together, so there should be no concern about the walking distance to the restaurant or lounge.

The Wawona Hotel is a peaceful alternative to lodging facilities in busy Yosemite Valley. The dining room retains its Victorian flavor with tall windows offering views out the front and side of the main building. Outside tables are also available. Although officially called a hotel, the Wawona is actually more of a resort. The hotel has a swimming pool, a tennis court, and a nine-hole golf course. A practice putting green is on the hotel's front lawn. The hotel sits adjacent to Pioneer Village, a collection of historic buildings that introduce visitors to some of the events shaping Yosemite's history. Included are a covered bridge, horse-drawn coaches, a homestead, and numerous other historic buildings. A free shuttle bus operates between the hotel and Mariposa Grove, the site of many giant sequoia trees.

- **ROOMS:** Mostly doubles, with a few triples and quads. About half the rooms have private baths. Rooms with private bath are often fully booked a year ahead during the busy seasons. Previous guests often request particular rooms, so be as specific as possible about the type and location of the room you want.

- **RATES:** Rooms without private baths ($$$); rooms with private baths ($$$$). Rates are quoted for two adults. Additional persons are $12.50 extra. Children under twelve years are free. Several vacation packages are offered for fall and winter.

- **LOCATION:** Four miles north of the south entrance to Yosemite National Park. The hotel is approximately 25 miles from Yosemite Valley.

- **SEASON:** Open Easter through the Thanksgiving holiday. Also open during Christmas holidays and from Thursday noon to Sunday noon January through March.

- **FOOD:** A beautiful dining room ($$$/$$$$) in the main building serves three meals a day. A continental breakfast is served from 10:00 to 11:00 A.M. A buffet only is offered for lunch. During the summer months an old-fashioned barbecue is served on Saturday night. A snack shop at the golf shop in the Annex offers sandwiches and beverages from spring to fall. A market with limited groceries is a short walk from the hotel.

- **FACILITIES:** Swimming pool, tennis court, nine-hole golf course, putting green, market, gift shop, post office, gas station, historic Pioneer Village.

- **ACTIVITIES:** Golf, tennis, horse rides, swimming, fishing, and hiking.

## TUOLUMNE MEADOWS LODGE

Yosemite National Park, CA 95389 • (209) 372–8413

Tuolumne Meadows Lodge is a group of sixty-nine canvas tent cabins situated high in the Sierras. The lodge offers stays of up to seven days and is an attractive location for individuals who plan to hike to other camps in the High Sierra Loop. Tuolumne Meadows also attracts people who want to avoid the crowds of Yosemite Valley. The tents sit on a hill to the east of a canvas lodge that houses the registration area and a dining room. The lodge is located about a mile off Tioga Road, 9 miles from the Tioga Pass Entrance on the east side of Yosemite National Park. It is 52 miles from Yosemite Valley.

The sixty-nine tents at Tuolumne Meadows are virtually identical to those at Curry Village in the valley. These tents are erected on a cement slab, and each unit has an inside wood stove for heat. Each canvas tent is equipped with either four single beds or one double bed plus two single beds. Sheets, pillows, and blankets are provided. The lodge also has maid service. The tents have no electricity or plumbing, so guests must use a common bathhouse with showers. Guests are also provided with candles for light, wood for the stove, and towels for the bathhouse. A large central parking lot is a moderate walk from many of the tent cabins.

*Tent Cabin at Tuolumne Meadows Lodge*

Tuolumne Meadows Lodge is in a lovely area of Yosemite National Park and is appropriate for someone who doesn't mind roughing it a little. The tent cabins sit near the Tuolumne River's Dana Fork, which runs through the largest subalpine meadow in the Sierra Nevada. No cooking or picnicking is permitted in or near the tent cabins. The nearby restaurant serves regular breakfast items and five or six dinner entrees at reasonable prices. Beer and wine are also available. Other facilities are available at Tuolumne Meadows Store, about 2 miles away on Tioga Road.

- **ROOMS:** Doubles, triples, and quads. No rooms have private baths.
- **RATES:** All tent cabins ($). Price is quoted for two adults. Additional adults are $6.50, and an additional child is $3.50.
- **LOCATION:** One mile south of Tioga Road, 9 miles west of the Tioga Pass entrance.
- **SEASON:** Late spring to early fall. Season depends on the weather.
- **FOOD:** A dining room ($$/$$$) in the registration/dining tent serves breakfast and dinner. Reservations are required for dinner. Fast food is available at Tuolumne Meadows Grill ($) from 7:30 A.M. to 6:00 P.M. The grill is 2 miles away on Tioga Road.
- **TRANSPORTATION:** No public transportation is available to the lodge.
- **FACILITIES:** Minimal gifts and necessities are sold near the registration desk. Tuolumne Meadows Store has a post office, market, gas station, climbing school, and stable.
- **ACTIVITIES:** Hiking, fishing, horseback riding, and rock climbing.

# WHITE WOLF LODGE

*Wooden Cabins at White Wolf Lodge*

Yosemite National Park 95389 • (209) 372–8416

White Wolf Lodge consists of a wooden registration/dining building that sits beside four wood cabins and in front of twenty-four canvas tent cabins. A central bathhouse with showers is located in the middle of the tent cabins. The lodge appeals primarily to people who want to get away from it all, especially the congestion of Yosemite Valley. White Wolf Lodge is at an altitude of 6,700 feet at an isolated location in the High Sierra just off Tioga Road. The lodge is approximately 30 miles east of Yosemite Valley.

The lodge has four wood cabins, each with two double beds, a wood-burning stove, electricity, and a full bath. The cabins have a small front porch and are built as duplexes. Parking is directly in front of the buildings, and the dining room is next door. The tent cabins at White Wolf Lodge are identical to the cabins described for Tuolumne Meadows Lodge. Each tent contains a wood stove, with wood provided.

White Wolf Lodge provides solitude in an attractive outdoor environment. This is a good place to meet other guests, because there are not many activities to divert their attention. The cozy restaurant has a stone fireplace and serves breakfast and dinner in small inside and outside dining areas.

- ■ **ROOMS:** Doubles, triples, and quads. Full bathrooms are only in the four wood cabins. A community bathhouse is available for guests in the tent cabins.

- ■ **RATES:** Tent cabins ($). Rate quoted for two adults. Additional adults are $6.50 each; additional child is $3.50. Wood cabins with private bath ($$). Rate quoted for one to four persons.

- **LOCATION:** Just north of Tioga Road, 30 miles east of Yosemite Valley.

- **SEASON:** Late spring to early fall, depending on the weather.

- **FOOD:** A small dining room ($$/$$$) serves regular breakfast items and four to five dinner entrees. Reservations are required for dinner.

- **TRANSPORTATION:** No public transportation is provided to White Wolf Lodge.

- **FACILITIES:** Small store and restaurant. Central bathhouse with showers.

- **ACTIVITIES:** Hiking.

# COLORADO

## MESA VERDE NATIONAL PARK

Mesa Verde National Park, CO 81330
(303) 529–4461 or 529–4475

Mesa Verde National Park comprises 52,000 acres, including the most notable and best-preserved pre-Columbian cliff dwellings in the United States. Your first stop should be the Far View Visitor Center, which is 15 miles from the park entrance. Mesa Verde National Park is in the southwestern corner of Colorado, 36 miles west of Durango on U.S. Highway 160. The park's entrance road from U.S. Highway 160 has steep grades and sharp curves. Trailers must be dropped off 4 miles inside the entrance, near the campground.

###  Lodging in Mesa Verde National Park

Mesa Verde has only a single lodging facility, which provides a total of 150 rooms in seventeen motel-style buildings. Far View Lodge is 15 miles from the park entrance station, near Far View Visitor Center and Far View Terrace. None of the park ruins are within walking distance of the lodge.

# MESA VERDE NATIONAL PARK

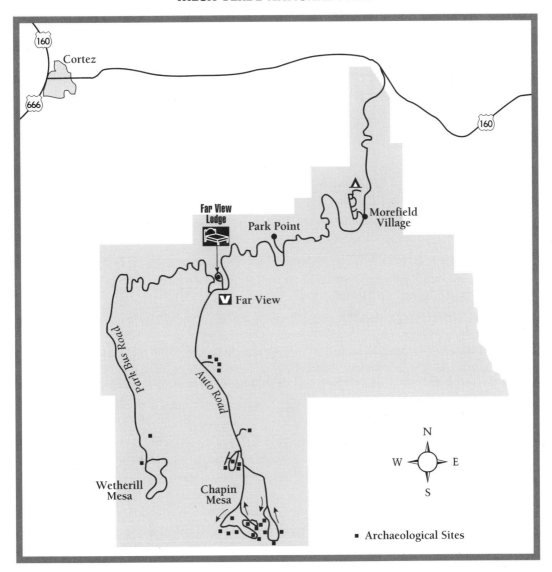

## FAR VIEW LODGE

P.O. Box 277 • Mancos, CO 81328 • (970) 529–4421

Far View Lodge features an attractive adobe building housing the registration desk, a dining room, a gift shop, and a cocktail lounge, with seventeen separate but nearby motel-type wooden buildings, each with from four to twenty rooms that generally offer great views. The lodge is 15 miles inside the park entrance, near the Far View Visitor Center. Paved roads near the lodge lead to the park ruins.

Far View Lodge is situated at 8,250 feet on a shoulder of the Mesa Verde. It provides an outstanding view of up to 100 miles and three states, Colorado, New Mexico, and Arizona (hence the name). The lodge offers 150 rooms that are virtually identical in every respect

*A Four-Unit Building at Far View Lodge*

other than the view and the bedding. Guests have a choice of one queen or two double beds, and each room has a bath with shower but no tub. Each room has heat and a clock radio but no telephone, television, or air conditioning.

All of the seventeen lodge buildings are one-level except for two that are two-story. The back of each room has a large window and a private balcony with two chairs. The buildings are situated on a hillside so that all the rooms offer a view of mesas and canyons. All rooms have at least a good view, but some are better than others. The best views are in rooms 131 through 140 (nonsmoking) and 111 through 120 (smoking). All these rooms are on the second floor of a two-story building. Adequate parking is available directly outside each building. A number of rooms are handicap accessible. Small pets are permitted, but a deposit is required.

Far View Lodge is ideally situated for visitors to Mesa Verde National Park. It is a short distance off the main road to Wetherill and Chapin Mesas, a quiet but handy location because most guests plan to visit both these areas. A quarter-mile paved trail from the lodge leads to the park's main visitor center, which contains exhibits of both prehistoric and historic Indians of the region, including native jewelry and pottery. Tickets for ranger-guided tours of Cliff Palace, Balcony House, and Long House can be purchased in the visitor center. Another quarter-mile along the same trail brings visitors to the Far View Terrace, which offers a cafeteria, gift shop, and gas station. Guided half-day and full-day bus tours of the park begin at the lodge, where tickets can be purchased. A small gift shop, a very nice restaurant (dinner only), and a lounge are located in the main registration building.

- **ROOMS:** Doubles, triples, and quads. Rates are quoted for two adults. All rooms have private baths with shower but no bathtub.

- **RESERVATIONS:** Far View Lodge, P.O. Box 277, Mancos, CO 81328. Phone (800) 449–2288; fax (970) 529–4411. Deposit required for one night's lodging. Cancellation notice of seventy-two hours required for refund of deposit.

- **RATES:** High-season from mid-June to early October ($$$); off-season from late April to mid-June and from early October to mid-October ($$). Rates are quoted for two adults. Extra persons each pay $6.00 per night. Children twelve and under stay free with adults.

- **LOCATION:** Fifteen miles inside the entrance to Mesa Verde National Park. The nearest major town is Cortez, Colorado, 10 miles west of the park entrance.

- **SEASON:** Far View Lodge is open from late April to the middle of October.

- **FOOD:** The registration building houses the attractively decorated Metate Room, which serves excellent dinners ($$/$$$). Many of the tables are situated to take advantage of the great view outside a wall of windows. Alcoholic beverages are served in the dining room and at a lounge on the second floor. A half-mile away Far View Terrace offers three meals a day ($) in a nice cafeteria. A small cafeteria offers breakfast and lunch ($) at Spruce Tree Terrace, and the Knife Edge Cafe offers snacks ($) all day at Morefield Village.

- **TRANSPORTATION:** Scheduled air service serves Cortez and Durango, where rental cars are available. The nearest train service is at Grand Junction, Colorado.

- **FACILITIES:** Dining room, gift shop, cocktail lounge. Eleven miles away Morefield Village has a Laundromat, gift shop, snack bar, gas station, and store with groceries, beer, wine, and camping supplies. A gas station (with diesel fuel), gift shop, and cafeteria are at Far View Terrace.

- **ACTIVITIES:** Full- and half-day guided tours of Mesa Verde Indian ruins originate from Far View Lodge. Ranger-guided tours of Cliff Palace, Balcony House, and Long House require tickets, which can be purchased at the visitor center. Chapin Mesa Museum offers Indian exhibits. Evening campground programs are presented at Morefield Campground. A multimedia tour of Mesa Verde (fee charged) is offered four times each evening at Far View Lodge. Brochures for self-guiding tours of the Ruins Road can be purchased at the visitor center. Trails of from 1.5 to nearly 8 miles are available for hikers.

*The Durango & Silverton Narrow Gauge Railroad offers scenic full-day train trips from Durango, Colorado, to the historic mining town of Silverton and back on tracks originally laid in the early 1880s. The authentic coal-burning, steam-powered locomotives were manufactured in the early 1920s for the Durango and Rio Grande Railroad. This is one of the finest historic train trips in the United States. Reservations are recommended. Write Durango & Silverton Narrow Gauge Railroad Company, 479 Main Avenue, Durango, CO 81301, or phone (970) 247–2733.*

# FLORIDA

## EVERGLADES NATIONAL PARK

40001 State Road 9336
Homestead, FL 33034
(305) 242–7700

Everglades National Park comprises more than 1.5 million acres of subtropical wilderness, including extensive freshwater and saltwater areas, open prairies, and mangrove forests. A large portion of the park is covered by a giant river only a few inches deep and 50 miles wide. A 38-mile paved road from the entrance station to Flamingo, the most developed portion of the park, provides access to numerous walking trails. The park is located across the southern tip of Florida, with main access from State Highway 9336. The entrance is 11 miles south of Florida City.

###  Lodging in Everglades National Park

The park's lodging consists of a single motel-style facility and cabins at Flamingo, near the terminus of the main park road. A restaurant and marina are nearby. No other accommodations or eating facilities are in the park. A variety of lodging and eating establishments are outside the park at Florida City and Homestead. Flamingo is approximately 83 miles southwest of Miami International Airport.

# EVERGLADES NATIONAL PARK

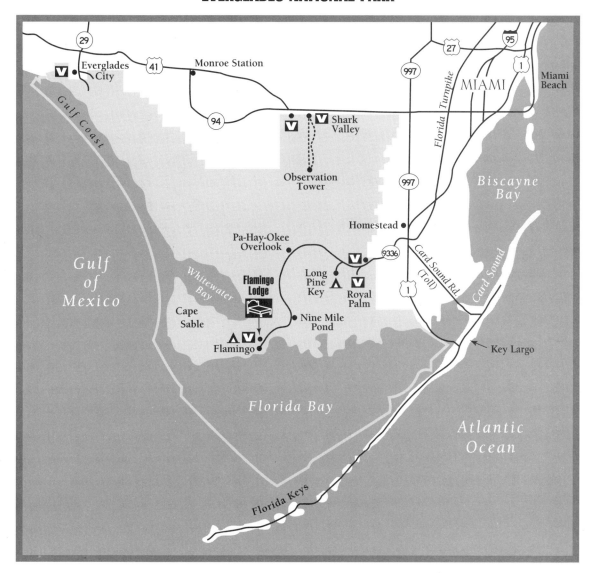

## FLAMINGO LODGE, MARINA, AND OUTPOST RESORT

1 Flamingo Lodge Highway • Flamingo, FL 33034 • (941) 695–3101

Flamingo Lodge is part of a resort complex consisting of motel buildings, multiple cottage units, a full-service marina with a store, and a main building with a restaurant, bar, cafe, and gift shop. The lodge provides a total of 126 rooms, most of which are in the motel buildings. The motel buildings and the cottages are separate from but only a short walk to the restaurant and marina. The resort sits on Florida Bay at the southern tip of Everglades National Park.

Accommodations at the lodge consist of 102 rooms in six cement motel buildings and twenty-four rooms in twelve wood duplex cottages. Rooms in the four one-story and two

*The Flamingo Lodge*

two-story motel buildings, have each a telephone, heat, air conditioning, and television. The rooms are carpeted and have two double beds and a private bathroom with a combination tub-shower. The forty-two rooms in the one-story buildings each have a back sliding-glass door. Sixty rooms in the two-story buildings have a large back window. One suite has one bedroom with two double beds, two baths, a kitchen, and a sitting/dining area with a sofa bed. Most of the motel rooms offer a view.

Twelve cottage buildings are constructed as duplex units to offer twenty-four rooms, each with a fully equipped kitchenette and one bedroom containing two double beds. These units do not have television. The kitchenette is fully equipped for cooking, and an attached sitting area has a sofa bed. All but the bathroom and kitchen are carpeted. The cottages have a private bath with a shower but no bathtub. One cottage is handicap accessible with a combination tub-shower. Adequate parking is available for both the motel units and the cottages.

Flamingo Lodge is a good place to stay while you explore one of our most unique national parks. The lodge enjoys a scenic location on Florida Bay and is close to a restaurant, cafe, and cocktail lounge. A National Park Service visitor center is also nearby. This is a pleasant place to walk, jog, or ride a bicycle. A screened pool that overlooks the bay is available for guests of both the motel units and the cottages. Houseboats, kayaks, and canoes are available for rent at the marina. Be warned that mosquitoes can get nasty in the wet season, which begins in late spring and continues through summer. The best time to visit is in winter, when the weather is mild and mosquitoes are less numerous.

- **ROOMS:** Doubles, triples, and quads. The suite and cottages can hold up to six. All rooms have a private bathroom.

- **RESERVATIONS:** Flamingo Lodge, 1 Flamingo Lodge Highway, Flamingo, FL 33034. Phone (800) 600–3813; fax (941) 695–3921. One night's deposit required within two weeks of making a reservation. Cancellation requires at least forty-eight hours' notice for refund of deposit.

- **RATES:** Motel room ($$$), cottages ($$$$$), and suite ($$$$$) during peak season from mid-December through the end of March. Prices reduced about 20 percent from November 1 through mid-December and during April. Further reductions from May through October. Rates quoted for two adults in motel units and four adults in cottages. Children under twelve years are free with an adult.

- **LOCATION:** Directly on Florida Bay at the southern tip of Everglades National Park. Flamingo is 38 miles southwest of the park's main visitor center.

- **SEASON:** Flamingo Lodge is open year-round. Peak season is during winter.

- **FOOD:** A full-service restaurant serves three meals a day during winter months but may be closed in spring and fall. A cafe in the same building is open year-round. Limited groceries are sold at the marina.

*The 38-mile road from the main visitor center to Flamingo provides access to many trails, both long and short, through the park. These trails offer the best chance to see wildlife close-up. Many of the trails are only a quarter- to a half-mile long. Longer trails near Flamingo lead deeper into the Everglades. The park also includes many miles of canoe trails.*

- **TRANSPORTATION:** Scheduled air, train, and bus service is available at Miami, about 85 miles northeast of Flamingo and 45 miles northeast of the park's main visitor center.

- **FACILITIES:** Restaurant, cocktail lounge, cafe, store, bicycle rentals, gift shop, full-service marina.

- **ACTIVITIES:** Swimming, fishing, bird-watching, hiking, boating, charter fishing, sightseeing boat tours, guided hikes.

# HAWAII

## HAWAII VOLCANOES NATIONAL PARK

Hawaii Volcanoes National Park, HI 96718
(808) 967–7311

Hawaii Volcanoes National Park comprises 220,000 acres of active volcanism, including 13,676-foot Mauna Loa and famous Kilauea, near where most of the park's activity is centered. An 11-mile paved road that circles the Kilauea caldera provides access to scenic stops and nature walks. Hawaii Volcanoes National Park is located in the southeastern corner of the island of Hawaii. The visitor center is approximately 29 miles southwest of Hilo, on Hawaii Highway 11, which bisects the park.

 ## Lodging in Hawaii Volcanoes National Park

Volcano House, with forty-two rooms, is the only hotel facility in the park. It sits just off Highway 11 on the north end of Crater Rim Drive, which circles Kilauea Crater. Ten camper cabins operated by the same firm are at Namakani Paio Campground, 3 miles west of the park entrance, on Highway 11. Additional lodging is available in nearby communities and in Hilo. Members of the military may find accommodations at Kilauea Military Camp, 1 mile west of Park Headquarters. Phone (800) 438–6707 from Oahu and (808) 967–8333 from out of state.

### VOLCANO HOUSE

P.O. Box 53 • Hawaii Volcanoes National Park, HI 96718 • (808) 967–7321

Volcano House is a rustic, two-story wood and stone hotel constructed in 1941 and added to in 1962. The hotel has since been completely renovated. It is the oldest continuously operated hotel in Hawaii. The dining room, gift shops, cocktail lounge, snack bar, lobby, and most of the accommodations are all in a single building that rests on the edge of Kilauea Crater. A separate two-story building with a small lobby houses ten garden-view rooms. Ten less expensive wood cabins without private bath are 3 miles from the hotel, in the Namakani Paio Campground. Volcano House is located just off Highway 11, on Crater Rim Drive, which circles Kilauea Caldera.

# HAWAII VOLCANOES NATIONAL PARK

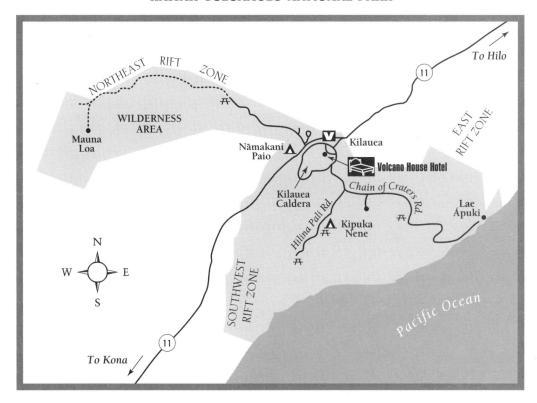

The hotel has a total of forty-two rooms, twenty of which offer a crater view. Twelve rooms without a crater view rent for about $25 less than rooms with the view. All of these rooms are approximately the same size. Ten somewhat smaller garden-view rooms in a separate building (the Ohia Wing) rent for approximately $50 less than crater-view rooms. Bedding varies from one king, to two doubles, to two twins. Three rooms have a queen plus two twin beds. All rooms are carpeted, are furnished with koa wood furniture, and include heat, telephone, and private bath with shower. Two handicap-accessible rooms have a tub.

The ten single-room wood cabins at Namakani Paio Campground, 3 miles from Volcano House, have each one double bed and two single bunk beds. The cabins also have an electric light (no outlets) and an outdoor grill and picnic table. Linens, pillows, and one blanket are provided when you check in at the Volcano House registration desk. You may wish to bring additional blankets. Cabin guests must use community bathroom facilities, which are situated among the cluster of cabins.

Volcano House is a convenient and interesting place to stay when you will be spending several days touring the Big Island, including a day in this unique national park. The location on the edge of the huge caldera is spectacular. The large lobby includes a famous fireplace that has been burning continuously for many years. The first-class restaurant serves three meals a day, including breakfast and lunch buffets.

■ **ROOMS:** Doubles, triples, and quads. All forty-two rooms in the hotel have a private bath. Cabins at Namakani Paio do not have private baths.

*The Volcano House*

- **RESERVATIONS:** Volcano House, P.O. Box 53, Hawaii Volcanoes National Park, HI 96718. Phone (808) 967–7321; fax (808) 967–8429. One night's deposit required within ten days of confirmation. Cancellation required seventy-two hours ahead of scheduled arrival.

- **RATES:** Crater view ($$$$$); no crater view ($$$$); Ohia Wing of Volcano House ($$$); Namakani Paio cabins ($). Rates are quoted for two adults. Additional adults are $10.00 each in Volcano House and $6.00 each in the cabins. Children twelve years and under are free with parents.

- **LOCATION:** Just off Highway 11 on the north section of Crater Rim Drive. Volcano House is 30 miles from Hilo.

- **SEASON:** Both Volcano House and Namakani Paio cabins are open year-round.

- **FOOD:** Ka Ohelo Dining Room ($$$$) serves daily breakfast and lunch buffets. Supper is ordered from a menu. A less expensive snack bar ($$) serves chili, salads, sandwiches, and beverages. Limited groceries are available in nearby Volcano Village.

- **TRANSPORTATION:** The nearest scheduled airline service is at Hilo, where rental cars are available. A city bus operates between Hilo and the park's visitor center, which is across the road from the hotel.

- **FACILITIES:** Restaurant, snack bar, cocktail lounge, gift shops, National Park Service visitor center, art center, golf course (1 mile away).

- **ACTIVITIES:** Hiking, interpretive programs, golf.

The original Volcano House was constructed in 1866 of grass and ohia poles. The first wooden hotel was built here eleven years later. This structure is across the road from the hotel and now serves as the Volcano Art Center. The main building of the hotel burned in 1940 and was replaced by the current Volcano House, which opened in November 1941.

# KENTUCKY

## MAMMOTH CAVE NATIONAL PARK

Mammoth Cave, KY 42259

(502) 758–2328

Mammoth Cave National Park comprises 52,714 acres, including the longest recorded cave system in the world. The park also includes rugged hillsides and beautiful rivers. A variety of guided cave tours are offered throughout the day. The park also offers 70 miles of hiking trails, a gravel bicycle trail, and scenic boat rides. Mammoth Cave National Park is located in central Kentucky, approximately 90 miles south of Louisville via Interstate 65.

### Lodging in Mammoth Cave National Park

A single lodging complex in the park offers a wide variety of accommodations that are all close to the visitor center and ticket sales area for cave tours. Buses near the visitor center provide transportation to the cave entrance.

## MAMMOTH CAVE HOTEL

Mammoth Cave, KY 42259–0027 • (502) 758–2225

Mammoth Cave Hotel is a lodging complex consisting of a two-story brick hotel, four one-story motel buildings, and thirty cottages; it provides ninety-two total lodging units. Registration for all the lodging is just inside the front entrance to the hotel, which also contains a gift shop, a lower lobby, a craft store, a meeting room, and several places to dine. The hotel, motel units, and cottages all sit in an expansive grassy area near the National Park Service visitor center, where tickets are sold for tours to this famous cave. Tours leave from just behind the visitor center, which is an easy walk from any of the rooms at the hotel. A big parking area is in front of the hotel. Mammoth Cave Hotel is located just off Highway 70, in the southeastern section of Mammoth Cave National Park. The park is just off Interstate 65 at either the Park City or the Cave City exit.

# MAMMOTH CAVE NATIONAL PARK

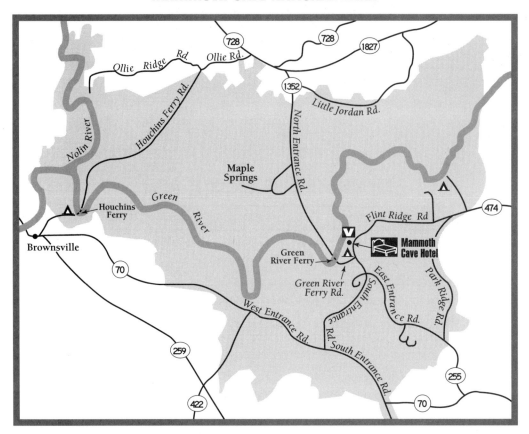

Four types of accommodations are available at Mammoth Cave Hotel. The least expensive lodging is the twenty Woodland Cottages, clustered on the north side of the visitor center. These rustic wooden structures were constructed in the 1930s and are available in one-, two-, three-, and four-bedroom units. Bedding in each bedroom ranges from a double bed to a double and a twin bed. Only one each of the three- and four-bedroom units are available. Each of these two large buildings has two bathrooms with showers but no tubs. The predominant units are two-bedroom, constructed with one bedroom on each side of a central bathroom. Each of these units has a ceiling fan but no air conditioning, telephone, or television. Keep this in mind if you will be staying during a period that is likely to be hot and humid.

Ten Hotel Cottages are located across the road from the main hotel. The small wood cabins, also constructed in the 1930s, sit in a semicircle along the top of a wooded hillside. Each cabin has air conditioning, a television, electric heat, carpeting, and a private bath with shower but no tub. Bedding ranges from one double bed to two double beds. The cottages have a small stone porch but no telephone. The Hotel Cottages are worth the $10 extra per night compared with the rates for Woodland Cottages because the interior is that much nicer, they have air conditioning, and the location is less crowded.

The main hotel, constructed in the 1960s, has thirty-eight rooms in a two-story brick building immediately next to the lobby/registration building. Four handicap-accessible

*Mammoth Cave Hotel*

rooms are near the lobby. Although separate, the two buildings sit so close together that they are essentially a single structure. The rooms all have a full bath with a combination tub-shower, and most have a private balcony or patio with chairs and a small table. These rooms have heat, air conditioning, telephone, and television and are nicely furnished. Bedding ranges from two twins to one king; a queen and a double plus a single are also available. Rooms on both floors are entered through an interior corridor that runs the length of the building. This building is the most convenient to the lobby and the dining facilities. Choose a back room on the second floor. The handicap-accessible rooms can be entered at ground level from the parking lot.

Four single-story motor lodge buildings constructed in the 1960s each house four or six large one-bedroom units. These units each have heat, air conditioning, a telephone, a television, and a full bath with a combination tub-shower. All the units have two double beds and are generally recommended for families. A nice grassy area in front of the units provides a good place for kids to play.

Mammoth Cave National Park offers more than the cave tours for which it is so famous. In fact, this is one of our favorite parks. The area in which the lodging facilities are located is very pleasant, with lots of trees and open grassy spaces. Most park visitors have completed their cave tours by the late afternoon so that evenings are perfect for a quiet walk. Inexpensive scenic boat rides on the Green River are operated several times each day. Hiking trails and ranger-led walks are also available. If you plan to take a ranger-led cave tour, be certain to check in at the visitor center behind the hotel as soon as possible after your arrival so that you can reserve a tour time. In fact, you may want to make a reservation (800–967–2283) prior to your arrival.

- **ROOMS:** Singles, doubles, triples, and quads. Only a couple of buildings will handle more than four. All rooms and cabins have private baths.

- **RESERVATIONS:** National Park Concessions, Mammoth Cave Hotel, Mammoth Cave, KY 42259–0027. Phone (502) 758–2225; fax (502) 758–2301. One night's deposit required. Refund of deposit requires forty-eight-hour cancellation notice. Animals are allowed only in the Woodland Cottages. A kennel is available without charge for animals brought by room guests.

- **RATES:** Woodland Cottages ($); Hotel Cottages ($); hotel ($$); motor lodge ($$). Rates quoted for two persons in cottages and hotel and for three persons in the motor lodge. Additional persons are $7.00 extra. Children under sixteen are free when extra bedding is not required.

- **LOCATION:** The lodging complex at Mammoth Cave is located near the visitor center in the eastern section of the park. From Interstate 65, take exit 53 when traveling south and exit 48 when traveling north.

- **SEASON:** The hotel and motel units are open all year. The Hotel Cottages are open from March to November, and the Woodland Cottages are open from May to October.

- **FOOD:** A dining room ($$) serves breakfast, lunch, and dinner. An adjacent coffee shop ($/$$) serves a late breakfast and lunch. A fast-food restaurant ($) is open from 10:30 A.M. to 5:00 P.M. during summer and on weekends in spring and fall. Limited groceries are available from May through October in the store near the campground.

- **TRANSPORTATION:** The nearest major airports are at Louisville, Kentucky, and Nashville, Tennessee, where rental vehicles are available. Scheduled bus service is available to nearby Cave City, Kentucky.

- **FACILITIES:** Gas station, pet kennels, restaurant, coffee shop, fast-food restaurant, gift shop, craft store, tennis courts, shuffleboard courts, nature trails, Laundromat, post office.

- **ACTIVITIES:** Hiking, cave tours, boat tours, tennis, fishing, evening campfire programs, ranger talks.

*Cave tours are the most popular activity at Mammoth Cave National Park. Approximately a dozen tours are offered, depending on the season and demand. Some tours are easy and last about an hour. Others are strenuous and last from three to six hours. A schedule of each day's cave tours is posted in the visitor center. Cave temperatures are in the fifties, and the paths can be slick, with many steps, so it is important to dress properly. Most tours fill rapidly, so, if possible, make a reservation by mail or phone (800–967–2283) prior to arrival. Reservations may be made up to five months in advance of the tour date you desire. If you arrive at the park without a reservation, be sure to head for the visitor center, where reservations can be made and tickets purchased. You will also be able to obtain information about the various tours that are offered.*

# MICHIGAN

## ISLE ROYALE NATIONAL PARK

800 East Lakeshore Drive
Houghton, MI 49931
(906) 482–0984

Isle Royale National Park comprises 572,000 acres, including the largest island in Lake Superior. Eighty percent of the park is under water. Isle Royale, approximately 45 miles long and 9 miles wide, is a roadless island of forests, lakes, and rugged shores. There are 166 miles of foot trails and numerous inland lakes on the island, where travel is via foot, boat, or floatplane. Isle Royale is located in northwestern Lake Superior, 22 miles southeast of Grand Portage, Minnesota. No roads or bridges provide access to the island.

## Lodging in Isle Royale National Park

The only overnight accommodations inside the park are at Rock Harbor, on the south shore of the northeastern tip of the island. Rock Harbor Lodge provides motel-type buildings and duplex housekeeping cabins, with a total of eighty rooms. Access to Rock Harbor is via seaplane or scheduled passenger boats from Houghton and Copper Harbor in Michigan's Upper Peninsula and from Grand Portage on Minnesota's north shore.

# ISLE ROYALE NATIONAL PARK

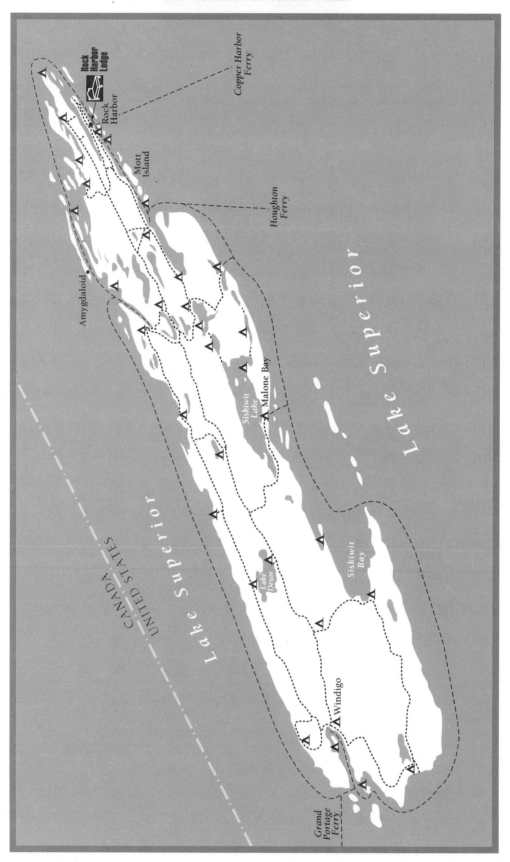

# ROCK HARBOR LODGE

P.O. Box 405 • Houghton, MI 49931-0405 • (906) 337–4993

*Rock Harbor Lodge*

Rock Harbor Lodge is a complex of four motel-type lodge buildings, twenty housekeeping cabins, a dining room, a meeting hall, a gift shop, a store, and a marina, all located on or near the shore of Lake Superior. The four two-story lodge buildings sit side by side on each side of a meeting hall (actually, an old lodge building) used as a gathering place for guests. All these buildings are directly on the shoreline. The dining room is a short distance behind the lodge buildings. The housekeeping cottages are nearby and convenient to the dining room and store.

The four identical lodge buildings house a total of sixty rooms, each with a private bath and combination tub-shower. The buildings have a stone and wood exterior and cement block interior walls. Lodge rooms have steam heat but no television or telephone. Bedding varies from one double, to two twins, to two doubles. Rooms on the first floor each have a balcony. Second-floor rooms have a better window view but no balcony. Three meals a day in the dining room are included in the rental of lodge rooms.

Ten stone and wood duplexes provide twenty housekeeping cottages, which each have an electric stove, a refrigerator, dishes, and utensils. These units have a double bed and two bunk beds, with linens, blankets, and electric heat but no maid service. The cottages are located near Tobin Harbor, a short distance from the four lodge buildings. An asphalt walkway connects the cottages with the dining room and lodge buildings. Units 1–12 have a view of the harbor, while units 13–20 are deeper in the woods. Meals are not included in cottage rentals, but guests are permitted to eat in the dining room at extra cost.

Isle Royale is an unusual national park that appeals to individuals who want to try something different. There are no roads, no vehicles, and few people. You won't pass through this park on your way to some other destination, and neither will anyone else. The lodge allows you to experience nature while enjoying nice accommodations and good food. The dining room serves three meals daily, while a marina store sells a variety of groceries, fishing equipment, and personal supplies. The nearby marina will accommodate boats of up to 65 feet. Motorboats and canoes are available for rent. Charter fishing boats and sightseeing boats are also at Rock Harbor.

- **ROOMS:** Doubles, triples, and quads. All rooms in the lodge buildings and housekeeping cottages have private baths.

- **RESERVATIONS:** From May through September, National Park Concessions, Rock Harbor Lodge, Isle Royale National Park, P.O. Box 405, Houghton, MI 49931–0405. Phone (906) 337–4993. From October through April, National Park Concessions, Inc., Mammoth Cave, KY 42259–0027. Phone (502) 773–2191.

- **RATES:** Lodge rooms with meals ($$$$$); housekeeping cottages without meals ($$$$). Rates are quoted for two adults. Additional persons are approximately $71.00 extra per night ($39.00 for children under twelve) in lodge rooms (meals included) and $33.50 extra in housekeeping cottages.

- **LOCATION:** South shore on the northeastern tip of Isle Royale.

- **SEASON:** The lodge is open from the second week in June through the first week in September. Housekeeping units are available from Memorial Day through mid-September.

- **FOOD:** A dining room serves three meals daily. Snack bar service is available throughout the day. Groceries can be purchased in the store.

- **TRANSPORTATION:** Passenger boats leave for Isle Royale from Copper Harbor and Houghton in Michigan's Upper Peninsula and from Grand Portage on Minnesota's north shore. Floatplanes leave from Houghton. One boat circumnavigates the island and will drop off and pick up passengers at various points.

- **FACILITIES:** Dining room, store, gift shop, marina with boat and canoe rentals.

- **ACTIVITIES:** Hiking, fishing, canoeing, charter fishing, and sightseeing via boat.

Isle Royale has a rich history to share with present-day visitors. Native Indians had mined copper here thousands of years earlier when the French claimed possession of Isle Royale in 1671. The island became a possession of the United States in 1783 and was identified as Chippewa Territory until the mid-1800s. Copper mining continued during the latter half of the 1800s, when large areas were burned and logged.

# MINNESOTA

## VOYAGEURS NATIONAL PARK

3131 Highway 53
International Falls, MN 56649–8904
(218) 283–9821

Voyageurs National Park preserves 218,000 acres of beautiful forested lake country that was once inhabited by French-Canadian fur traders. The south side of the Kabetogama Peninsula is dotted with numerous islands, while the north shore is broken with many coves and small bays. One of the park's visitor centers is in its southwest corner, on Highway 123. Voyageurs National Park stretches 55 miles along the U.S.–Canadian border, east of International Falls in northern Minnesota. Summer travel within the park is confined to watercraft or floatplane.

###  Lodging in Voyageurs National Park

Overnight accommodations within Voyageurs National Park are available only at the hotel at Kettle Falls. Kettle Falls, in the northeast corner of the park, is reached via private boat, by ferry from Ash River, or by tour boat from the Kabetogama Lake Visitor Center and Rainy Lake Visitor Center. Accommodations are available outside the park in Ash River, Crane Lake, Kabetogama Lake, and International Falls.

# VOYAGEURS NATIONAL PARK

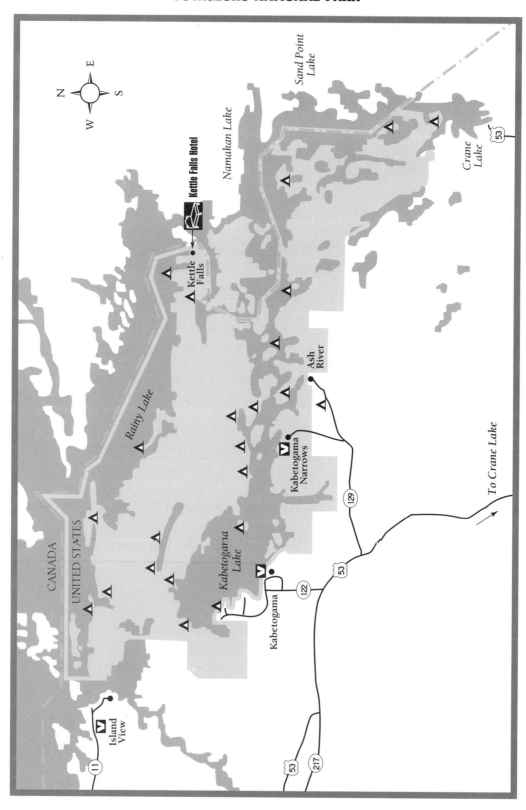

# KETTLE FALLS HOTEL

10502 Gamma Road • Ray, Minnesota 56669 • (888) 534–6835

*Kettle Falls Hotel*

Kettle Falls is a relatively small lodging complex consisting of an historic frame two-story hotel plus three newer nearby wooden lodges that each contain from two to four lodging units. The hotel is part of a National Register of Historic Places District that also includes the historic dam, a dam tenders cabins, and other sites or features. A total of twenty-two rooms are available at Kettle Falls. The hotel has a dining room and saloon on the first floor and twelve overnight rooms on the second floor. The hotel sits in a small clearing surrounded by woods and the lodges overlook the rocky shore of Rainy Lake. Only the hotel is open during the winter season. A quarter-mile gravel road leads from the dock to the hotel. Transportation from dockside to the lodging complex is available. Kettle Falls Hotel sits in the northeast corner of Voyageurs National Park and is reached only by boat or seaplane. Scheduled boat service to Kettle Falls is available from Ash River and Kabetogama via tour boats.

Several types of rooms are available at Kettle Falls. None of the rooms have a telephone or television although a telephone is in the hotel lobby and a large screen television is in the saloon. The least expensive rooms, all without private bath, are in the hotel, which was constructed from 1910 through 1913 to house construction workers on the nearby dam. The twelve hotel rooms are furnished with antiques and have either one double bed or two single beds. All these rooms are approximately the same size. The twelve hotel rooms and three centrally located community bathrooms with showers are on the second floor of the hotel. Coffee and rolls are served on the second floor each morning.

Kettle Falls also offers ten units in three separate lodge buildings on the Rainy Lake side of the Kettle Falls dam. These buildings, constructed in the early 1990s, are finished with a pine and oak decor. Each unit has a screened porch and a private ceramic-tiled bathroom that includes a shower. One single-story lodge building with two units is handicap accessible (as is the first floor of the hotel). The other two lodge buildings each have two first-floor units and two second-floor units. Five of the villas have a fully equipped kitchen, including utensils. Bedding in the lodge units ranges from bunk beds to full-size beds. The units can sleep up to ten persons when an adjoining door is used to convert two units to a suite. While the lodge rooms are newer and nicer than rooms in the hotel, you will save some money and probably enjoy a more intimate lodging experience by choosing to stay in the hotel. Keep in mind that guests who stay in the hotel must use community bathrooms.

Staying at Kettle Falls Hotel is a restful and refreshing experience in a historic location where fur traders and trappers once portaged canoes and goods. If you want to get away from it all, and do so in the great outdoors, this may be just the place. The hotel has a large screened veranda where guests can sit and drink coffee or have a meal. Most activities center on the water, where fishing and canoeing are the most popular activities. Guide service is available, and boats and canoes can be rented.

*Voyageurs National Park was named in honor of the French-Canadian traders who moved animal pelts and other trade goods through this area during the late eighteenth and early nineteenth centuries. The voyageurs used canoes to transport their goods between Montreal and the Canadian Northwest. A 1783 treaty established the U.S.–Canadian boundary along the waterway used by the voyageurs. Kettle Falls Hotel is situated a short walk north of the present international boundary. Here you can look south into Canada.*

- **ROOMS:** Singles, doubles, triples, and quads. Lodge units with connecting doors can be converted to suites that accommodate up to ten people. All suites have private baths. Guests at the main hotel have access to community bathrooms.

- **RESERVATIONS:** Kettle Falls Hotel, 10502 Gamma Road, Ray, MN 56669. Phone (888) 534–6835 or (218) 374–4404; (218) 875–2070 during the off-season.

- **RATES:** Hotel rooms ($$); lodge rooms ($$$); lodge rooms with kitchenette ($$$$$). Hotel room rates are quoted for one adult. Extra adults are $20 each, and extra children under twelve are $15 each. Children under two are free. Lodge units are quoted for four adults.

- **LOCATION:** Kettle Falls Hotel is in the northeast corner of Voyageurs National Park.

- **SEASON:** Mid-May through the first week of October. Winter season is from late December until mid-March. Only the hotel is open during the winter season.

- **FOOD:** A hotel dining room ($$/$$$) serves meals from 7:00 A.M. to 9:00 P.M. daily. Morning coffee and rolls are served to guests of the hotel. Limited groceries are available at the trading post.

- **TRANSPORTATION:** The nearest scheduled air service is 50 miles from Kettle Falls, at International Falls, Minnesota, where rental cars are available. With advance notice the hotel will arrange for pickup at the airport. Scheduled boat service is available to Kettle Falls from Ash River and Kabetogama Lake Visitor Center.

- **FACILITIES:** Dining room, saloon, boat rental, fishing bait, trading post with souvenirs, gifts, and groceries.

- **ACTIVITIES:** Hiking, bird-watching, fishing, canoeing, kayaking.

# MISSOURI

## OZARK NATIONAL SCENIC RIVERWAYS

P.O. Box 490

Van Buren, MO 63965

(573) 323–4236

Ozark National Scenic Riverways comprises nearly 80,000 acres of forested hills and mountains along 134 miles of the beautiful Current and Jacks Fork Rivers. The rivers are especially popular for fishing and for float trips in canoes, rafts, kayaks, and inner tubes, all of which can be rented. The riverways includes large freshwater springs and caverns. Ozark National Scenic Riverways is located in southeastern Missouri, 150 miles south of St. Louis.

 ## Lodging in Ozark National Scenic Riverways

The riverways has a single lodging facility at Big Spring, 4 miles south of the town of Van Buren. Other accommodations are available outside park boundaries in Eminence, Mountain View, and Van Buren.

# OZARK NATIONAL SCENIC RIVERWAYS

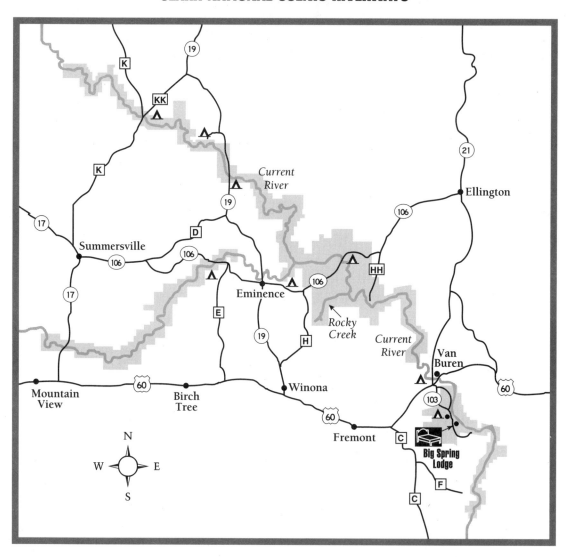

# BIG SPRING LODGE

P.O. Box 130 • Van Buren, MO 63965 • (573) 323–4332

*Cabin at Big Spring Lodge*

**B**ig Spring Lodge consists of a main lodge building plus fourteen freestanding cabins. The timber and stone lodge building houses the registration desk and dining room on a bluff overlooking the Current River. The cozy dining room has a small wing with windows that provide a view of the river. The wood and stone cabins on a hill above the lodge building provide the only overnight accommodations at Big Spring. A paved road leads up the hill from the lodge to the cabins. Adequate parking is beside each of the cabins. The lodge building and cabins were constructed by the Civilian Conservation Corps in the 1930s; the entire complex sits amid a thick forest of hardwood trees. Big Spring Lodge is in southeastern Missouri, 4 miles south of the small town of Van Buren on Highway 103.

The fourteen cabins at Big Spring are available in four sizes that sleep two, four, six, or eight persons. The rate charged is determined by the cabin that is rented, not by the number of persons who stay in the cabin. Thus, two people who rent a six-person cabin must pay the same price as a family of four who rent the same cabin.

All the cabins have a private bath with shower but no bathtub. The cabins are quite roomy, with hardwood floors, stained wood walls, and a private screened porch. They also have fans but no air conditioning, telephone, or television. All except the two six-person cabins have kitchen facilities and a stone fireplace. Wood is provided for a nominal fee. The kitchens have a cooktop stove, refrigerator, and freezer but no oven or utensils. Outside each cabin are a grill and picnic table. The cabins are widely spaced along both sides of a paved road to provide relative privacy.

Big Spring Lodge, a small lodging complex in a quiet rural area of Missouri, is a good place to get away from the hustle and bustle. Plan to read a few books, play some cards, and do a little hiking. On a rainy day you can sit in front of the stone fireplace in the small lobby area of the lodge building. Another stone fireplace is in the dining room. Van Buren is an especially good place to visit if you enjoy a leisurely float down a beautiful river. The Ozark National Scenic Riverways includes 134 miles of clear, spring-fed streams, including the Current River, which flows past Big Spring Lodge.

- **ROOMS:** From doubles to eight persons per unit. All cabins have a private bath with a shower but no tub.

- **RESERVATIONS:** Big Spring Lodge, P.O. Box 130, Van Buren, MO 63965. Phone (573) 323–4332. A two-night-minimum stay may be required on weekends. A three-day cancellation is requested.

- **RATES:** Two-person cabin ($); four- or six-person cabin ($$); eight-person cabin ($$$). Weekend rates are increased by $15 to $20 per day.

- **LOCATION:** In southeast Missouri, 4 miles south of the town of Van Buren on Highway 103.

- **SEASON:** April through October.

- **FOOD:** A cozy dining room ($/$$) serves breakfast, lunch, and dinner. Groceries are available in Van Buren.

- **TRANSPORTATION:** The nearest scheduled airline service is at St. Louis and Springfield, Missouri.

- **FACILITIES:** Dining room.

- **ACTIVITIES:** Hiking, fishing, canoeing, tubing, swimming.

Many of the visitors to Ozark National Scenic Riverways come here in order to float on one or both of the Class II rivers. Nineteen National Park Service-authorized concessionaires rent canoes at or near Alley Spring, Big Spring, Pulltite, Round Spring, Two Rivers, and Watercress. Inner tubes are available for rent at several locations. Floaters are permitted to camp overnight on the river gravel bars.

# MONTANA

## GLACIER NATIONAL PARK

West Glacier, MT 59936

(406) 888–5441

Glacier National Park comprises more than one million acres of beautiful wilderness area, including sparkling lakes, tall mountains, and nearly fifty glaciers. Glacier is one of the United States' most beautiful national parks. The park is bisected by 50-mile "Going-to-the-Sun Road," which is one of America's most spectacular drives. The park is in northwestern Montana. The west entrance is 32 miles east of Kalispell, Montana.

###  Lodging in Glacier National Park

Six facilities offer guest accommodations within Glacier National Park. Three of the facilities are on the west side of the park near Apgar, one is toward the east side on the Going-to-the-Sun Road, and two are at Many Glacier on the park's east side. We have also included two special lodges that are near the park. Beautiful Glacier Park Lodge is just outside the park's east boundary in the town of East Glacier. Glacier's sister national park just across the border in Canada, Waterton Lakes, has one of the most beautiful lodges to be found anywhere.

# GLACIER NATIONAL PARK

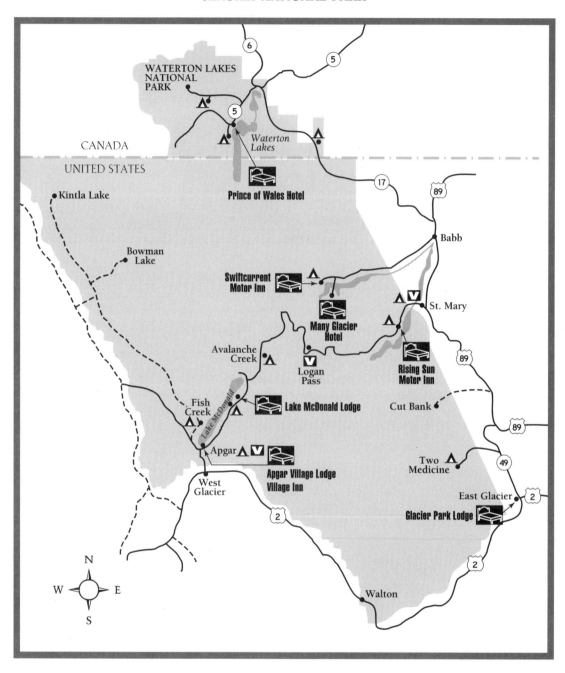

# APGAR VILLAGE LODGE

200 Going-to-the-Sun Road • Apgar, MT 59936 • (406) 888–5484

*Cabin at Apgar Village Lodge*

Apgar Village Lodge is a cluster of two motel buildings and twenty-eight rustic cabins. The wooden structures were constructed over a period of years, with the oldest cabin dating to 1893. The motel units were built in the early 1940s. The complex covers a fairly large area between the road through Apgar Village and McDonald Creek, which empties into Lake McDonald. One motel building and seven cabins provide a view of the creek. The other motel unit is on the dead-end road that leads to the lake. None of the lodging units are on Lake McDonald, although the entire complex is only about a half-block away from the lake. No pets are permitted. Apgar Village Lodge is in Apgar Village, 3 miles inside the west entrance to Glacier National Park. The lodge is just up the street from Village Inn, another Glacier Park lodge.

Apgar Village Lodge offers a wide variety of accommodations. All the rooms have electric heat, television (except motel rooms near the creek), and private baths with showers but no air conditioning or telephone. Picnic tables are scattered about the complex. The least expensive rooms are in the motel building on the creek. Eleven older small rooms have bedding that varies from one double bed, to one queen bed, to one double bed and a single. The beds pretty much fill the room. The other motel unit on Apgar Road has eleven rooms facing the road that offer a partial view of the lake. These rooms are somewhat larger (but still not large) than the rooms in the other motel unit. Bedding varies from one queen or double to two queen beds. Two rooms have a bath and two bedrooms with one queen bed and two twin beds.

All but two of the twenty-eight cabins have a kitchen with refrigerator, stove, oven, and sink. The oldest log cabins were mostly constructed in the very early 1900s; other cabins were built in the 1910s and 1930s. All of the cabins have knotty pine interior walls. The smallest of the cabins has one double bed and no kitchen, while the largest cabin has a kitchen and two bedrooms with five queen beds. Cabins 6, 7, and 8 have kitchens and sit directly on

McDonald Creek. Four other cabins with kitchens (cabins 10, 11, 12, and 22) sit across a parking area from the creek. Most of the cabins have adjacent parking.

Apgar Village Lodge offers rustic buildings in a relatively quiet setting. Although the buildings are fairly close together, the complex tends to be quiet and is suited for people who like this type of environment. Walks, viewing and wading in the lake, and boating are several of the activities that are available here. The National Park Service visitor center is about a half-block away. Although the lodge doesn't have its own eating facility, a deli and a restaurant flank the building. Gift shops and a grocery are a short walk away.

- **ROOMS:** Singles, doubles, triples, and quads. A few large cabins can hold six or more persons. All rooms have private baths with showers but no bathtubs.

- **RESERVATIONS:** Apgar Village Lodge, P.O. Box 398, West Glacier, MT 59936. Phone (406) 888–5484; fax (406) 888–5273.

- **RATES:** Riverview Motel units ($$); Lakeview Motel units ($$$); cabins without kitchens ($$); cabins with kitchens ($$$/$$$$); three-room cabin ($$$$$). Rates for motel units and small cabins are quoted for two adults. Rates on medium and large cabins are quoted for four adults.

- **LOCATION:** In the small village of Apgar, Montana, 3 miles from the West Glacier entrance station.

- **SEASON:** Early May through mid-October.

- **FOOD:** No food service is available at Apgar Village Lodge. The Village Deli next door serves sandwiches, ice cream, and drinks from 9:30 A.M. to 8:30 P.M. On the opposite side of the lodge, Eddie's Cafe ($$) serves breakfast, lunch, and dinner from 7:00 A.M. to 9:30 P.M. Depending on the weather, both restaurants are open from mid-May through most of September. A store sells limited grocery items, beer, and wine.

Milo Apgar, an early homesteader in the area where Apgar Village now stands, arrived soon after the Great Northern Railway reached Belton (now called West Glacier) in the early 1890s. Unable to make it as a farmer, Apgar started offering overnight accommodations for miners and visitors to this beautiful area. Some of Apgar's original cabins are still standing as part of Apgar Village Lodge. Cabin 21 was part of Apgar's first home.

- **TRANSPORTATION:** Scheduled airlines serve Kalispell, Montana, where rental cars are available. An airport shuttle service from Kalispell serves West Glacier. Tours of the park can be arranged from West Glacier. Amtrak service is available to Belton/West Glacier (800–872–7245). A rental car agency is across the street from the Amtrak station. A private shuttle provides service throughout the park, including Apgar, from July 1 through August.

- **FACILITIES:** The village of Apgar has gift shops, a restaurant, a deli, an ice cream shop, bicycle rentals, boat rentals, and a National Park Service visitor center. An ATM machine is next door in a gift shop.

- **ACTIVITIES:** Nightly ranger/naturalist talks at the Apgar campground, boating, swimming (very cool water), fishing, hiking, horseback riding. Sightseeing tours of the park leave from Apgar.

# GLACIER PARK LODGE

East Glacier, MT 59434 • (406) 226–9311

*Glacier Park Lodge*

Glacier Park Lodge is one of the classic Great Northern Railway park lodges. In fact, freight and passenger trains still operate little more than a stone's throw in front of the impressive hotel entry. The main lodge building was constructed during 1912–13 and the adjacent annex building was built in 1913–14. The two buildings have a similar outside appearance and are connected by a large covered walkway. The massive three-story lobby with 40-inch-diameter fir and cedar pillars and surrounded by interior balconies consumes most of the first floor of the main building. The annex contains more than twice as many guest rooms. A large grassy front lawn has flowers from the entrance to the train station. Adequate parking is near the hotel, but you will want to drop off luggage at the front door. No elevators are in the hotel, but bellhops are available to assist with luggage. The lodge is in the southeast corner of Glacier National Park, in the town of East Glacier, Montana. It is at the intersection of Highways 2 and 49.

Glacier Park Lodge has 161 guest rooms that fall into a number of classifications. Rates are set by room size and not by view. Rooms on the west have a view of the Rocky Mountains, while rooms on the east view the front lawn and distant rolling hills. All the rooms have heat, telephone, and private bath with a shower or shower-tub combination. None of the rooms have air conditioning or television. Bedding in nearly all the rooms varies from two twins to two double beds. Some of the rooms have balconies and some do not.

All of the fifty rooms in the main building are on the second and third floors. Thirty-four are the hotel's least expensive "value" rooms, which tend to be relatively small. This building also houses ten larger lodge rooms that rent for about $20 per night more than the value rooms. Four corner "Big Sky" rooms on the third floor have two queens and are quite a bit larger. The other two rooms in this building are very large suites, with one king bed and a sitting area with a sofa bed. The suites also have a balcony.

The majority of 111 rooms in the annex are classified as "annex rooms" and are a nice size, with bedding that ranges from two twins to two doubles. The annex rooms are a little bigger and rent for slightly more than the main lodge rooms. Three family rooms are very large, with three double beds. Six corner minisuites have one queen bed. The annex also contains one handicap-accessible room. Our choice would be a value room facing the west in the main lodge building. Ask for one with a balcony.

Glacier Park Lodge is a handy place to spend a night or more on the east side of Glacier National Park. It's perfect if you travel on the train, because the station is only a short walk from the hotel entrance. It is also a good place to stay if you plan to take a day trip across the park's Going-to-the-Sun Road. The hotel has a nine-hole golf course and a pitch and putt for those who are so inclined. Horseback riding and hayrides are also available. If food in the hotel restaurant isn't to your liking or you consider it too expensive, a short walk takes you to several restaurants and a grocery in the town of East Glacier. The lodge is one of the few where you will find a swimming pool. You might also be interested in signing up for a park tour in one of the red "Jammers."

- **ROOMS:** Singles, doubles, triples, and quads. Three family rooms hold up to six persons. All rooms have a private bath.

- **RESERVATIONS:** Glacier Park Lodges, 1850 North Central, Mail Station 0928, Phoenix, AZ 85077–0928. Phone (602) 207–6000.

- **RATES:** Value rooms ($$$$); all other rooms ($$$$$). Rates are quoted for two adults. Children eleven and under are free. Extra adults are charged $6.00 per night. Rates are reduced from mid-May to mid-June and during mid-September.

- **LOCATION:** In East Glacier, Montana, at the intersection of Highways 2 and 49. The lodge is at the southeast corner of the park.

- **SEASON:** Mid-May to mid-September.

Glacier National Park is famous for the red "Jammer" motor coaches that transport people between the park hotels and sites. The coaches, built by the White Motor Company between 1933 and 1939, have black canvas tops that can be rolled back for greater visibility of occupants. The coaches derive their name from the drivers who at one time had to "jam" the gears to get up the mountain roads of Glacier. The Jammers are now used to offer circle tours of the park and one-way transportation between lodges and hotels.

- **FOOD:** The dining room serves a buffet breakfast, lunch, and dinner until 10:00 P.M. A snack shop in the lobby sells hot dogs, ice cream, and drinks. Additional restaurants and a grocery are nearby in the town of East Glacier.

- **TRANSPORTATION:** Great Falls and Kalispell, Montana, have scheduled air service and rental vehicles. Amtrak stops directly across the street from the hotel.

- **FACILITIES:** Restaurant, cocktail lounge, gift shop, swimming pool, golf course, ATM. Restaurants, gas stations, and a grocery store are across the road in the town of East Glacier.

- **ACTIVITIES:** Hiking, horseback riding, swimming, golf, evening entertainment by employees.

# LAKE McDONALD LODGE

P.O. Box 210052 • Lake McDonald, MT 59921–0052 • (406) 888–5431

*Lake McDonald Lodge*

Lake McDonald Lodge is a complex consisting of a large main lodge building, fourteen structures with cabin accommodations, two two-story motel units, and several support buildings for employee housing, a store, and a gas station. The main structure is a classic old national park lodge with a terrific lobby and restaurant on the main floor, and guest rooms on the second and third floors. The main lodge building, which sits on a small hill overlooking Lake McDonald, was constructed in 1913 and partially renovated in 1988. It is an attractive building with comfortable guest rooms. A huge stone fireplace dominates the three-story lobby with log beams and interior balconies. A covered back patio has chairs and benches for relaxing while viewing Glacier National Park's largest lake.

Lake McDonald Lodge offers rooms of various sizes and bedding in the main lodge, cabins, and motel-type buildings. All the rooms have heat, a telephone, and a private bath with a shower (no tub) but no air conditioning or television. The main lodge has thirty-two rooms, nearly all of which are on the second and third floors. Two handicap-accessible rooms are on the first floor. The building has no elevator. Rooms in the lodge are priced the same regardless of the variation in size, bedding, and view. Some enjoy a great view of the lake, while others have no view at all. Bedding ranges from one double bed to two double beds. Rooms 202, 212, 302, and 312 are large corner rooms with two windows. Rooms 201, 213, 301, and 313 are quite large, with windows toward the lake.

Fourteen separate buildings, some log and some frame, house a total of thirty-eight cabin rooms. Most of these buildings contain two, three, or four cabin rooms, although one building has six units. While all of the cabins are on the lake, trees and plants obscure most views. Bedding in the cabins ranges from one double bed to two double beds. Twenty-one smaller cabin accommodations rent for about half the price of seventeen larger cabin rooms. All the cabins are furnished pretty much the same except for the bedding.

Two wooden two-story motel buildings sit parallel to one another and offer a total of thirty rooms. Both the buildings and the rooms are pretty ordinary. One of the buildings has an interior hallway for entry to the rooms. The other building has entry from an outside balcony and walkway. The motel rooms rent for more than the small cabins and are probably the least desirable rooms at Lake McDonald Lodge. Our first choice would be the larger lakeside rooms in the main lodge. The best value is the small cabins.

Lake McDonald Lodge is a great place to spend a vacation in Glacier National Park. It is a beautiful lodge with attractive rooms in both the main lodge and the cabins. The lake offers boating and fishing, although the water is a little cool for swimming. Boat tours of the lake leave from the back of the lodge. The complex also includes a general store with gifts, supplies, and limited groceries, as well as a gas station (regular unleaded only) and post office. An attractive restaurant with a decor similar to that of the lobby has large windows that overlook the lake. This restaurant offers three meals a day, with breakfast being buffet only, while a smaller restaurant across the road has a more limited and less expensive menu.

- **ROOMS:** Singles, doubles, triples, and quads. All rooms have a private bath with a tub but no shower.

- **RESERVATIONS:** Glacier Park, Inc., 1850 North Central, Mail Station 0928, Phoenix, AZ 85077–0928. Phone (602) 207–6000.

- **RATES:** Main lodge ($$$$); small cabins ($$); large cabins ($$$$); motor inn ($$$).

- **LOCATION:** Ten miles inside the west entrance to Glacier National Park. The lodge is on Lake McDonald, just off the Going-to-the-Sun Road.

- **SEASON:** Early June to late September.

- **FOOD:** A restaurant ($$$) in the main lodge serves breakfast, lunch, and dinner until 10:00 P.M. No reservations are taken. Across the road Russell's Trails Inn Family Restaurant ($$) is open from 7:00 A.M. to 9:30 P.M. with a somewhat limited menu for breakfast, lunch, and dinner. Russell's also has a take-out counter ($/$$). The Stockade Lounge in the main lodge serves snacks. Limited groceries, beer, and wine are sold in the general store.

The site where Lake McDonald now sits was homesteaded in 1895 by George Snyder, who built a small hotel here. Ownership later passed to John Lewis, who operated a fishing and tourist camp. In 1910 Lewis built the log cabins, and three years later he added the present lodge building at a cost of $48,000. The fireplace was originally used as both a kitchen and a furnace for the lodge. His many hunting trophies remain on display in the lodge lobby. The two motel units, additional cabins, and the camp store were added later. The lodge was included in the National Register of Historic Places in 1978.

- **TRANSPORTATION:** The nearest scheduled airline service is to Kalispell, Montana, where rental cars are available. Amtrak and buses serve West Glacier. A park shuttle stops at Lake McDonald Lodge during July and August.

- **FACILITIES:** Restaurants, gift shop, post office, ATM machine, cocktail lounge, boat rental.

- **ACTIVITIES:** Boating, hiking, fishing, boat tours of Lake McDonald, horseback riding, evening ranger programs.

# MANY GLACIER HOTEL

P.O. Box 147 • East Glacier, MT 59434 • (406) 732–4411

*Many Glacier Hotel*

Many Glacier Hotel is a classic old national park lodge. The five-story wooden structure with shake roof and numerous gables and balconies sits on the edge of Swiftcurrent Lake. Although it appears as a single structure, the hotel is actually two separate buildings connected by an enclosed walkway. The main floor is highlighted by an outstanding four-story lobby with log beams, interior balconies, and a huge conical metal fireplace suspended from the roof. The lobby also has a traditional stone fireplace. Many guest rooms in both the main hotel and the annex have an outstanding view of Swiftcurrent Lake and the surrounding mountains. Parking is on a steep hill above the hotel, so register and drop off luggage before parking your vehicle. No elevators are in the hotel, but bellhops are on duty to assist with luggage. Many Glacier Hotel is in the northeastern section of Glacier National Park, 11 miles west of Babb on Many Glacier Road.

The hotel offers a total of 211 rooms of varying size, bedding, and view. All of the rooms have heat, telephone, and a private bath but no television. Most rooms fall into three categories: Lakeside, Standard, and Value. A sloping roof causes rooms on the fourth floor of both buildings to offer less headroom. Surprisingly, basement-level rooms have been assigned 500 room numbers. Lakeside and the slightly less expensive Standard rooms are virtually identical except for the view. Size and bedding for these rooms varies considerably, although each of the rooms in a category rents for the same price. Also, some rooms have balconies with chairs, while other rooms do not. Bedding varies from two twin beds to one double plus a single bed. Bigger lakeside rooms in the annex with balconies include rooms 102, 104, 112, 114, and corresponding rooms on the second and third floors. Sixty-seven Value rooms, which rent for about $10 less per night than a Standard, are smaller, have an obscured view, or both. The hotel has three handicap-accessible rooms on the first floor. One is a Value room, and two are Lakeside rooms.

Six family rooms consist of two bedrooms and a bath. One bedroom has a double plus a single bed, while the other bedroom has a double bed. Three are Lakeside and three are not, although all six rooms rent for the same price, which is about $52 per night more than a Standard room. Two suites each consist of a bedroom with a king bed and a living room with a sleep sofa. These corner rooms also have a private bath. Lakeside rooms with a great view of the lake are worth the difference in price.

Many Glacier Lodge is a wonderful old hotel. In addition to the spectacular lobby, an inviting restaurant at one end of the building has a large stone fireplace and big windows that allow diners to look out over Swiftcurrent Lake. Two lounge areas, one of which is nonsmoking, are just outside the restaurant. Nightly entertainment (fee charged) is offered by employees of the lodge. Take a few steps outside the hotel and you can canoe, fish, or enjoy a boat tour accompanied by a park naturalist. Or perhaps you would rather relax in one of the chairs or benches on the large porch that wraps around two sides of the first floor. A stable next to the parking area offers horseback riding. Evening natural history programs are presented in the hotel basement by National Park Service rangers. All in all, this is a great place to spend several days or a week.

*Construction on Many Glacier Hotel commenced in 1914 and the first guests were welcomed on July 4 of the following year. The annex next door was completed two years later. The Great Northern Railway, which built the hotel, placed a sawmill and drying kiln near the site to process timber used in the construction. Trees for the lobby columns were harvested from the upper end of nearby Lake Josephine. Even though most of the timber and rocks came from the local area, the high cost of fixtures, glass, and boilers resulted in construction costs of $500,000. A swimming pool that sat beside the dining room and a stone fountain near the current St. Moritz Room have both been removed. The hotel once had its own hydroelectric plant at Swift Current Falls, but the unit was put permanently out of operation by a 1964 flood.*

- **ROOMS:** Singles, doubles, triples, and quads. Six family rooms hold five persons. All the hotel rooms have private baths.

- **RESERVATIONS:** Glacier Park, Inc., 1850 North Central, Mail Station 0928, Phoenix, AZ 85077–0928. Phone (602) 207–6000.

- **RATES:** Value rooms ($$$); Lakeside and Standard ($$$$); family rooms and suites ($$$$$). Room rates quoted for two adults. Extra adults are $6.00 each per night. Children eleven years and under are free.

- **LOCATION:** In the northeast section of the park, at the end of Many Glacier Road, 11 miles east of Babb, Montana.

- **SEASON:** Mid-June to mid-September.

- **FOOD:** A restaurant ($$$$) offers a breakfast buffet, lunch, and dinner. A small store sells hot dogs, ice cream, yogurt, snacks, drinks, and wine from 6:30 A.M. to 11:00 P.M. Limited groceries are available in a general store 1 mile up the road at Swiftcurrent Motor Inn. The motor inn also has a less expensive restaurant.

- **TRANSPORTATION:** The nearest scheduled air service is at Kalispell, Montana, where rental vehicles are available. Commercial bus service is available in Great Falls and Kalispell, Montana. Amtrak stops in East Glacier, Montana.

- **FACILITIES:** Restaurant, cocktail lounge, snack bar, gift shop, tour desk in lobby, horse stable, boat rentals, ATM.

- **ACTIVITIES:** Hiking, fishing, boating, horseback riding, evening naturalist programs, evening talent shows, boat tours of Swiftcurrent Lake and Lake Josephine.

## PRINCE OF WALES HOTEL

Waterton, Alberta, Canada TOK2MO • (403) 859–2231

*Prince of Wales Hotel*

The Prince of Wales Hotel is a single seven-story alpine chalet that may be the most picturesque of all the national park lodging facilities. The only Canadian park lodge constructed by the Great Northern Railway, the hotel opened in 1927. It sits high on a hill overlooking Waterton Lake and the quaint town of Waterton. Two-story windows across one end of the five-story lobby provide a spectacular view of glacier-carved Waterton Lake and the surrounding mountains. Interior balconies on each floor and huge timbers near the roof highlight an attractive lobby filled with chairs, tables, and sofas. The hotel is about 48 miles northwest of the town of St. Mary, Montana, via Highway 89 and the Chief Mountain International Highway, which turns off 4 miles north of Babb, Montana. You must pass through a Canadian port of entry and pay a Canadian park fee to enter Waterton Lakes National Park, where the hotel is located.

The hotel has eighty-seven rooms, each with heat, telephone, and private bath. None have television or air conditioning. A small elevator (the oldest in Alberta) in the lobby stops at floors 2, 3, and 4. Most rooms in the hotel fall into two classifications: Lakeside or Standard. Lakeside rooms offer a view of Waterton Lake, while Standard rooms, which rent for about $15 per night less, do not. These rooms are a nice size and offer two twins, one double, or one double plus a twin. Lakeside and Standard rooms comprise all of the accommodations on the second, third, and fourth floors. All third-floor rooms have balconies, and smoking is permitted. Second- and fourth-floor rooms are nonsmoking, and only some have balconies. The wind is generally strong enough that you won't want to spend much time on the balconies, so a balcony shouldn't be a major consideration in choosing a room.

*Waterton Lakes and Glacier National Park were joined as Waterton-Glacier International Peace Park in 1932, largely as a result of work by local chapters of Rotary International. The park was designated one of 400 World Heritage Sites in 1995. The designation recognizes the unique nature of the park's natural and cultural heritage. Note, however, that even though the two parks were joined as one, visitors are required to pay separate entrance fees for each park.*

The hotel offers twenty fifth-floor Value rooms that are smaller, with variable views. About half face Waterton Lake. These rooms require climbing an additional flight of stairs, and the hotel's sloping roofline reduces headspace in some of these rooms, which rent for about $20 less than the Lakeside and Standard rooms. Value rooms have one double or two singles. Bathrooms have a shower but no tub. Keep in mind that the lobby elevator does not provide access to the fifth floor. On the positive side, rooms on the fifth floor tend to be quieter. The hotel's sixth floor (yet another flight of stairs) has four rooms, two of which have two bedrooms and one bath. The other two rooms have a single bedroom. One in each category is Lakeside and the other is not. These are really neat rooms if you don't mind the additional stairs. The hotel also offers one suite that is a very large L-shaped room with a king bed, and a sofa bed and chairs in the living room area.

The Prince of Wales Hotel allows you to experience the beauty of the Canadian Rockies, combined with a touch of English tradition. Tea is served each afternoon in the lobby, where you can relax and look out over Waterton Lake. The hotel's main floor has a restaurant and a cocktail lounge, both of which provide great views of the surrounding landscape. A gift shop is also on the main floor. The small town of Waterton, with additional restaurants, clothing stores, and gift shops, is a modest walk down the hill. Keep in mind that lodging rates are quoted in Canadian dollars, which in recent years have traded at a discount to U.S. dollars. Pay for everything with a credit card and you won't have to worry about obtaining Canadian currency or getting a bad exchange rate when paying with U.S. dollars.

- **ROOMS:** Singles, doubles, triples, and quads. All rooms have private baths.

- **RESERVATIONS:** Glacier Park, Inc., 1850 North Central, Mail Station 0928, Phoenix, AZ 57077–0928. Phone (602) 207–6000.

- **RATES:** Most rooms ($$$$$); Value rooms without view and sixth-floor with one bedroom ($$$$). Rates are for two adults. Additional adults $10 each per night. Children eleven and under are free with an adult. Rates are reduced during the month prior to mid-June and the week after mid-September. Rates are quoted in Canadian dollars.

- **LOCATION:** In Canada's Waterton Lakes National Park, about 48 miles northwest of St. Mary, Montana.

- **SEASON:** Mid-May to late September.

- **FOOD:** A restaurant ($$$$) serves a breakfast buffet, lunch, and dinner. The lobby tearoom serves a continental breakfast from 8:30 to 11:00 A.M. and an afternoon tea. A variety of restaurants are within walking distance in the town of Waterton.

- **TRANSPORTATION:** Scheduled air service is available to Calgary and Lethbridge, Alberta, and Great Falls and Kalispell, Montana, where vehicles can be rented.

- **FACILITIES:** Gift shop, restaurant, cocktail lounge. Additional facilities are in the town of Waterton, a short distance away.

- **ACTIVITIES:** Hiking, golf, tennis, horseback riding, boat rentals, lake cruises, and national park programs are offered in Waterton.

## RISING SUN MOTOR INN

P.O. Box 147 • East Glacier, MT 59434 • (406) 732–5523

Rising Sun Motor Inn, initially known as East Glacier Auto Camp, is a complex of wooden buildings, including a main registration/restaurant building without guest rooms, a separate general store with attached lodging rooms, nineteen cabins, and two motel-type structures. A total of seventy-two rooms are offered at this location, where guests first arrived in 1941 to find nineteen cabins that are still in use. Registration for all guest rooms is in the building that houses a restaurant and a small gift shop. The early-1940s–era general store is across the parking lot, and the cabins and motel buildings are up a small hill but within easy walking distance of both main buildings. Rising Sun is in a scenic area overlooking St. Mary Lake and surrounded by tall mountains. Rising Sun Motor Inn is located on the east side of the park on the Going-to-the-Sun Road, 6 miles from the park entrance at St. Mary.

Rising Sun offers three types of rooms. All the rooms have heat and private baths with showers but no bathtubs. No air conditioning, telephone, or television is in any of the rooms. The least expensive rooms are thirty-five duplex cabin units that sit fairly close to one another. The cabins are all the same size, with varnished plywood interiors. Bedding varies from one double bed to two double beds. The toilet and shower are in a small bathroom, and the sink is in the bedroom. The cabins provide fair to good views of the mountains from relatively small windows.

The general store houses nine rooms that are accessed from an interior hallway. Bedding varies from a double to two double beds. These rooms cost about $10 per night more than the cabin units. The most expensive rooms at Rising Sun, only a few dollars more than rooms

*Cabin at Rising Sun Motor Inn*

at the store, are in two one-story motel-type buildings that hold twenty-eight rooms. These rooms are basically identical except for bedding, which varies from one double to two double beds. Units 8 through 14 in one building and 22 through 28 provide good views of the mountains and a fair view of St. Mary Lake. Two handicap-accessible rooms are in these units. The cabins appear to offer the best value at Rising Sun Motor Inn. The nine rooms in the general store are the least desirable.

Rising Sun Motor Inn is in a very scenic location, where the blue waters of St. Mary Lake glimmer from down a hill. The lake is mostly out of direct view of the lodging units, and the surrounding mountains are only partially visible from some of the units. Still, this is a quiet place to relax in a natural setting. Walk a short distance from your room and gaze at some of the prettiest landscape in the United States. Rising Sun certainly isn't a busy or congested area, since most people on the Going-to-the-Sun Road drive right by. The restaurant, with a vaulted ceiling and large windows facing the lake and mountains, offers three meals a day.

*The 52-mile Going-to-the-Sun Road, one of the country's most scenic drives, is the product of more than a decade of work that commenced in 1921. Although several routes were considered, 6,664-foot Logan Pass was chosen, partially because greater exposure to the sun would help clear the road of snow. It takes up to two months each spring to clear the road of snow that can reach a depth of 80 feet in places. The road provides spectacular views of mountains, lakes, waterfalls, and glacial valleys in the heart of Glacier National Park. The road is winding and quite narrow. Vehicles longer than 21 feet and wider than 8 feet are prohibited from travel between Avalanche Campground and the Sun Point parking area.*

The general store has limited groceries, camping supplies, fishing supplies, and many, many T-shirts. You can hike, fish, or just experience nature without bumping into hundreds of other vacationers. You can also take a boat tour of St. Mary Lake. No pets are permitted at the inn.

- **ROOMS:** Singles, doubles, triples, and quads. All rooms have a private bath with a shower but no bathtub.

- **RESERVATIONS:** Glacier Park, Inc., 1850 North Central, Mail Station 0928, Phoenix, AZ 85077–0928. Phone (602) 207–6000.

- **RATES:** Cottages ($$); store motel rooms ($$); motel-type units ($$$). Rates are for two adults. Children eleven years and under are free. Extra persons are $5.00 each per night.

- **LOCATION:** East side of Glacier National Park, 6 miles west of the park entrance station at St. Mary.

- **SEASON:** Early June to mid-September.

- **FOOD:** A coffee shop/grill ($$/$$$) in the main building serves three meals daily. Limited groceries are sold in the general store.

- **TRANSPORTATION:** The nearest airport is at Kalispell, Montana, on the west side of the park. Amtrak provides service to East Glacier, where rental cars are available. Rising Sun is served by a park shuttle that operates in July and August.

- **FACILITIES:** Restaurant, gift shop, general store with camping and fishing supplies and limited groceries.

- **ACTIVITIES:** Hiking, fishing, boating, boat tour of St. Mary Lake, National Park Service evening naturalist program in campground amphitheater.

## SWIFTCURRENT MOTOR INN

P.O. Box 147 • East Glacier Park, MT 59434 • (406) 732–5531

Swiftcurrent Motor Inn is a complex consisting of a registration building that also houses a store and restaurant, four motel buildings, twenty-six cabins, and a central bathhouse. In all, Swiftcurrent offers eighty-eight lodging rooms. The cabins and motel units sit behind and to the side of the registration building, which contains no accommodations. Plenty of parking is available outside the registration building and beside the cabins and motel units. The cabins were constructed in 1937 after a fire destroyed cabins built several years earlier. The motel-type buildings were constructed in 1955. Swiftcurrent Motor Inn is in the northeast section of Glacier National Park, at the end of Many Glacier Road, 12 miles west of the town of Babb.

Two types of accommodations are available at Swiftcurrent. Both types have electric heat but no air conditioning, television, or telephone. The least expensive lodging is in cabins without bath. A community bathroom has toilets and pay showers. The cabins are quite rustic but nicely spaced, and all are single units (no duplex units, common among other lodges). Eighteen small one-bedroom cabins each have a double bed in one room and a sink (cold water only) and small picnic table in a separate room. Two one-bedroom cabins with a private bath rent for about $20 per night more than the one-bedroom units without a bath. Six two-bedroom cabins have a small bedroom with a double bed on each side of a small room,

*One-Bedroon Cabin without Bath at Swiftcurrent Motor Inn*

with a sink and picnic table. These cabins do not have a private bathroom. The two-bedroom units rent for about $10 per night more than the one-bedroom units without bath. Cabins in Loop C are closest to the community bathhouse.

Four one-story motel buildings have a total of sixty-two rooms. The Pinetop unit, near the front of the complex, has twenty rooms, all but two of which have two double beds and a private bath with a shower but no bathtub. The rooms are entered from a central hallway that runs the length of the building. Three additional one-story motel units, near the back of the complex, each have fourteen rooms that are slightly larger and about $10 more expensive than the Pinetop rooms. Each room has two double beds and a private bath with shower but no tub. Two handicap-accessible rooms have two twin beds. Rooms in these buildings back up to one another and are entered from an outside doorway. A small cement porch runs the length of each side of the buildings, but there are no outside chairs.

Swiftcurrent offers lodging at a reasonable price in a very beautiful area of Glacier National Park. In fact, the one-bedroom cabins without bath are about as cheap accommodations as you will find in any national park area. The complex sits across from a campground and only a mile down the road from the fancier and more

> A number of interesting hikes begin from the Many Glacier/Swiftcurrent area. Grinnell Glacier Trail leads 5.5 miles to one of the park's best-known and most visible glaciers. Tour boats on Swiftcurrent and Josephine Lakes can be used to reduce the length of the hike. Another 4.7-mile trail from Swiftcurrent Motor Inn leads to Iceberg Lake, on which icebergs can be seen well into the summer.

expensive Many Glacier Hotel. The registration building has a small lobby area and a large covered porch with chairs. All of the lodging buildings at Swiftcurrent Motor Inn are surrounded by trees, so you won't have any great vistas from your room. On the other hand,

Swiftcurrent is a pleasant and relatively inexpensive place to stay. The restaurant serves three meals a day, and a modest walk takes you to more elegant dining at Many Glacier Hotel. Hikers frequently choose Swiftcurrent because of the many trails that originate in the Many Glacier area.

- **ROOMS:** Singles, doubles, triples, and quads. All the motel rooms have private baths. Most cabin guests must use a community bathroom.

- **RESERVATIONS:** Glacier Park, Inc., 1850 North Central, Mail Station 0928, Phoenix, AZ 85077–0928. Phone (602) 207–6000.

- **RATES:** Cabins ($); motel units ($$). Room rates are quoted for two adults. Extra adults are charged $5.00 per night each. Children eleven years and under are free with an adult.

- **LOCATION:** In the northeast section of the Glacier National Park at the end of Many Glacier Road, 12 miles east of Babb, Montana.

- **SEASON:** Mid-June to mid-September.

- **FOOD:** A restaurant ($$) in the registration building offers breakfast, lunch, and dinner. Lunch and dinner have the same menu. Limited groceries are available in the general store.

- **TRANSPORTATION:** The nearest scheduled air service is at Kalispell, Montana, where rental vehicles are available. Commercial bus service is available in Great Falls and Kalispell, Montana. Amtrak stops in East Glacier, Montana.

- **FACILITIES:** Restaurant, Laundromat, and camp store with gifts, groceries, and supplies.

- **ACTIVITIES:** Hiking, fishing, horseback riding, evening campfire programs, boat tours of Swiftcurrent Lake and Lake Josephine.

# VILLAGE INN

1038 Apgar Street • Apgar, MT 59936 • (406) 888–5632

Village Inn is a long, two-story motel-style wooden building that offers a total of thirty-six rooms. The inn sits at the end of a short road, directly on the shore of scenic Lake McDonald. The building, constructed in 1956, was flooded and remodeled in the mid-1960s. Each room enjoys an excellent view of the lake and the mountains beyond. The small registration area at the front of the building offers coffee but no chairs or lobby area. The inn also has no restaurant, although two eating establishments are a short walk up the street. Village Inn is located in Apgar, Montana, 3 miles inside the west entrance to Glacier National Park.

The inn offers four types of rooms. All the rooms are nicely furnished and have heat and a full bath but no air conditioning, telephone, or television. They have wood paneling throughout, and each room has a large window and an outside balcony or patio that offer excellent views of Lake McDonald. The rooms all have doors that open to the balcony or patio. Larger rooms on the first floor can also be entered from the parking lot behind the

*The Village Inn*

building. Unless you specifically desire one of the kitchen units, we recommend a second-floor room for increased privacy and a better view of the lake. The twelve least expensive rooms sit at one end of the building, six on the second floor and six on the ground floor. Half the rooms have one double bed, and the other half have two twin beds.

Ten two-bedroom family units, all on the second floor, have a double bed in one bedroom and either a double and twin bed or a double bed and a sofa bed. These rooms cost $20 to $25 more per night and are quite a bit larger than the least expensive rooms described above. On the first floor twelve rooms have a bedroom and a kitchen with a refrigerator, sink, oven, and stove. These are the same size as the two-bedroom units on the second floor and substitute the kitchen in place of the second bedroom. The inn also offers two suites at each end of the second floor that have a living room and two back bedrooms, each with a double bed. A sofa bed is in the living room. The two suites cost about $10 extra per night compared with the two-bedroom and kitchen units.

Famous western artist Charles Russell had a home built beside Lake McDonald in 1908 by Dimon Apgar, Sr. Russell's studio, which still stands, was constructed eight years later.

Village Inn is a quiet place to spend a night or two on the west side of Glacier National Park. The inn's location at the end of a short road allows you to avoid the crowds while enjoying a view of Lake McDonald and some of the park's scenic mountains. A gravel beach just outside the rooms leads to the cool waters of the lake. The inn is located less than a block from both a deli and a restaurant that each serves good food at reasonable prices. It is also a short walk from a National Park Service visitor center that offers exhibits and an audiovisual program. Park Service rangers are at the visitor center to answer questions about the park. You will also find three gift shops and a couple of ice cream shops nearby. A store offers limited groceries, beer, and wine.

- **ROOMS:** Singles, doubles, triples, and quads. Some of the family units and the two suites can hold up to six persons. All rooms have private baths.

- **RESERVATIONS:** Glacier Park, Inc., 1850 North Central, Mail Station 0928, Phoenix, AZ 85077–0928. Phone (602) 207–6000.

- **RATES:** Standard rooms ($$$) single or double; kitchen units ($$$$) single or double; two-bedroom family units and three-room suites ($$$$). Rates are quoted for two adults. Children eleven and under are free with an adult. Additional adults are $6.00.

- **LOCATION:** In the small village of Apgar, Montana, 3 miles from the West Glacier entrance station.

- **SEASON:** Mid-May through late September.

- **FOOD:** No food service is available at Village Inn. Less than a block away, Village Deli serves sandwiches, ice cream, and drinks from 9:30 A.M. to 8:30 P.M. Within 1 block Eddie's Cafe ($$) serves breakfast, lunch, and dinner from 7:00 A.M. to 9:30 P.M. Depending on the weather, both restaurants are open from mid-May through most of September. A store sells limited grocery items, beer, and wine.

- **TRANSPORTATION:** Scheduled airlines serve Kalispell, Montana, where rental cars are available. An airport shuttle service from Kalispell goes to West Glacier. Tours of the park can be arranged from West Glacier. Amtrak service is available to Belton/West Glacier (800–872–7245), where rental cars are across the street from the station. A private shuttle serves various points in the park, including Apgar, from July 1 through the end of August.

- **FACILITIES:** The village of Apgar has gift shops, a restaurant, a deli, an ice cream shop, bicycle rentals, boat rentals, and a National Park Service visitor center.

- **ACTIVITIES:** Nightly ranger/naturalist talks at the Apgar campground, boating, swimming (very cool water), fishing, hiking, horseback riding. Sightseeing tours of the park leave from Apgar.

# NEVADA

## LAKE MEAD NATIONAL RECREATION AREA

601 Nevada Highway
Boulder City, NV 89005
(702) 293–8906

Lake Mead National Recreation Area comprises nearly 1.5 million acres of desert landscape surrounding Lake Mead and Lake Mohave. The 290 square miles of clear water in the two lakes is supplied by the Colorado River. Lake Mead is 110 miles long and results from the famous Hoover Dam near Boulder City, Nevada. Farther south, 67-mile-long Lake Mohave is formed by Davis Dam near Bullhead City, Arizona. The recreation area is particularly popular for water-related activities such as boating, fishing, and waterskiing. Areas near the lake are often five to ten degrees warmer than Las Vegas, which means that summer temperatures frequently rise to 110 degrees Farenheit and above. The recreation area is located in southern Nevada and northwestern Arizona. Main access is via U.S. 93, which connects Las Vegas, Nevada, and Kingman, Arizona.

###  Lodging in Lake Mead National Recreation Area

Five lodging facilities are scattered throughout Lake Mead National Recreation Area. Echo Bay Resort, Lake Mead Resort at Boulder Beach, and Temple Bar Resort are each on Lake Mead in the northern half of the recreation area. Cottonwood Cove Marina and Lake Mohave Resort at Katherine Landing are on Lake Mohave in the southern half of the recreation area. The three facilities on Lake Mead and Lake Mohave Resort on Lake Mohave are operated by Seven Crown Resorts of Irvine, California. All five facilities are designed for individuals interested in water-based activities, in particular boating and fishing.

# LAKE MEAD NATIONAL RECREATION AREA

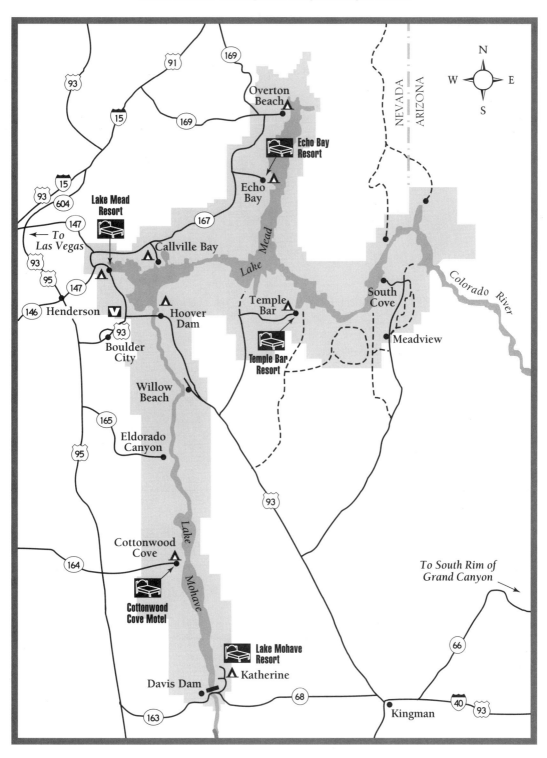

# COTTONWOOD COVE MARINA

Box 1000 • Cottonwood Cove, NV 89046 • (702) 297–1464

*Cottonwood Cove Motel*

Cottonwood Cove is a family resort with overnight accommodations, a restaurant, and a large marina, all on the Nevada shoreline of Lake Mohave. The cement block motel building, with twenty-four guest rooms, was renovated in 1995. The separate restaurant was renovated in 1996. Cottonwood Cove Resort is on the west side of Lake Mohave, 14 miles east of the intersection of Highway 164 and U.S. Highway 95. It is 70 miles southeast of Las Vegas, Nevada, via U.S. 95.

The one-story motel's twenty-four guest rooms each provide lake views. The rooms have either one king bed or two double beds and a private bath with a combination tub-shower. All rooms are the same size, and those with a king bed cost about $5.00 extra. Each room has a patio that provides access to a swimming beach and harbor.

- **ROOMS:** Doubles, triples, and quads. All rooms have a full bath.

- **RESERVATIONS:** Cottonwood Cove Marina, P.O. Box 1000, Cottonwood Cove, NV 89046. Phone (702) 297–1464.

- **RATES:** All rooms ($$$) from March 16 through the end of October; ($$) during Value Season, from November 1 through March 15. Value Season rates not applicable during national holidays. Rates are quoted for two adults. Extra persons are $8.00 per night. Rollaway beds are $6.00 extra. Children five years and under are free.

- **LOCATION:** Fourteen miles east of Searchlight, Nevada, on Highway 164. The resort is approximately 70 miles southeast of Las Vegas, Nevada.

- **SEASON:** The resort is open year-round. High season is from March 16 to October 31, when rates are highest.

- **FOOD:** A full-service restaurant ($$/$$$) serves three meals daily. A store sells groceries and supplies.

- **TRANSPORTATION:** No public transportation serves Cottonwood Cove. The nearest major airport is at Las Vegas, where rental vehicles are available. An airport is also at Laughlin, Nevada.

- **FACILITIES:** Restaurant, convenience store, full-service marina.

- **ACTIVITIES:** Fishing, boating, and waterskiing. Numerous casinos are about forty-five minutes away in Laughlin, Nevada.

## ECHO BAY RESORT

Overton, NV 89040 • (702) 394–4000

*Echo Bay Resort*

A marina complex, Echo Bay Resort includes a 1970s two-story cement block motel that sits on a hill overlooking the west side of the Overton Arm of Lake Mead. Approximately half the resort's fifty-two rooms face the water; a marina is in front. The motel, with several nearby palm trees, has an appearance similar to what you might expect near the Florida coast. A large wooden deck on the lake side is accessed from the second floor. Plentiful parking is directly beside the building and close to the main entrance to the registration area. Pets are permitted with a $25.00 deposit and an additional daily charge of $5.00. The resort is 60 miles northeast of Las Vegas, Nevada, and the farthest north of the five lodging facilities in Lake Mead National Recreation Area. It sits at the end of a paved road, 5 miles east of Highway 167.

All of the rooms at Echo Bay have air conditioning, heat, television, and a telephone. Furniture incudes a dresser, a table, and three chairs. Nearly all of the rooms have two chairs on a private balcony or patio. Rooms on both sides of the building are accessed through a central corridor that can be entered at either end of the building or near the registration area on the main floor. Three categories of rooms are offered. The least expensive rooms have two double beds and face west, toward the parking lot. A few face a large cement block wall and have no balcony or patio—try to avoid these. Twenty-five rooms face the water and have a single king bed; these cost about $10 more than rooms on the opposite side of the building. Three extra-large rooms have two double beds and a Hide-A-Bed. Several rooms on the south side of the building appear to have considerably more floor space than the other rooms but rent for the same daily rate.

Echo Bay is a water-based resort that appeals primarily to individuals who boat and fish. A National Park Service ranger station and campground are nearby, but most facilities are some distance away. A marina rents boats of all types, from personal watercraft to large houseboats. The main resort building has a 2,500-square-foot conference room on the second floor. A restaurant has a nautical decor, with a wall of large windows that provides a view of the lake. A cocktail lounge located next to the restaurant is accessed through the same outside door. A snack bar/store with supplies and limited groceries is at the marina.

**M**any people who visit Lake Mead National Recreation Area are interested in houseboat rentals, which are available at the marinas. Most houseboats are about 14 feet wide, with lengths that range from 40 to nearly 60 feet. The smaller units sleep six or eight persons, while the larger units can sleep a dozen or more. Be forewarned that houseboats aren't cheap to rent. Smaller houseboats often cost $200 to $300 per night for weeklong rentals and more for shorter rentals. Larger houseboats that hold up to ten or twelve persons rent for $400 to $500 per night for weeklong rentals and even more for two- or three-night rentals. Rental fees are often reduced during the off-season of mid-September to mid-June (excluding Memorial Day weekend). Houseboats are available at 7:00 A.M. on the first day and need to be returned by 4:00 P.M. on the last day. Reservations and deposits are required.

- **ROOMS:** Doubles, triples, and quads. All rooms have a full bath.

- **RESERVATIONS:** Seven Crown Resorts, P.O. Box 16247, Irvine, CA 92623–0068. Phone (800) 752–9669. Reservations require a one-night deposit. A seventy-two-hour cancellation is required for deposit refund.

- **RATES:** Rates ($$$) are quoted for two adults per room, except extra-large rooms, which are quoted for four adults. Extra persons and rollaway beds are $6.00 additional. Children five years and under are free.

- **LOCATION:** Sixty miles northeast of Las Vegas via Highways 147 and 167. The resort is at the end of a paved road, 5 miles east of Highway 167.

- **SEASON:** The resort is open year-round except Christmas Day. High season is during summer months, when the resort often fills on weekends.

- **FOOD:** A full-service restaurant ($$/$$$) serves three full meals daily and is open from 7:00 A.M. to 9:00 P.M. in-season. Hours can change during the off-season. The cocktail lounge is open from 4:00 P.M. to midnight. A snack bar/store at the marina is open from 7:00 A.M. to 8:00 P.M.

- **TRANSPORTATION:** The nearest major airport is at Las Vegas, where rental cars are available. An asphalt landing strip 3 miles from Echo Bay provides access for private planes. The resort has a free pickup service when called ahead.

- **FACILITIES:** A restaurant, cocktail lounge, and conference room are in the main building. An adjacent gas station sells unleaded gasoline, diesel fuel, and propane. A Laundromat is at the nearby RV park. A full-service marina rents a variety of boats, including houseboats.

- **ACTIVITIES:** Fishing, waterskiing, boating.

## LAKE MEAD RESORT

322 Lake Shore Road • Boulder City, NV 89005 • (702) 293–2074

*Lake Mead Resort and Marina*

Lake Mead Resort is a complex of three one-story cement block buildings on a hill overlooking the Boulder Basin section of Lake Mead, with a floating marina and restaurant situated a quarter-mile down the road. The buildings sit in a grassy area a short distance back from the parking lot. Lake Mead Resort is located at Boulder Beach, 6 miles north of

Boulder City, Nevada. Of the five lodging facilities in Lake Mead National Recreation Area, this is the nearest to Las Vegas (30 miles).

Most of the resort's forty-three rooms are in a U-shaped building that sits parallel to the shoreline of Boulder Basin. Rooms in this building are relatively small and have one double bed. A smaller adjacent building houses the registration office and a very nice suite with a living room, bedroom, and complete kitchen. A separate annex has eight larger rooms with two queen beds. All the rooms have heat, air conditioning, and television (with cable). One handicap-accessible room is available. A swimming pool is on the opposite side of the parking lot.

*Lake Mead, with 550 miles of shoreline, is formed by famous Hoover Dam. The dam, completed in 1935, tamed this portion of the often wild Colorado River. The giant concrete structure required more than 5,000 men to work around the clock for five years. Downstream, Davis Dam was completed in 1953. Guided tours of Hoover Dam are offered daily. Self-guiding tours of Davis Dam are also available.*

- **ROOMS:** Mostly doubles, with some triples, and quads. All rooms have a private bath.

- **RESERVATIONS:** Seven Crown Resorts, P.O. Box 16247, Irvine, CA 92623–0068. Phone (800) 752–9669. Reservations require a one-night deposit. A seventy-two-hour cancellation is required for deposit refund.

- **RATES:** All regular and deluxe rooms ($$); suites ($$$$). Rates are quoted for two adults per room. Extra persons and rollaway beds are $6.00 additional. Children five years and under are free.

- **LOCATION:** Six miles north of Boulder City, Nevada, on Lakeshore Scenic Drive. The resort is 30 miles southeast of Las Vegas.

- **SEASON:** The resort is open year-round except Christmas Day. High season is during summer months when the resort often fills on weekends.

- **FOOD:** A full-service restaurant ($$/$$$) at the marina serves three full meals. The cocktail lounge and store are also at the marina.

- **TRANSPORTATION:** The nearest major airport is at Las Vegas, where rental cars are available.

- **FACILITIES:** Swimming pool. A restaurant, cocktail lounge, and store are at the full-service marina where boat rentals are available.

- **ACTIVITIES:** Fishing, waterskiing, boating.

# TEMPLE BAR RESORT

Temple Bar, AZ 86443 • (520) 767–3211

*Temple Bar Resort*

Temple Bar Resort consists of an eighteen-unit wood and concrete block motel, four free-standing fishing cabins, a restaurant, and an adjacent store. The complex also includes a full-service marina and a paved 3,500-foot airstrip. The resort sits on the south shoreline of Lake Mead within view of a large monolith called The Temple. Temple Bar Resort is located 28 miles northeast of U.S. Highway 93, which connects Las Vegas, Nevada, with Kingman, Arizona. It is 78 miles east of Las Vegas.

All of the motel rooms at Temple Bar have heat, air conditioning, telephone, television, and a private bathroom. Twelve of the eighteen motel rooms have two double beds. Six of these units have a view of the lake. Three of the remaining six rooms offer a double bed and double hideaway. One of these has a kitchen. Two kitchen suites have two double beds and a hideaway bed. One deluxe room has two double beds. The four wood fishing cabins have a kitchen but no bath.

- **ROOMS:** Doubles, triples, and quads. Suites hold up to six adults. All rooms except fishing cabins have a full bath.

- **RESERVATIONS:** Seven Crown Resorts, P.O. Box 16247, Irvine, CA 92623–0068. Phone (800) 752–9669. Reservations require a one-night deposit. A seventy-two-hour notification is required for a full refund.

- **RATES:** Regular motel rooms ($$); kitchen unit and kitchen suites ($$$); fishing cabins ($). Rates are quoted for two adults in regular units and for three adults in kitchen suites. Extra persons and rollaway beds are $6.00 additional. Children five years and under are free.

- **LOCATION:** The resort is 78 miles east of Las Vegas, Nevada. It is at the end of a paved road 28 miles northeast of Highway 93.

- **SEASON:** The resort is open year-round except for Christmas Day. High season is during summer, and the resort often fills on summer weekends.

- **FOOD:** A full-service restaurant ($$/$$$) serves three full meals daily. A convenience store sells groceries and supplies.

- **TRANSPORTATION:** Kingman, Arizona, and Las Vegas, Nevada, both have airports with rental car service.

- **FACILITIES:** Restaurant, cocktail lounge, store, marina. A Laundromat is at the nearby RV park.

- **ACTIVITIES:** Fishing, boating, and waterskiing.

## LAKE MOHAVE RESORT AT KATHERINE LANDING

Bullhead City, AZ 86430 • (520) 754–3245

*Lake Mohave Resort at Katherine Landing*

Lake Mohave Resort is a marina complex that sits on a hill above Lake Mohave. The two-story motel, constructed of wood and cement block in the early 1970s, provides a total of fifty-two rooms in a large grassy area landscaped with palm trees. The resort is located at the south end of Lake Mohave, just off Highway 68, north of Davis Dam. It is the southernmost lodging facility in Lake Mead National Recreation Area. Lake Mohave Resort is 32 miles west of Kingman, Arizona.

The resort offers five types of accommodations. All of the rooms include air conditioning, heat, a telephone, a television, a full bathroom, and a private balcony or patio. Twelve of the resort's least expensive rooms have one king bed. Thirty-one rooms have two double beds. Six of these rooms include a kitchen and rent for an additional $4.00 per night. Eight rooms classified as kitchen suites have two queen beds. A single deluxe rental house, which sleeps up to ten persons, includes three bedrooms, two baths, and a kitchen. The rental house is attached to the end of the main building.

As is the case with its sister resorts on Lake Mead, activities at Lake Mohave Resort center on the water and primarily appeal to individuals who enjoy fishing, waterskiing, and boating. A full marina provides slips, moorage, a gas dock, and repair facilities. The main building of the resort houses a full-service restaurant and lounge. A Laundromat is in the nearby RV park, and a convenience store and tackle shop are adjacent to the restaurant. The booming town of Laughlin, Nevada, and its many casinos is a short drive from the resort.

- **ROOMS:** Doubles, triples, and quads. All rooms have a full bath.

- **RESERVATIONS:** Seven Crown Resorts, P.O. Box 16247, Irvine, CA 92623–0068. Phone (800) 752–9669. A seventy-two-hour notification is required for a full refund.

- **RATES:** Rates ($$) are quoted for two adults per room, except kitchen units and suites, which are quoted for three adults per room. Rollaway beds are $6.00 extra. Children five years and under are free.

- **LOCATION:** The resort is located on the shore of Lake Mohave, 32 miles west of Kingman, Arizona. It is 3 miles off Highway 68.

> Lake Mead and Lake Mohave offer excellent fishing and have open season on all species of fish year-round. Largemouth bass, rainbow trout, channel catfish, black crappie, and bluegill are in both lakes. Lake Mead is noted for an abundance of striped bass, some weighing fifty pounds and more. Rainbow trout are the most popular catch in Lake Mohave. Fishing from shore requires an appropriate state fishing license. Fishing from a boat requires a fishing license from either Nevada or Arizona and a special use stamp from the other state. Licenses and stamps are sold at most of the marinas.

- **SEASON:** The resort is open year-round except for Christmas Day. High season is during summer, and the resort often fills on summer weekends.

- **FOOD:** A full-service restaurant ($$/$$$) serves three full meals daily. A store adjacent to the restaurant sells groceries and supplies.

- **TRANSPORTATION:** Kingman, Arizona, and Las Vegas, Nevada, both have airports with rental car service.

- **FACILITIES:** A restaurant and cocktail lounge are in the main building. A Laundromat is at the nearby RV park. A full-service marina with houseboat rentals is in front of the lodge building.

- **ACTIVITIES:** Fishing, boating, and waterskiing. Numerous casinos are a short distance away in Laughlin, Nevada.

# NORTH CAROLINA

## BLUE RIDGE PARKWAY

200 BBB&T Building
Asheville, NC 28801
(704) 259–0710

The Blue Ridge Parkway comprises 81,000 acres in a narrow strip alongside 470 miles of winding road that follows the crest of the Blue Ridge Mountains. The parkway provides access to craft centers, campgrounds, scenic overlooks, log cabins, rail fences, and beautiful mountain vistas. The Blue Ridge Parkway is especially beautiful in the spring and fall. The parkway is located in western North Carolina and western Virginia. The north end of the parkway connects with Shenandoah National Park, and the south end leads to Great Smoky Mountains National Park.

###  Lodging Along the Blue Ridge Parkway

Four lodging facilities are within the boundaries of the Blue Ridge Parkway. Accommodations range from very nice two-story lodges to very rustic cabins with private bath. The facilities are scattered along the parkway from mile marker 86 in the north to very near the south entrance and Great Smoky Mountains National Park.

# BLUE RIDGE PARKWAY

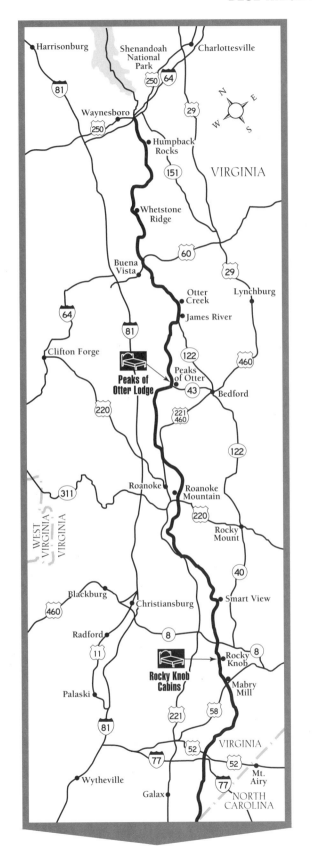

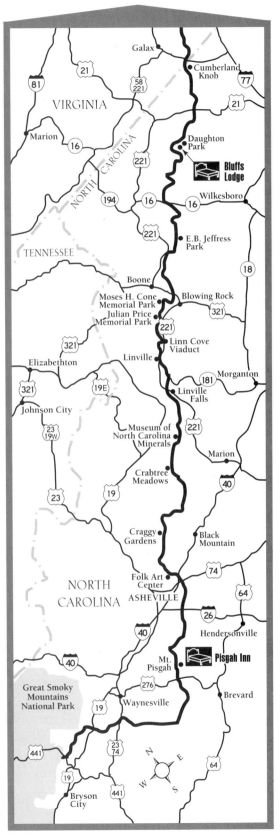

# BLUFFS LODGE

Route 1, Box 266 • Laurel Springs, NC 28644–9716 • (919) 372–4499

*Bluffs Lodge*

Bluffs Lodge consists of two identical two-story lodge buildings that sit on a grassy hillside overlooking a meadow and surrounding hillside. No other buildings are connected to the lodge, although a coffee shop and gas station are a quarter-mile away on the parkway. Each lodge building contains twelve rooms, four on each floor of the back side facing the meadow and four rooms on the front facing the parking lot. A balcony runs across the second floor on the back side. Rock walkways are on the front side and the bottom floor of the back side. The buildings opened in 1949 but are well maintained. Bluffs Lodge is located in northern North Carolina in the Doughton Park area of the Blue Ridge Parkway. It is at milepost 241, about midway between the north and south entrances to the parkway.

All the rooms at Bluffs Lodge are nearly identical except for the bedding and the views. The rooms each have hot-water heat and a full bath with a combination tub-shower but no air conditioning, telephone, or television. Each room has a desk and several chairs. The eight second-floor back-side rooms have two twin beds except corner rooms 203A and 203B, which have one double. Bedding in other rooms varies from a double bed, to a double plus a twin, to three twins, to one room that has two double beds. The best bet is to try for a second-floor room on the back side, which has a superior view. All rooms rent for the same rate.

Bluffs Lodge is a quiet place in a lovely setting. It is a quarter-mile off the Blue Ridge Parkway, so you won't be bothered by traffic noise, and since no restaurant or visitor center is at the site, there is no congestion of people or vehicles. You will have to walk (or drive) a quarter-mile to the coffee shop in order to eat, but that isn't so bad. Besides, the old-fashioned coffee shop (it still has counter service) with its vaulted ceiling is kind of neat. A nice rock patio area between the two buildings has a large outdoor stone fireplace and many chairs and tables for viewing the scenery or visiting.

- **ROOMS:** Singles, doubles, triples, and one quad. All rooms have a private bath with a combination tub-shower.

- **RESERVATIONS:** National Park Concessions, Bluffs Lodge, Route 1, Box 266, Laurel Springs, NC 28644–9716. Phone (919) 372–4499. During the off-season write Bluffs Lodge, P.O. Box 397, Jefferson, NC 28640. Reservations require one night's deposit. Cancellation of forty-eight hours required for full refund of deposit.

- **RATES:** All rooms ($$). Rates are quoted for two adults. Additional persons are charged $7 each. Children twelve and under stay free.

- **LOCATION:** In northern North Carolina, near the midpoint of the Blue Ridge Parkway at milepost 241. The lodge is a quarter-mile off the parkway.

- **SEASON:** End of April through the end of October.

- **FOOD:** A coffee shop ($/$$) a quarter-mile from the lodge serves breakfast, lunch, and dinner. A special is offered each evening. Snacks are sold at a gas station next to the coffee shop.

- **TRANSPORTATION:** The nearest scheduled airline serves Greensboro, North Carolina, about two hours from the lodge. A major airport is three hours away at Charlotte, North Carolina.

- **FACILITIES:** No facilities are at the lodge. A coffee shop, gift shop, and gas station are a quarter-mile away on the Blue Ridge Parkway.

- **ACTIVITIES:** Hiking. Park Service rangers present programs on the lodge patio each Sunday evening. Programs are presented on Friday and Saturday nights at the nearby campground.

Lodges, overlooks, restaurants, and other major points of interest along the Blue Ridge Parkway can be located according to milepost markers alongside the road. Mile marker 0 is at Rockfish Gap near Waynesboro, Virginia, the northern entrance to the parkway. Each mile is numbered progressively southward. Be certain to stop at a visitor center and pick up a copy of the parkway folder that provides a map along with the locations of points of interest on the parkway.

# PEAKS OF OTTER LODGE

P.O. Box 489 • Bedford, VA 24523 • (540) 586–1081

*Peaks of Otter Lodge*

Peaks of Otter Lodge consists of a main registration and dining building and three adjacent two-story lodging buildings that provide a total of sixty-three overnight rooms. All four of the wood and cement block buildings were constructed in the mid-1960s and have a similar appearance. The three buildings with rooms (a few rooms are in the main building) are identical. The buildings sit side by side on the grassy bank of Abbott Lake, and all the rooms provide an excellent view of this small but pretty body of water. Peaks of Otter Lodge is located about 35 miles north of Roanoke, Virginia, at mile marker 85 on the Blue Ridge Parkway. It is the farthest north of the four lodging facilities on the parkway.

The twenty rooms in each of the three lodging buildings are identical. They are roomy and nicely furnished. Three suites in the main building are also available. The regular rooms each have two double beds and a full bath with a combination shower-tub. Each room has electric heat and air conditioning but no television or telephone. Second-floor rooms have a private balcony and first-floor rooms a patio with table and chairs that face the lake. Two rooms without a balcony are offered at a discount. Two handicap-accessible rooms are available. The three suites in the main registration building are each different and rent for $15 to $25 more than a regular room. One suite with a queen, two twins, and a sofa bed can sleep up to six adults.

Peaks of Otter Lodge is a very nice facility that is perfect for a weekend getaway. Plan to do a lot of reading and hiking while you visit. A paved walking trail circles Abbott Lake. Three other loop trails are nearby. Daily bus trips to Sharp Top Mountain (nominal fee) leave hourly from the nearby camp store when weather permits. Sitting on one side of small Abbott Lake with a background of tree-covered hills and mountains makes for a tranquil setting. You can even fish in the lake, so long as you use artificial lures. The main lodge has a small lobby with a large stone fireplace and ceiling-height windows that provide a view of the lake and hills. The country-style dining room serves three meals a day, including a special buffet each Sunday. It is best known for its trout dinners. A coffee shop serves sandwiches and light meals all day. The main building also contains a gift shop, a coffee shop, and a downstairs cocktail lounge.

- **ROOMS:** Singles, doubles, triples, and quads. One suite will accommodate up to six adults. All rooms have a private bath with a combination tub-shower.

- **RESERVATIONS:** Peaks of Otter Lodge, P.O. Box 489, Bedford, VA 24523. Phone (800) 542–5927. One night's deposit required via check or money order. Cancellation of twenty-four hours required for full refund.

- **RATES:** Regular rooms ($$); suites ($$$). Rates are slightly higher on holiday weekends and during all of October. Discounts and packages are offered from November 1 to Easter.

- **LOCATION:** Thirty-five miles north of Roanoke, Virginia, at mileposts 84/87 of the Blue Ridge Parkway.

- **SEASON:** Open year-round.

- **FOOD:** A dining room serves breakfast, lunch, and dinner, including a special Sunday buffet. A coffee shop in the main building is open for breakfast and sandwiches. A nearby camp store has limited groceries.

- **TRANSPORTATION:** Nearby Roanoke and Lynchburg, Virginia, each provide scheduled airline service. Rental cars are available in each town.

*Several short- and intermediate-length hiking trails are near Peaks of Otter Lodge. The nearest is the 1-mile loop trail around Abbott Lake. Directly across the parkway a 2-mile loop trail leads to Johnson Farm, where living history demonstrations are presented on a seasonal basis. The same trail connects with the 3.3-mile Harkening Hill Loop Trail, which leads to a ridge where distant views are possible. The most popular trail leads 1.6 miles from the camp store to the summit of Sharp Top Mountain. The summit offers a 360-degree view of the area. A map and description of these and other trails can be obtained at the lodge or at the National Park Service visitor center across the road.*

- **FACILITIES:** Restaurant, coffee shop, cocktail lounge, gift shop, gas station, camp store, National Park Service visitor center.

- **ACTIVITIES:** Hiking, fishing, interpretive programs, National Park Service campfire programs on weekend evenings.

# THE PISGAH INN

P.O. Box 749 • Waynesville, NC 28786 • (704) 235–8228

*The Pisgah Inn*

The Pisgah Inn consists of three buildings with accommodations, a separate building with a restaurant and gift shop, a gas station, and a store. A National Park Service campground is across the road. All of the buildings are of wood and masonry construction. The registration desk is at the end of the lodging building nearest the restaurant. The three two-story buildings with lodging provide a total of fifty-one rooms, including one suite. All of the rooms are a short walk from the dining room. Each of the rooms provides an excellent view of the distant mountains. The three lodge buildings and the restaurant sit alongside one another at 5,000 feet on the side of 5,749-foot Mt. Pisgah. The gas station and camp store are nearby. The inn was constructed in the mid-1960s. The Pisgah Inn is in southwest North Carolina, approximately 25 miles south of Asheville, North Carolina. It is the farthest south of the four lodging facilities on the Blue Ridge Parkway, at milepost 408.

Two types of rooms and one suite are offered at the inn. The only difference between the two categories of rooms is that thirty rooms labeled "deluxe" are slightly larger and were remodeled in 1993. These have a nicer appearance, including a new carpet. Twenty rooms rent as "standard" at $5.00 per night less. All of the rooms have heat, a full bathroom with a combination tub-shower, and a color television but no air conditioning or telephone. Each room has a private balcony with rocking chairs. Most of the rooms have two double beds, and some have one queen. Three handicap-accessible rooms with one queen bed are available. Great views from the back windows or balcony are available from each of the rooms. Rooms are entered from an outside door facing the parking lot. More than enough parking is available and close to each of the rooms. The single suite has one large room with a sitting area, one king bed, and the only fireplace of any room at the inn.

The Pisgah Inn is a nice place to spend a restful weekend. Temperatures are generally cool, even during summer. The views are great, and the facility is comfortable. The restaurant has ceiling-high windows on three walls that provide views from nearly any table. This is an excellent area for hiking, and good fishing is about 10 miles away. National Park Service rangers offer evening weekend programs across the road at the campground amphitheater.

- **ROOMS:** Singles, doubles, triples, and quads. All rooms have a private bath with a combination tub-shower.

- **RESERVATIONS:** The Pisgah Inn, P.O. Box 749, Waynesville, NC 28786. Phone (704) 235–8228. One night's deposit is required. Refund requires cancellation forty-eight hours ahead of arrival.

- **RATES:** All standard and deluxe rooms ($$); suite ($$$$). An extra $5.00 per night charged during holidays. Extra persons are $6.00 each. Children twelve years and younger are free with an adult.

- **LOCATION:** Southwest North Carolina, 25 miles south of Asheville on the Blue Ridge Parkway.

- **SEASON:** Early April through early November.

- **FOOD:** An attractive restaurant ($$/$$$) serves breakfast, lunch, and dinner. A nearby camp store sells limited groceries.

- **TRANSPORTATION:** The nearest scheduled airline service is at Asheville, where rental vehicles are available. No public transportation services the inn.

- **FACILITIES:** Restaurant, gift shop, Laundromat, gas station, camp store.

- **ACTIVITIES:** Hiking, evening weekend programs at the nearby campground amphitheater.

*The Biltmore Estate near Asheville, North Carolina, is one of this region's major visitor attractions. The 250-room mansion was constructed in the late 1800s by George Washington Vanderbilt, grandson of railroad tycoon Cornelius Vanderbilt. Allow at least a half-day for the full self-guiding tour (fee charged) of the home, winery, gardens, and greenhouse. The Biltmore Estate is 3 blocks north of Interstate 40 (exit 50) on U.S. Highway 25.*

# ROCKY KNOB CABINS

Route 1, Box 5 • Meadows of Dan, VA 24120–9603 • (540) 593–3503

*Duplex Unit at Rocky Knob Cabins*

Rocky Knob Cabins is a small complex consisting of one registration office/manager's cabin, a central bathhouse, and five older wooden buildings that sit in a semicircle in back of the bathhouse. Two of the buildings are constructed as duplex units, resulting in a total of seven rental cabins. The cabins are in a meadow surrounded by heavily wooded hills. There are no lobby, no dining room, and no recreation hall. The buildings sit all by themselves in as remote a setting as there is in any national park area. The wooden buildings were all built in the 1930s, during construction of the parkway. Rocky Knob Cabins is in southern Virginia, at milepost 174 on the Blue Ridge Parkway. It is 54 miles south of Roanoke, Virginia.

The seven cabins at Rocky Knob Cabins are virtually identical, with two double beds, electricity, and a kitchen with an oven and stove, refrigerator, and sink with cold water only. Linens and utensils, including pots, pans, plates, cups, and silverware, are provided. There is no heat (other than a stone fireplace in two of the cabins), air conditioning, telephone, or television. Each cabin has a kitchen table and chairs and also an outside porch with table and chairs. None of the cabins have a bathroom, and guests must use the central bathhouse, which has sinks, toilets, and showers. Two of the buildings are constructed as duplex units, with one unit in each duplex having a stone fireplace (wood not provided). None of the other cabins have a fireplace or heat of any kind. The three other buildings are freestanding cabins.

Rocky Knob Cabins is certainly one of the unique lodging units in the national park system. Staying there is like returning to Appalachia in years past—many years past. The cabins are old but clean and comfortable. The deciding factor for many travelers is whether a community bath is a viable alternative. If you don't mind this inconvenience and you want to stay overnight in a very rural setting, Rocky Knob may be your place. Also, Rocky Knob has no planned activities or other facilities; you are on your own for something to do. You will also enjoy a sense of solitude that many seek in a vacation. If you don't want to cook, a restaurant is a mile down the road. In addition, Mabry Mill, a famous stop on the Blue Ridge Parkway, is 2 miles south.

- **ROOMS:** Doubles, triples, and quads. None of the cabins have a private bath.

- **RESERVATIONS:** Rocky Knob Cabins, Route 1, Box 5, Meadows of Dan, VA 24120–9603. Phone (540) 593–3503; during the off-season write Rocky Knob Cabins, P.O. Box 27, Mammoth Cave, KY 42259. One night's deposit required. Cancellation notice of 48 hours required for full refund.

- **RATES:** All cabins ($). Rates are quoted for two adults. Extra adults are $5.00 each.

- **LOCATION:** Southern Virginia, 1 mile off the Blue Ridge Parkway at milepost 174. The cabins are approximately 55 miles south of Roanoke, Virginia.

- **SEASON:** Last week of May through Labor Day.

- **FOOD:** No dining facilities are available. A restaurant is about a mile up the road. A coffee shop is at Mabry Mill, 2 miles south on the Blue Ridge Parkway.

- **TRANSPORTATION:** Scheduled airlines serve Roanoke, Virginia, where rental vehicles are available.

- **FACILITIES:** Community bathhouse.

- **ACTIVITIES:** Hiking.

Mabry Mill, at milepost 176, is a favorite stop for travelers on the Blue Ridge Parkway. The mill, operated by E. B. Mabry from 1910 to 1935, today serves country ham, barbecue, and corn and buckwheat pancakes. Native handicrafts, including pottery, woodcraft, and metalcraft, are available for purchase. A trail takes you to the original gristmill, sawmill, blacksmith shop, and other outdoor exhibits. Demonstrations are presented in summer and fall.

# OREGON

## CRATER LAKE NATIONAL PARK

P.O. Box 7

Crater Lake, OR 97604

(503) 594–2211

Crater Lake National Park is comprised of 183,000 acres, including a deep blue lake that resulted from a collapse of Mt. Mazama, an ancient 12,000-foot volcano. A 33-mile paved road circles the lake. At 7,100 feet the days can be cool and the nights quite chilly. Heavy winter snowfall that averages 533 inches can keep portions of the Rim Road closed until July. Crater Lake is located in southern Oregon, 57 miles north of Klamath Falls. The major road into the park is Oregon Highway 62, which enters through the southwest corner.

###  Lodging in Crater Lake National Park

The park has two very different facilities that provide overnight accommodations. Crater Lake Lodge offer seventy-one rooms in an old but newly remodeled four-story wooden lodge that sits on the rim of Crater Lake. Mazama Village Motor Inn offers forty basic and less expensive rooms 7 miles south of the rim. While Crater Lake Lodge is one of the classic national park lodges, with a back patio, a large lobby, and two fireplaces, Mazama Village Motor Inn is more of a motel unit. Both locations have eating facilities. Crater Lake Lodge sits 1,000 feet higher than Mazama Village, resulting in lower temperatures.

# CRATER LAKE NATIONAL PARK

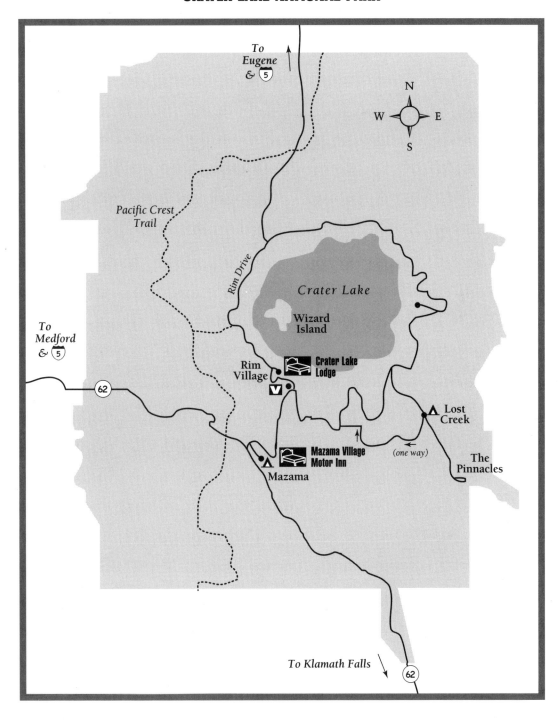

# CRATER LAKE LODGE

Crater Lake National Park, OR 97604 • (541) 594–2255, ext. 3014

*Crater Lake Lodge*

Crater Lake Lodge provides a total of seventy-one rooms in a fine old national park hotel that has been completely renovated. The four-story stone and wood building was originally completed in 1915 and reopened in 1995 after a six-year total renovation. The building sits on the rim of Crater Lake, allowing guests to view what many consider to be America's most beautiful lake from the window of some rooms. The lodge building has a cozy dining room on the first floor, which also contains the registration desk, lobby, and Great Hall with a massive stone fireplace. Another stone fireplace is in the registration lobby. The entire hotel is nonsmoking. Two elevators are near the registration area on the first floor. Parking may involve a short walk, so it is best to unload your luggage from a loading zone in front of the entrance and then locate a parking spot. Bell service is available. Crater Lake Lodge sits on the south rim of Crater Lake, at the east end of Rim Village. The lodge is 15 miles from both the west and the north entrances to the park.

All the rooms in the lodge vary by size, view, and bedding. The remodeled rooms look much newer than the exterior of the lodge would lead you to expect. All the rooms are nicely furnished and have heat but no air conditioning, telephone, or television. A few rooms have bathtubs but no showers. Rooms are entered from a center corridor that is accessed from elevators or a stairway near the registration desk. Bedding varies from one queen bed to two queen beds. Views vary from looking directly at the lake from the hotel's back-side rooms to looking across the parking lot toward mountains from the hotel's front rooms. Prices are established according to view and room size. Windows are largest on the second floor. Third-floor windows are high (your chin may rest on the windowsill), and fourth-floor windows are smaller but have window seats. The few first-floor rooms have virtually no view. Room 401, with one queen bed, allows a lake view from the claw-footed bathtub. Room 410 is quite large and has two window seats that provide a lake view. Room 220 has one queen bed in a large room that faces the lake. Room 221, a corner room with two queens, provides good views of both Crater Lake and Garfield Peak. Four loft suites, each with one bathroom, have bedrooms on two floors and windows that face both the front and the back of the building. These rent for about 50 percent more than view rooms with one bedroom.

Crater Lake Lodge is a comfortable place to stay during a trip to one of America's oldest national parks. The large back porch across most of the length of the original hotel has rocking chairs for relaxing while looking out over the deep blue water of Crater Lake. The Great Hall off the main lobby is covered in pine sheathing and has large windows that provide a terrific lake view. The large stone fireplace has gas logs that are lit each evening. An intimate dining room is just off the Great Hall. All in all, this is one of the nicest lodges of the national park system. Although the rooms have been remodeled enough to lose some of their rustic charm, the lodge building itself radiates its long history.

*Construction on Crater Lake Lodge commenced about a decade after Crater Lake became a national park in 1900. The building, while impressive from the outside, had many structural faults. Over the years major maintenance, including the installation of big columns to support the ceiling and walls in the Great Hall, was required to keep the lodge in operation. The National Park Service assumed ownership of the lodge in 1967 and in the early 1980s started considering its demise. The lodge was closed to visitors in 1988, but public and political pressure resulted in congressional support for a $15 million rehabilitation that included everything from a new foundation to a new roof frame. Essentially, the lodge was torn down and completely rebuilt from the ground up for a reopening in May 1995.*

- **ROOMS:** Doubles, triples, and quads. All rooms have a private bath, most with a tub-shower combination.

- **RESERVATIONS:** Crater Lake Lodge, Crater Lake National Park, 1211 Avenue C, White City, OR 97503. Phone (541) 830–8700; fax (541) 830–8514.

- **RATES:** Most rooms ($$$$); suites ($$$$$). Rates quoted for two adults except suites, which are for four adults. Children twelve years and under are free in the same room with an adult.

- **LOCATION:** On the south rim of Crater Lake, 15 miles from the west entrance to Crater Lake National Park.

- **SEASON:** Mid-May to mid-October, depending on the weather. The lodge will generally sell out from mid-June to the end of the season.

- **FOOD:** A small dining room ($$$/$$$$) offers breakfast, lunch, and dinner. Make dinner reservations early unless you are willing to eat very early or very late. A nearby cafeteria ($) at Rim Village offers complete breakfasts, sandwiches, pizza, and salads from 8:00 A.M. to 8:00 P.M. One floor above the cafeteria, a chalet-style restaurant ($$) is open for lunch and dinner from noon to 10:00 P.M.

- **TRANSPORTATION:** Scheduled airline service is available to Klamath Falls, Medford, and Eugene, Oregon, where vehicles can be rented.

- **FACILITIES:** A dining room. Rim Village, a short walk from the lodge, has a cafeteria, a restaurant, and a large gift shop. A National Park Service visitor center is on the rim near the lodge.

- **ACTIVITIES:** Boat tours of Crater Lake, hiking, fishing, and ranger-guided walks.

## MAZAMA VILLAGE MOTOR INN

Crater Lake National Park, OR 97604 • (541) 594–2255, ext. 3704

*Mazama Village Motor Inn*

**M**azama Village Motor Inn provides a total of forty rooms in ten modern chalet-style wooden buildings constructed in 1993. The one-story buildings each contain four guest rooms and sit around the outside of a paved one-way loop drive. Ample parking is directly in front of each building where the entry doors are located. The lodging complex sits in a heavily wooded area a short distance from facilities in Mazama Village that include a market and snack bar. Mazama Village Motor Inn is in the southern part of the park, at the intersection of Highway 62 and the road to Rim Drive. It is 7 miles from the rim and 8 miles from the west entrance of Crater Lake National Park. At an altitude of 6,000 feet, here it is warmer than at the higher rim area.

All of the rooms at Mazama Village Motor Inn are identical in size, bedding, and layout except for several that are handicap accessible. The rooms are nice and new, but this is basic motel-style lodging. Each room is relatively small and has two queen beds. The private bath has a shower but no tub. Each room has an entrance door in the front and a medium-size window in the back. No particularly good views are available from any of the rooms, and so no one room or building is preferable to any other. Each building has a picnic table in front. The handicap-accessible rooms have one queen bed and a bathroom that is somewhat larger than in the regular rooms.

The motor inn is a convenient place to stay on a one- or two-day visit to Crater Lake National Park. The rooms are basic but relatively close to places in the park you are likely to want to visit—in particular, the rim. The motor inn is within walking distance of Mazama Village, which includes a gas station, a market/snack bar, public showers, and a Laundromat. Evening programs are presented by National Park Service rangers at the nearby campground amphitheater, which is within easy walking distance. The motor inn is only an 8-mile drive from Rim Village, which has several restaurants and attractive Crater Lake Lodge.

- **ROOMS:** Doubles, triples, and quads. All rooms have private baths with showers only.

- **RESERVATIONS:** Crater Lake Company, Crater Lake National Park, 1211 Avenue C, White City, OR 97503. Phone (541) 830–8700; fax (541) 830–8514.

- **RATES:** For all rooms ($$$). Rate is quoted for two adults. Extra persons pay $6.00 per night. Children twelve years and under are free when staying with an adult.

- **LOCATION:** On the south side of Crater Lake National Park, 8 miles inside the west entrance.

- **SEASON:** Mid-May to mid-October, depending on the weather.

- **FOOD:** A snack bar ($) inside the market is open daily from 7:00 A.M. to 10:00 P.M. The snack bar serves pizza, sandwiches, ice cream, and beverages. Restaurants are at Rim Village, 8 miles from the inn.

- **TRANSPORTATION:** Scheduled airline service is available to Medford, Klamath Falls, and Eugene, Oregon, where cars may be rented.

- **FACILITIES:** Grocery store, Laundromat, snack bar, public showers, gas station.

- **ACTIVITIES:** Hiking and evening naturalist programs.

Mazama Village derives its name from the ancient volcano that self-destructed into what is now Crater Lake. This dormant volcano is a member of the Cascade Range, a string of volcanoes that extend from Lassen Peak in the south to Mt. Girabaldi near Vancouver, British Columbia. Mt. Mazama may once have towered to 12,000 feet above sea level before a violent eruption occurred about 7,700 years ago. After the chamber inside the mountain was emptied, the walls of the volcano collapsed in on itself to form a caldera that filled with water from rain and snow and resulted in the nation's deepest lake, at 1,932 feet.

# OREGON CAVES NATIONAL MONUMENT

19000 Caves Highway
Cave Junction, OR 97523 • (503) 592–2100

Oregon Caves National Monument was established in 1909 to protect eleven small caves and a 3-mile cave that has rare bats and all of the earth's six main rock types. The monument contains 480 acres of old-growth forest, including part of the most diverse conifer forest in the world. The national monument is located in southwestern Oregon, 20 miles east of Cave Junction via Oregon Highway 46. Although Highway 46 is paved, the last 8 miles are crooked and hilly. Motor homes and vehicles pulling trailers should avoid the road. Trailers can be dropped off at the Illinois Valley Visitor Center in Cave Junction or at Grayback Campground on Highway 46.

## Lodging in Oregon Caves National Monument

A wonderful six-story lodge with twenty-two guest rooms is the only lodging facility in this relatively small national monument. The lodge is at the end of the road near the entrance to the cave. Motels and restaurants are in the town of Cave Junction.

## OREGON CAVES NATIONAL MONUMENT

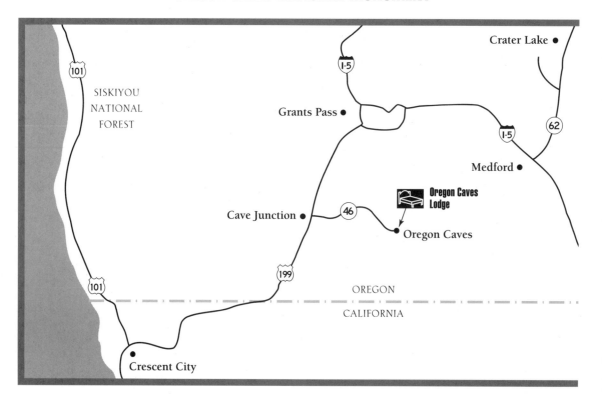

# OREGON CAVES LODGE

P.O. Box 128 • Cave Junction, OR 97523 • (541) 592–3400

*Oregon Caves Lodge*

For most travelers Oregon Caves Lodge remains one of the undiscovered jewels of the national park system. The facility not only calls itself a lodge but really is a lodge. The registration area, lobby, dining room, coffee shop, and all the overnight rooms are in the same Alpine-style wooden building that was constructed in 1934 and became a National Historic Landmark in 1987. The lobby is entered on the building's fourth floor (which the lodge calls the first floor), and overnight rooms are on that floor and the two floors above. A restaurant and coffee shop are one floor below. No smoking is permitted anywhere in the lodge. Oregon Caves Lodge is located at the end of Highway 46, 20 miles east of Cave Junction, Oregon.

Six-story Oregon Caves Lodge retains a coziness and warmth that modern hotels lack. It is completely covered with cedar bark sheathing, and wood shakes top the roof with its many gables. The large lobby area, with huge log supports and giant beams across the ceiling, is dominated by a double-hearth marble fireplace. Some of the original furnishings, including, chairs, card tables, writing desks, and a piano, remain in the lobby. Original furnish-

The first wood buildings, including the original chalet, were constructed here in 1923 by a group of businessmen who hoped to profit from curious tourists drawn to this area by the caves. The original chalet was expanded in 1941–42 and currently serves as the gift shop and cave ticket office. The bottom story is the original chalet while the added story now houses employees. The current Oregon Caves Lodge was finished at a total cost of $50,000 in 1934 after three years of work. The lodge remains relatively unchanged since its construction was completed.

ings are also in guest rooms on the second and third floors. Parking is directly in front of the lodge. The lodge sometimes fills on summer weekends, but rooms are likely to be available on most weekdays.

All of the twenty-two guest rooms offer heat but no air conditioning, telephone, or television. The rooms all differ with respect to bedding, size, interior layout, or view. Some rooms are much bigger than others. Some rooms have one queen bed, while others have a double bed and a single bed. A few have two double beds or two queen beds. Front rooms face the road or parking lot, while rooms in the back look out over a tree-covered ravine. Several rooms on the top floor are snuggled under gables. In general, the lodge offers three room classifications. Rooms with a full bath and good view rent for about $20 more per day than rooms with a lesser view or rooms with a bathtub but no shower. Three suites, composed of two bedrooms and one bath, rent for about $10 daily more than the view rooms, but the rate is for up to four occupants. Try for one of the rooms at the back of the lodge; these offer more quiet and better views. On the front side several rooms are near a small pond with a waterfall that provides a nice sound and decent view. Keep in mind there is no elevator so you will most likely have to climb stairs to your room.

Oregon Caves Lodge is a great place to spend several peaceful days in a wonderful facility. Spend the first afternoon taking one of the cave tours and the next day walking along the trails. The ticket office for the cave tour is directly across from the lodge. Arrive early enough and you may be able to do the cave tour and some hiking in the same day. On the other hand, maybe you would prefer sitting in the lobby and reading a good mystery. The lodge offers all the facilities you will need for a pleasant stay. The attractive dining room has large windows that look out over the ravine. A 1930s-era coffee shop is on the same floor. Giant logs provide support for the wooden stairway from the lobby to the second floor.

*Suite 309–310 of Oregon Caves Lodge is thought by some guests and employees to be haunted. In 1942 a newly married Elizabeth and her husband were staying in the lodge on their honeymoon. Unfortunately, she discovered her husband with a maid, became distraught, and committed suicide by hanging herself in her room. Since the hanging, housekeepers and guests have reported lights mysteriously turned on after being turned off and windows opened after being closed. On rare occasions piano music has been heard from the lobby area when no one appeared to be around.*

- **ROOMS:** Doubles, triples, and quads. Three suites will hold up to seven persons. All rooms have a private bath, although some have a tub but no shower.

- **RESERVATIONS:** Oregon Caves Company, P.O. Box 128, Cave Junction, OR 97523. Phone (541) 592–3400; fax (541) 592–6654.

- **RATES:** Standard rooms with full bath ($$$); rooms with no shower or lesser view ($$); suites ($$$). Rates for nonsuites quoted for two adults. Children six years and under with an adult are free. Extra persons are $10 each.

- **LOCATION:** Twenty miles south of Cave Junction, Oregon, at the end of Highway 46.

- **SEASON:** The lodge is open from May through October. Cave tours are offered year-round.

- **FOOD:** An attractive dining room ($$/$$$) is open from 5:00 to 9:00 P.M. for dinner only. Reservations are recommended but not required. A 1930s-era coffee shop ($) on the same floor serves breakfast, sandwiches, real milk shakes, and snacks from 7:00 A.M. to 5:00 P.M. A snack bar in the gift shop serves ice cream and beverages. Beer and wine are available at the registration desk.

- **TRANSPORTATION:** The nearest scheduled air service is at Grants Pass, Oregon, about 50 miles away. A shuttle (fee charged) operates from the lodge to Cave Junction visitor center and the Cave Junction airport.

- **FACILITIES:** Gift shop, restaurant, and coffee shop.

- **ACTIVITIES:** Cave tours, evening naturalist programs, and hiking. Three major trails begin at the lodge.

# SOUTH DAKOTA

## BADLANDS NATIONAL PARK

P.O. Box 6

Interior, SD 57750

(605) 433–5361

Badlands National Park comprises 243,000 acres of prairie grassland and scenic eroded landscape created millions of years ago by slow-moving streams. The park is located in southwest South Dakota, with the Pinnacles entrance 57 miles east of Rapid City off Interstate 90. Highway 240 provides access to the visitor center and much of the park. Three other National Park Service units—Jewel Cave National Monument, Wind Cave National Park, and world-famous Mount Rushmore National Memorial—are south of Rapid City.

 ## Lodging in Badlands National Park

Cedar Pass Lodge is the only facility providing accommodations in Badlands National Park. The lodge offers twenty-four individual cabins, a dining room, and a gift shop near the park visitor center on the park's east end. The lodge is 8 miles south of Interstate 90 on Highway 80.

# BADLANDS NATIONAL PARK

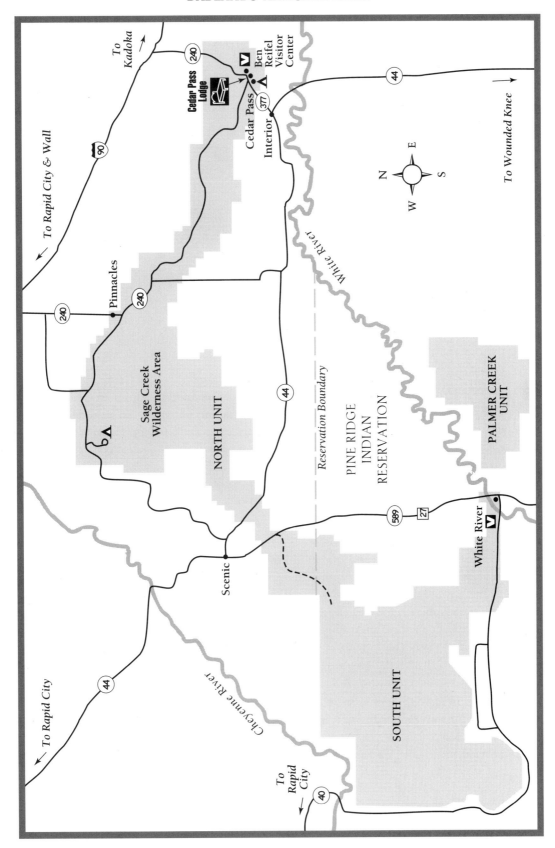

To Kadoka

240

To Rapid City & Wall

90

240

Pinnacles

240

Sage Creek Wilderness Area

NORTH UNIT

Cedar Pass Lodge

Ben Reifel Visitor Center

Cedar Pass

Interior

377

44

White River

Reservation Boundary

PINE RIDGE INDIAN RESERVATION

44

To Wounded Knee

N E S W

PALMER CREEK UNIT

589

27

White River

Scenic

Cheyenne River

To Rapid City

44

SOUTH UNIT

To Rapid City

40

# CEDAR PASS LODGE

1 Cedar Street • P.O. Box 5 • Interior, SD 57750 • (605) 433–5460

*Cabin at Cedar Pass Lodge*

Cedar Pass Lodge is a complex of freestanding cabins situated behind a wood and stucco registration building that also houses a restaurant and gift shop. No accommodations are in the main building, but all the cabins are a short walk from the registration desk and restaurant. Adequate parking is beside each cabin and the restaurant. Cedar Pass Lodge is operated by the Oglala Sioux Tribe. The lodge sits in a relatively barren area at the east end of Badlands National Park, within view of the Badlands. It is 8.5 miles south of Interstate 90, just south of the park's main visitor center.

The lodge offers twenty-four individual cabins with heat and air conditioning but not telephone or television. The cabins are carpeted and have wood-paneled walls. Each cabin has a small front porch with chairs but no patio. Bedding ranges from a queen bed, to a double and a single, to two double beds. All the cabins have a private bath, most with a shower but no tub. A few units have a combination tub-shower. Three two-bedroom units have either a queen and two double beds or three double beds.

Cedar Pass Lodge is an interesting and convenient place to stay during your trip to Badlands National Park. The lodge is a short walk from the park's main visitor center, which has exhibits on the Badlands. The lodge is also near the park campground, where evening programs are presented by National Park Service rangers. An 80-mile loop drive through the park to the small town of Scenic and then back through Buffalo Gap National Grassland on Highway 44 offers an interesting day of sightseeing and potential hiking. A side trip to the small town of Wall (north of the Pinnacles entrance to the park on Interstate 90) takes you to unique Wall Drug.

- **ROOMS:** Singles, doubles, triples, and quads. Three units with connecting bedrooms will hold up to six adults. All cabins have a private bathroom, some with a shower and others with a combination tub-shower.

- **RESERVATIONS:** Cedar Pass Lodge, Box 5, Interior, SD 57750. Phone (605) 433–5460; fax (605) 433–5560. Deposit of 50 percent of first night's lodging required. Cancellation requires twenty-four hours' notice.

- **RATES:** All single cabins ($); cabins with connecting bedrooms ($$). Rates are reduced about $8 per night from opening to May 15 and from September 17 through closing.

- **LOCATION:** At the eastern end of Badlands National Park, 8.5 miles south of Interstate 90 at exit 131.

- **SEASON:** April 15 through October.

- **FOOD:** A restaurant ($/$$) serves three meals daily from a menu that includes buffalo burgers and Indian tacos.

- **TRANSPORTATION:** Rapid City, South Dakota, is the nearest main town where airline service and rental vehicles are available.

- **FACILITIES:** Restaurant, gift shop, National Park Service visitor center.

- **ACTIVITIES:** Hiking, evening interpretive programs.

Cedar Pass Camp was opened here in 1928 to provide refreshments to the growing number of sightseers to this area. By the 1930s the facility had become an important stop for Badlands travelers. The owner, Ben Millard, died here in 1956, and Cedar Pass Lodge was purchased by the National Park Service in 1964. Cedar Pass Lodge has been operated by the Oglala Sioux Tribe of the Pine Ridge Indian Reservation since 1971.

# TEXAS

## BIG BEND NATIONAL PARK

Big Bend National Park, TX 79834

(915) 477–2251

Big Bend National Park comprises 801,000 acres of wild and scenic desert, mountain ranges, steep-walled canyons, and ribbons of green plant life along the fabled Rio Grande. The remote location causes this park to be less heavily used compared with many of its sister parks. Popular activities at Big Bend include bird-watching, hiking, and rafting on the Rio Grande. The park is located on the Mexican border in southwestern Texas.

### Lodging in Big Bend National Park

Chisos Mountains Lodge in the park's Basin area provides the only lodging in Big Bend National Park. The road to the Basin is not recommended for trailers exceeding 20 feet and RVs exceeding 24 feet. A trailer village at Rio Grande Village is available for individuals with trailers and motor homes.

# BIG BEND NATIONAL PARK

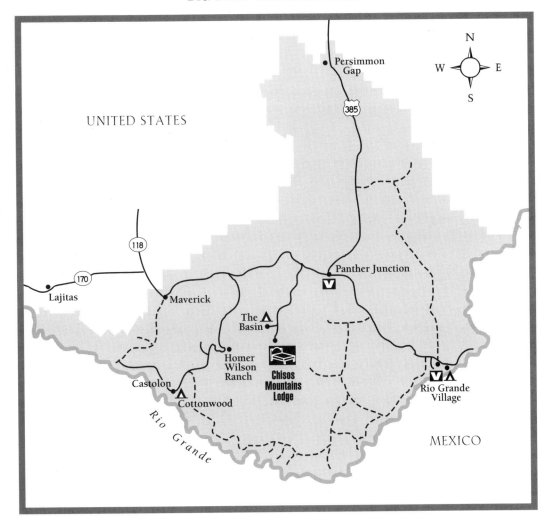

## CHISOS MOUNTAINS LODGE

Big Bend National Park, TX 79834–9999 • (915) 477–2291

Chisos Mountains Lodge is a group of modern motel-type units and older stone and adobe cabins and lodge units in the scenic Basin area of Big Bend National Park. All the lodging units rent for about the same price and are open year-round. The Basin area of Big Bend is approximately 40 miles inside the north park entrance, which itself is 40 miles south of Highway 90. In other words, this is a pretty remote lodge in a very remote national park. The good news is that the Basin area of the park provides breathtaking scenery along with the outdoor experience you are probably seeking in a national park visit. The lodge is at an altitude of 5,400 feet, which results in moderate summer temperatures when much of the rest of the park swelters in the desert heat. Scenery is provided by the Chisos Mountains, which surround and tower 2,000 to 3,000 feet above the Basin.

*Casa Grande Motor Lodge at Chisos Mountains Lodge*

Chisos Mountains Lodge is actually a combination of a main registration and food service building and four types of separate lodging units that provide a total of seventy-two rooms. Approximately half the rooms are in three two-story motor-lodge-type buildings (called Casa Grande units) that offer private rear balconies with an excellent view of the surrounding mountains. Most of these units, built in 1989, have two double beds, although a limited number of rooms offer a combination of a queen and a single, or a double and a single bed. Each room has a full bath and air conditioning.

Two one-story motel-type buildings constructed in the late 1970s each have ten rooms that back up to one another. That is, five rooms are located on each side of the building. As a result, the rooms do not have balconies and views are not as good as those in the Casa Grande section. These rooms have two double beds, a full bath, heat, and air conditioning. They are somewhat smaller than the rooms in Casa Grande.

The stone and adobe buildings offer a quieter setting a short distance away from the other lodging. One duplex and four freestanding cottages each have three double beds. These buildings, constructed in the late 1930s, have a shower but no tub. They also lack air conditioning. The thick construction and cross-ventilation generally result in a

*Bird-watching is a major activity at Big Bend National Park, where more than 450 species of birds have been identified. Although most are migrants that pass through on their way from wintering in Latin America, occasional rare species end up in Big Bend after wandering off-course. The Chisos Mountains of Big Bend are the only location in the United States where the Colima warbler can be observed. Multiday seminars on birding are regularly sponsored by the Big Bend Natural History Association.*

comfortable inside temperature. Most popular with frequent visitors to Big Bend are cabins 102 and 103, which offer the best mountain views of any of the park's lodging facilities. Cabin 100 is isolated and makes a nice honeymoon cottage. Eight nice 1950s-era stone lodge units situated near the cabins each contain one single and one double bed, a full bath, and heat. These units are in two buildings, each with four units. Access to one of the buildings involves climbing quite a few steps.

None of the rooms have a television or telephone, although a number of pay phones are scattered throughout the Basin area. Four Casa Grande motor lodge rooms are handicap accessible. Ice machines are scattered throughout the lodging area. Nonsmoking rooms are available in each of the four types of lodging units. Although you will probably be pleased with any of the lodging facilities, we recommend the Casa Grande units in buildings A, B, and C. Rooms in all three buildings are large, offer great views, and cost about the same as rooms in the other units. Choosing the second floor results in an improved view and additional privacy.

Other than the cabins and stone lodge units that are located a short distance from the main Basin area, the units are arranged in a circular fashion near the lodge building that houses registration, a small gift shop, and eating facilities. Adequate parking is available near each of the buildings, although a couple of the Casa Grande units require a climb of approximately thirty steps to reach the second floor. If stairs are a problem, you should note this in your reservation request. The stone cabins and lodge units are about a quarter-mile away from the other units, but everything in the Basin is within walking distance. Also in the Basin is a small store with a limited selection of groceries and camping supplies, and a small visitor center. A variety of hikes and nature programs are offered in-season. A self-guiding trail and access to several other trails originate near the lodge.

*Although the Rio Grande is one of the major natural features of Big Bend National Park, by the time the river forms the southern boundary of the park, most of the water is supplied by the Rio Conchos, which flows out of Mexico, rather than the headwaters of the Rio Grande. Much of the water of the Rio Grande has evaporated or been diverted for irrigation by the time the river reaches the western border of the park. Abrasive particles carried in the water give the river its impressive power to carve the canyons that have formed along its path.*

The Chisos Mountains Basin is only a small piece of a very large national park that offers much to attract visitors, especially during the spring and fall, when temperatures are mild. The main National Park Service visitor facilities are at Panther Junction. Here you will find the main visitor center and a host of facilities including a post office and gas station. Other major activity areas of the park center on Rio Grande Village, 20 miles southeast of park headquarters, which offers hiking, camping, a trailer park, a coin laundry, showers, groceries, general merchandise, gasoline, propane, and a visitor center. Castolon, a historic district 35 miles southwest of the visitor center, offers a campground, a ranger station, historic exhibits, and a frontier store that sells picnic supplies, groceries, and general merchandise.

- **ROOMS:** Doubles, triples, and quads. A few units sleep up to six. All rooms have private baths.

- **RESERVATIONS:** National Park Concessions, Inc., Chisos Mountains Lodge, Big Bend National Park, TX 79834–9999. Phone (915) 477–2291; fax (915) 477–2352. Reservations in any calendar year may be made at the beginning of the previous year.

- **RATES:** All rooms ($$). Rates are quoted for two adults. Each additional person $10.

- **LOCATION:** Approximately 40 miles south of the north park entrance station and 30 miles east of the west entrance station.

- **SEASON:** All of the lodging units are open year-round. Heaviest season is in the spring up to Memorial Day and in the fall following Labor Day. The lodge is heavily booked during Thanksgiving and Christmas holidays.

- **FOOD:** A full-service restaurant ($/$$) serves three meals a day in two-hour segments. Breakfast begins at 7:00 A.M., and dinner seating ends at 8:00 P.M. An adjoining coffee shop is open during periods the restaurant is closed. The restaurant is located in the main lodge building and is within walking distance of all the rooms.

- **TRANSPORTATION:** No public transportation is available to or through the park. Train and bus service is provided to the town of Alpine, approximately 110 miles north of the park. Airlines serve Del Rio, Midland-Odessa, and El Paso, where vehicles can be rented.

- **FACILITIES:** The Chisos Basin offers a store, visitor center, restaurant, and gift shop. All are within walking distance of the lodging units. A gas station, post office, and grocery are at Panther Junction. A variety of supplies and services are at Rio Grande Village, 20 miles southeast of the visitor center.

- **ACTIVITIES:** Hiking, bird-watching, guided walks, and National Park Service programs. Float trips on the Rio Grande are available with your own equipment (permit required) or through one of four local services approved by the Park Service.

# U.S. VIRGIN ISLANDS

## VIRGIN ISLANDS NATIONAL PARK

6010 Estate Nazareth
St. Thomas, VI 00802
(809) 776–6450

Virgin Islands National Park comprises nearly 14,700 acres of tropical island and water that include quiet coves, blue-green waters, and white sandy beaches fringed by lush green hills. The park is located on St. John Island and can be reached via hourly ferry service across Pillsbury Sound from Red Hook, St. Thomas. Ferry service also operates from Charlotte Amalie. Major airlines fly from the U.S. mainland to St. Thomas and St. Croix.

### Lodging in Virgin Islands National Park

Although a variety of lodging is available on the island, Cinnamon Bay Campground, with tents and cottages, offers the only accommodations within the national park. Cinnamon Bay is on St. John Island's north shore, approximately midway across the island via North Shore Road. The campground is a fifteen-minute taxi ride from the town of Cruz Bay, where the ferries dock.

# VIRGIN ISLANDS NATIONAL PARK

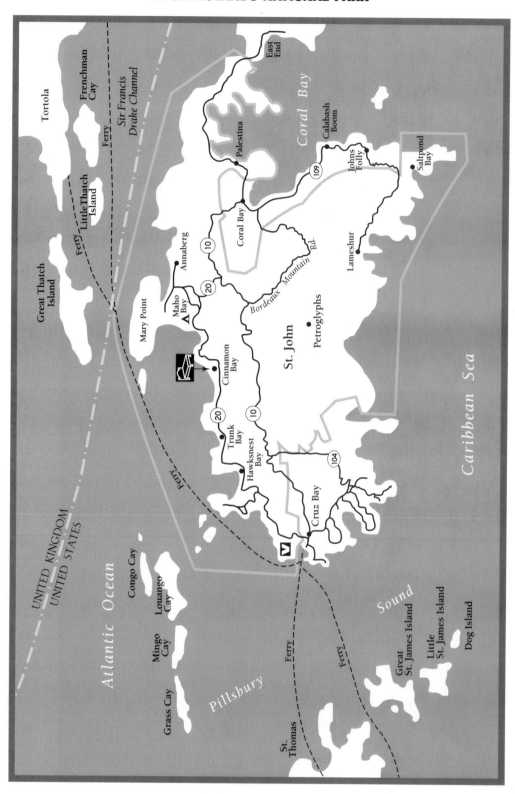

# CINNAMON BAY CAMPGROUND

P.O. Box 720 • Cruz Bay, St. John • U.S. Virgin Islands 00831 • (809) 776–6330

*Cottages at Cinnamon Bay Campground*

Cinnamon Bay Campground is a complex of cottages, tents, separate bathhouses, and a separate main building that houses a registration area, restaurant, and general store. The cottages and tents are grouped separately, with bathhouses available in each grouping. All the buildings are located in a natural area of trees a short walk from half-mile-long Cinnamon Bay Beach. The campground does not have a lodge with accommodations or the wood cabins you might expect to find at a Park Service lodging facility.

The forty cottages are 15 by 15 feet and constructed of cement sides and floor with front, and back screening to allow breezes from the trade winds. Each cottage is equipped with electric lights, table and chairs, ceiling fan, picnic table, charcoal grill, propane stove, ice chest, water container, and eating and cooking utensils. Bedding consists of four twin beds that are made by the guest on the day of arrival. Additional linens can be obtained twice a week at the front desk.

Forty-four tents, which rent for $15 to $20 less per night (depending on the season) than cottages, have a wood floor and are 10 by 14 feet. Each tent includes four cots with a 3-inch mattress, propane stove, charcoal grill, gas lantern, ice chest, water container, and utensils. A picnic table is under a large canvas flap that extends from the front roof. As with the cottages, beds are made on the day of arrival and fresh linens are available at the front desk twice a week.

Staying at Cinnamon Bay Campground provides a different national park experience, one in which the accommodations permit a full appreciation of the natural surroundings. Sleeping in canvas-sided structures tends to unite the occupants with nature. Both the cottages and the tents are a short walk from Cinnamon Bay Beach. Phones, safe-deposit boxes, and storage lockers are near the lodging facilities. A general store carries grocery items if you are interested in cooking some or all of your own meals. A restaurant is available when you choose to eat out. No Laundromat is in the campground. Not surprisingly, water-based activities such as snorkeling are popular and sailboards, sea kayaks, and sailboats are available for rent at a water sports center. Park rangers offer daily park tours.

- **ROOMS:** Doubles, triples, and quads. None of the cottages or tents have a private bathroom.

- **RESERVATIONS:** Cinnamon Bay Campground, P.O. Box 720, Cruz Bay, St. John, U.S. Virgin Islands 00831. Phone (800) 539–9998; (809) 776–6330; fax (809) 776–6458. Reservations can be guaranteed with a credit card. Personal checks are accepted only for reservation guarantees. Cancellations are required at least thirty days prior to arrival for a full refund. Meal packages are available.

- **RATES:** Cottages ($$) from May 1 through December 14, ($$$) from December 15 through April 30; tents ($) from May 1 through December 14, ($$) from December 15 through April 30. Rates are quoted for two adults. Children under three years are free with an adult. Additional adults are $15 each.

- **LOCATION:** On the north shore of St. John Island, approximately 4 miles (fifteen minutes) from the town of Cruz Bay on the island's west end.

- **SEASON:** Open year-round.

- **FOOD:** A restaurant ($/$$) serves three meals daily. A snack bar offers breakfast and lunch only. Groceries are available at a general store. Full and modified American plans are available at extra charge.

- **TRANSPORTATION:** Ferries ($3 one-way) for Cruz Bay, St. John, leave from Red Hook and Charlotte Amalie on St. Thomas. Taxis (approximately $3 per person) provide transportation from Cruz Bay to the campground.

- **FACILITIES:** Restaurant, general store, beach shop, water sports center with boat rentals.

- **ACTIVITIES:** Swimming, snorkeling, fishing, hiking, guided tours.

Rosewood Hotels & Resorts, the firm that manages Cinnamon Bay Campground, also operates exclusive Caneel Bay on the same island. Although separated by two bays and only a few miles, in cost and accommodations these two facilities are a world apart. For example, rooms at Caneel Bay run from $400 to $900 daily, depending on season and type of accommodation. The 171 rooms include wall safes, personal bars, and handcrafted furniture. Three restaurants provide a choice of formal, eclectic, and casual dining.

# UTAH

## BRYCE CANYON NATIONAL PARK

Bryce Canyon, UT 84717

(801) 834–5322

Bryce Canyon National Park comprises nearly 36,000 acres highlighted by numerous alcoves cut into cliffs along the eastern edge of the Paunsaugunt Plateau. The cliffs are bordered by badlands of vivid colors and strange shapes called hoodoos for which this park is most famous. A paved road with numerous scenic pullouts leads 18 miles south from the entrance to Rainbow Point. Trailers are not permitted beyond Sunrise Point, which lies about 3 miles inside the park entrance. The park is in southwestern Utah and most easily reached via U.S. 89 to Utah Highways 12 and 63.

## Lodging in Bryce Canyon

Bryce Canyon Lodge, with several types of accommodations, provides the only lodging in Bryce Canyon National Park. All of the rooms are comfortable and within easy walking distance of both the main lodge and spectacular Bryce Canyon. The lodge is in the northern section of the park, about 1.5 miles south of the park entrance and the visitor center. Privately operated motels are just outside the park entrance.

## BRYCE CANYON LODGE

1 Bryce Canyon Lodge • Bryce Canyon National Park, UT 84717 • (801) 834–5361

Bryce Canyon Lodge offers a total of 114 rooms in a complex of two motor lodge units, fifteen multiunit cabin buildings with forty rooms, and an impressive wood and stone main lodge building that houses the restaurant, registration area, and four overnight rooms. The main lodge was constructed in the 1920s and has been completely renovated to its original appearance. The lodge was designed by the same person who designed the Ahwahnee Hotel in Yosemite, Zion Lodge, and Grand Canyon Lodge on the North Rim. The attractive lobby area has a huge stone fireplace surrounded by chairs. A large brick porch with chairs and benches stretches across the entire front of the building and offers guests a

# BRYCE CANYON NATIONAL PARK

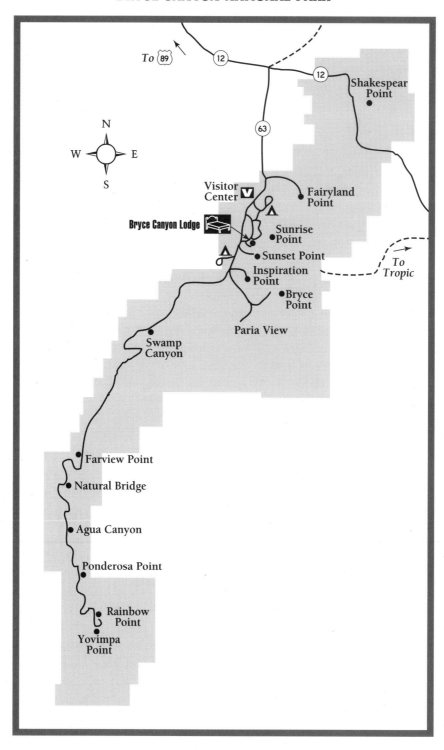

*Main Lodge at Bryce Canyon*

pleasant place to spend idle time. The porch faces a wooded area that separates the lodge from the canyon rim. Bryce Canyon Lodge is located near the rim of the canyon, about 1.5 miles south of the park visitor center and entrance station.

Each of the three types of lodging facilities at Bryce Canyon Lodge is first-class. All of the rooms have heat but no air conditioning or television. Forty western cabins, some two to a building and others four to a building, each contain two queen beds, a gas fireplace, a telephone, a table, a desk, three chairs, and a full bath. The log and limestone cabins, constructed in the 1930s, are roomy and nicely finished. Each has a private front porch. Cabins 506, 517, 525, 533, and 539 have porches that face a large wooded area but are a walk from the parking area. Two two-story motor lodge buildings contain a total of 70 rooms, each of which has two queen beds (a few have one queen bed), a full bath, a desk, a table, three chairs, and a telephone. These units each have a private balcony with a table and two chairs. Rooms are on each side of the building and are entered through a central corridor that can be accessed at either end or in the middle. Although the lodge classifies these as "motel" units, they are actually much nicer and more attractive than most motels. Rooms on the second floor and in the back of the building provide the most privacy and best view but are more distant from the parking areas. Two motel rooms are handicap accessible.

The main lodge building houses three second-floor suites and one studio apartment. These are the only sleeping rooms in the main lodge. The suites each have a bedroom with one queen bed and a separate sitting area with a wicker desk, a lounge chair, and two rocking chairs; both rooms have ceiling fans. The suites also have a full bath but no balcony. These rooms are quite nice and roomy, and it is convenient to stay in the main lodge, where the restaurant and lobby are located. The single studio is identical to the suites but without a separate sitting room.

Bryce Canyon Lodge is a pleasant place to spend several relaxing days while you explore this unique national park. It sits in a heavily treed area with attractive vistas and numerous outdoor activities. The lodge is near Bryce Canyon. A short walking trail from the front porch of the lodge leads to a spectacular overlook along the rim. A tour desk in the hotel lobby provides information on the area and several tours that originate near the lodge. The main lodge building, with a restaurant and gift shop, is within easy walking distance of all the lodging facilities. The attractive restaurant has two large stone fireplaces and serves three meals daily at reasonable prices.

- **ROOMS:** Doubles, triples, and quads. All rooms have a full bath.

- **RESERVATIONS:** TW Recreational Services, Inc., AmFac Parks and Resorts, 14001 East Iliff Avenue, Suite 600, Aurora, CO 80014. Phone (303) 297–2757; fax (303) 297–3175. Reservations may be made up to twenty-three months in advance.

- **RATES:** Western cabins ($$$); motel units ($$$); suites ($$$$); studio ($$$). Children under sixteen are free with an adult.

- **LOCATION:** The lodge is near the north end of Bryce Canyon National Park, approximately 1.5 miles south of the visitor center that is located near the park entrance station. The lodge sits within walking distance of the rim of the canyon.

- **SEASON:** Bryce Canyon Lodge is open from April 1 through November 1. The park is open year-round.

- **FOOD:** A full-service restaurant ($$$) serves breakfast, lunch, and dinner. Groceries and snacks are available at a general store at Sunrise Point, about 1 mile from the lodge.

- **TRANSPORTATION:** Airlines serve Cedar City, St. George, and Salt Lake City, Utah, and Las Vegas, Nevada. Rental cars are available at each of these airports. Greyhound/Trailways serves St. George and Cedar City. Amtrak serves Salt Lake City.

- **FACILITIES:** A full-service dining room, gift shop, and post office are in the main lodge building. A general store 1 mile north of the lodge near Sunrise Point has snacks and groceries.

- **ACTIVITIES:** The National Park Service conducts a variety of lectures, nature walks and talks, and slide presentations. A schedule with times is posted at the visitor center. Two-hour and half-day mule and horse trips into the canyon are offered daily. Van tours along the canyon road are also offered daily. Information on these and other activities is available at the tour desk located in the lobby.

Bryce Canyon is named for Ebenezer Bryce, who assisted in the settlement of this area of Utah and came here to live and harvest timber in 1875. Neighbors called the canyon behind his home Bryce Canyon, a name that carried over to the park when it was incorporated into the national park system in 1928. One of the suites in the main lodge building is named after Ebenezer Bryce.

# ZION NATIONAL PARK

Springdale, UT 84767

(801) 722–3256

Zion National Park comprises approximately 147,000 acres of colorful canyons and mesas that create phenomenal shapes and landscapes. Scenic drives and trails provide access to canyons, sculpted rocks, cliffs, and rivers in one of the most beautiful areas operated by the National Park Service. Zion is in southwestern Utah, with the southwest entrance approximately 150 miles northeast of Las Vegas, Nevada.

## Lodging in Zion National Park

Zion has only one lodging facility inside the park. Zion Lodge is located on Zion Canyon Scenic Drive, north of Highway 9, which crosses the southeastern section of the park. Additional lodging is available in the town of Springdale, just outside the southwest entrance.

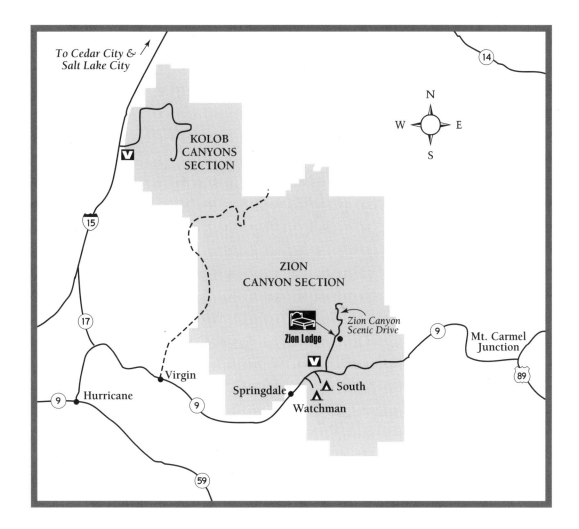

# ZION LODGE

Zion National Park • Springdale, UT 84767 • (801) 772–3213

*Motel Units at Zion Lodge*

Zion Lodge comprises a central lodge building that houses registration and dining facilities, plus seventeen separate but nearby buildings that provide a total of 121 rooms for overnight accommodations. No overnight rooms are in the main lodge building. The lodge is situated in a grassy area of cottonwood trees surrounded by the beautiful red sandstone cliffs that make this such a spectacular national park. The North Fork of the Virgin River is across the road from the lodge. The wood and Navajo sandstone main lodge building is a one- and two-story, V-shaped, ranch-style structure that was constructed in 1966 on the site of the original lodge, which burned earlier in the year. The new lodge is attractive but does not have the majestic look of its sister lodges at Bryce Canyon and the North Rim of the Grand Canyon. Zion Lodge is located 3 miles north of the main park road, on Zion Canyon Scenic Drive. The lodge is approximately 3.5 miles north of the National Park Service visitor center.

Three types of accommodations are available at Zion Lodge. All of the lodging is separate from but near the main lodge building. All the rooms have air conditioning, heat, and a telephone but no television. Forty Western Cabins each offer two double beds, a gas fireplace, a table, a desk, three chairs, and a full bath. The cabins were constructed either two or four units to a building, in the 1930s. These cabins, of wood construction, are very similar to the Western Cabins in both Bryce Canyon and the North Rim of the Grand Canyon. The cabins are closely clustered in the front and at the end of one of the motel buildings south of the main lodge. Each cabin has a private porch. Cabins that face west toward the parking lot offer a better location and view. These include cabins 503, 505, 509, 517, 518, 520, and 523.

Seventy-five motel-type rooms are in two large, two-story motor lodge builidngs. A big stone fireplace is in the central lobby area of the larger motel building. These rooms have two queen beds (some have only a single queen), a dresser, a nightstand, a table, and two chairs. Each room has a private balcony or patio with two chairs and a table. The rooms are accessed from an interior corridor that runs the length of each building. The best rooms are on the second floor of each building's back side. These are all odd-numbered rooms. Two motel-type rooms are handicap accessible. Six suites located on the second floor of the motor lodge buildings each have two rooms, one with a king bed and the other with two chairs, a sofa, a refrigerator, a desk, and a chair. The two rooms are separated by a bathroom. More than two occupants require a rollaway, which entails an extra charge.

Zion Lodge is a comfortable, quiet place to spend one or more days while you explore magnificant Zion National Park. The setting for the lodge is both attractive and convenient. Be forewarned that summer months generally bring hot days to Zion, and daytime temperatures often reach one hundred degrees and above. The main lodge contains most of the facilities you will need for a stay in the park. A large grassy area in front of the lodge provides a nice place to read a book, eat a picnic lunch, or lie on a blanket under a cottonwood tree. A spacious, wood-paneled restaurant on the second floor serves three full meals a day. The restaurant has large windows that provide a view of the front grounds of the lodge. A patio area is available for outside dining. A snack bar at the north end of the main lodge building serves light sandwiches and beverages. The lodge also houses a tour desk, auditorium, post office, and gift shop with jewelry, books, and T-shirts. A 0.6-mile paved trail to Lower Emerald Pools begins opposite Zion Lodge. The longer, 2-mile walk leads to Middle Emerald Pools. An inexpensive hourly guided tram tour of Zion Canyon Scenic Road leaves each hour from Zion Lodge.

*Navajo sandstone, which forms the canyon walls in Zion National Park, is a porous rock that absorbs rainfall. The moisture percolates through the rock and may require many decades (some say centuries) to reach the base of a large cliff. Perhaps the best example in Zion of this phenomenon is 2,000-foot Weeping Rock, where you can walk under the rock and feel the water dripping. Moisture seeping from the rock results in hanging gardens and spring wildflowers. Weeping Rock is accessed via a quarter-mile trail from Zion Canyon Scenic Drive north of Zion Lodge. This is a stop on the tram tour.*

- **ROOMS:** Doubles, triples, and quads. All rooms have a full bath.

- **RESERVATIONS:** TW Recreational Services, AmFac Parks and Resorts, 14001 East Iliff Avenue, Suite 300, Aurora, CO 80014. Phone (303) 297–2757; fax (303) 297–3175.

- **RATES:** Western cabins ($$$); motel ($$$); suites ($$$$). All rates are for two adults. Children twelve years and younger are free.

- **LOCATION:** Three miles north of the main park highway on Zion Canyon Scenic Drive.

- **SEASON:** All of the units of Zion Lodge are open year-round. The lodge is generally full from early April through October.

- **FOOD:** An attractive restaurant ($$$) on the second floor of the main lodge building serves three full meals daily. Breakfast includes a buffet. Dinner reservations are required. A snack bar ($) at the north end of the main lodge building serves light breakfasts, sandwiches, ice cream, and beverages from 7:00 A.M. to 9:00 P.M.

- **TRANSPORTATION:** Scheduled airlines serve Cedar City, St. George, and Salt Lake City, Utah, and Las Vegas, Nevada, where rental cars are available. Scheduled bus service is available to St. George and Cedar City. Amtrak serves Salt Lake City.

- **FACILITIES:** Post office, gift shop, restaurant, and snack bar. Groceries and numerous restaurants are in Springdale, Utah, a short distance outside the park's southwest entrance.

- **ACTIVITIES:** A tour desk in the main lodge building can arrange horseback rides and guided tram tours. Naturalist programs are offered throughout the park by National Park Service personnel. Schedules are posted at the front desk of the lodge and in the visitor center, which shows a fifteen-minute orientation film. Hiking is a popular activity in Zion National Park.

# VIRGINIA

## SHENANDOAH NATIONAL PARK

Route 4, Box 348

Luray, VA 22835

(540) 999–3500

Shenandoah National Park comprises 195,000 acres of forested mountains through an 80-mile stretch of the Blue Ridge Mountains. Most of the park's features lie alongside 105-mile Skyline Drive, which winds along much of the crest of the mountain range. Visitor centers are at Dickey Ridge near the north entrance and at Big Meadows. The park is located in northern Virginia, with the northern entrance approximately 60 miles west of Washington, D.C. The south entrance connects with the north end of Blue Ridge Parkway.

## Lodging in Shenandoah National Park

Three locations in Shenandoah National Park provide lodging facilities, all of which are in the central section between mile markers 40 and 60. Big Meadows and Skyland are relatively large complexes with modern lodges and cabins, while Lewis Mountain is a very small facility with cabins only. All three facilities are operated by the same firm.

- **RESERVATIONS FOR ALL LODGING FACILITIES:** ARAMARK Virginia Sky-Line Company, P.O. Box 727, Luray, VA 22835. Phone (800) 999–4714 or (540) 743–5108; fax (540) 743–7883. The first night's deposit by check is required within ten days of booking a reservation. Full refund of deposit requires a seventy-two-hour advance cancellation.

- **TRANSPORTATION:** Scheduled airline service is available to several towns surrounding Shenandoah National Park, including Washington, D.C. (use Dulles), and Charlottesville and Harrisonburg, Virginia. Bus service is available to Waynesboro, just outside the south entrance to the park, and Amtrak (800–872–7245) provides passenger rail service to Charlottesville, Virginia. No public transportation is available in the park.

# SHENANDOAH NATIONAL PARK

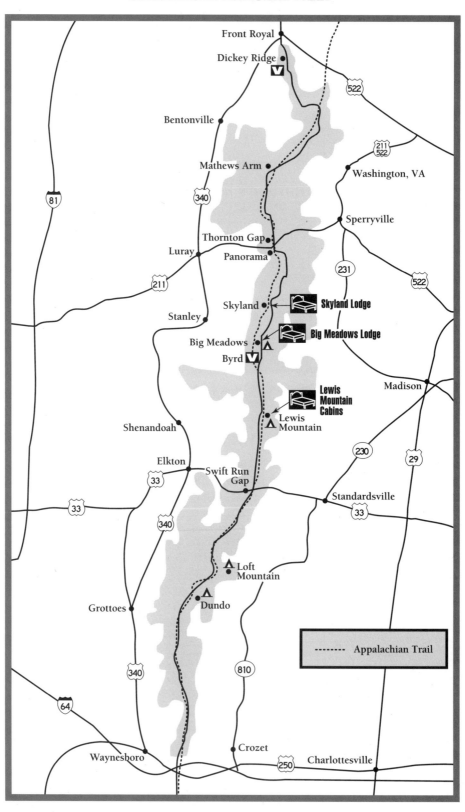

--------- Appalachian Trail

# BIG MEADOWS LODGE

P.O. Box 727 • Luray, VA 22835 • (540) 999–2221

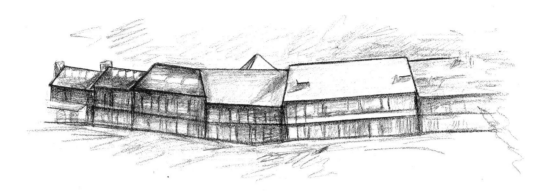

*Main Lodge Building Big Meadows*

Big Meadows Lodge is a complex consisting of a main lodge building constructed in 1939 and eleven separate but nearby cabins and one- and two-story wooden lodge buildings that provide a total of ninety-two rooms. Registration is just inside the main lodge building, which also houses the dining room and a large lobby that each provide spectacular views of the valley below Big Meadows. Registration parking is just outside the building, and adequate parking is near each of the lodging units. No pets are permitted. The main lodge building also contains a limited number of overnight rooms, six of which provide great valley views. All the lodging facilities at Big Meadows are within close walking distance of the dining room. Big Meadows sits in a heavily forested area at an altitude of 3,640 feet and is located at milepost 51, about midway between the north and south entrances to Shenandoah National Park. The northern entry point to Big Meadows is via Highway 211 from Luray, Virginia. The lodge is 15 miles north of Swift Run Gap Entrance and U.S. Route 33.

Big Meadows Lodge offers five categories of accommodations. All of the units have heat and a private bath but no air conditioning or telephone. Some of the units have a fireplace (wood provided), and minisuites in one of the buildings have television. The least expensive option is the main lodge, which has twenty relatively small rooms in a two-story wing of the building. Most of these rooms have one double bed or two twin beds and will accommodate two persons only. Two rooms have two double beds, and one has a queen bed. Each room has a private bath with a tub, a shower, or both. Some of the lodge rooms are on the second floor, and some are on the first floor. Six rooms on the back side of the building provide good views of the valley.

Six one- and two-story lodge buildings provide a total of sixty-two rooms in a combination of six suites, ten minisuites, and forty-six regular rooms. Four one-story buildings are in a wooded area south of the main lodge, while two newer two-story lodge buildings (Rapidan and Doubletop) sit on a bluff overlooking the valley. The regular lodge units each have two double beds and a private bath with a combination tub-shower. These rooms have either a balcony or a patio. Eight minisuites in the Cresent Rock building rent for about $10 daily more than the regular lodge rooms and each has one large room with a king bed and a sofa bed. Two other minisuites in the same building, with one double bed, are handicap accessible. Each of these units has a wood fireplace. Six regular suites with a separate sitting room have either one king bed or two double beds and a sofa bed. These units have a fireplace and a porch and rent for about $20 more than the minisuites.

Ten cabin rooms are constructed two or three to a building in a grassy area between the parking lot and two lodge buildings. Each of the rooms has one double bed, a fireplace, and a private bath with a shower but no tub. The cabins sit relatively close together and do not offer views.

Big Meadows Lodge is a relaxing place to spend several days. The views are terrific, and the fall colors can be spectacular. The great room in the main lodge, with a large stone fireplace and many stuffed chairs, sofas, and wooden rockers, is a pleasant place for reading, playing board and card games, and gazing out the large windows at the valley below. A large balcony runs across the back of the building. The country-style restaurant serves three meals a day at reasonable prices. You can enjoy a hike or participate in programs presented by National Park Service rangers. One of the park's main visitor centers near the lodge has exhibits and film programs.

- **ROOMS:** Doubles, triples, and quads. Suites will accommodate up to six adults. All rooms have a private bath, although some have only a shower or a tub.

- **RATES:** Main lodge ($$); cabins ($$); lodge units ($$$); minisuites ($$$); suites ($$$$). Slightly higher rates for weekends and daily in October.

- **LOCATION:** At milepost 51, about midway on Skyline Drive between the north and south entrances to Shenandoah National Park.

- **SEASON:** Last week in April to first week of November.

- **FOOD:** A full-service dining room ($$/$$$) serves breakfast, lunch, and dinner. A coffee shop and a camp store with limited groceries are just outside the entrance to Big Meadows.

- **FACILITIES:** Restaurant, gift and craft shop, taproom, and conference room. A gas station, coffee shop, camp store, nature trail, and National Park Service visitor center are at the nearby Big Meadows Wayside.

- **ACTIVITIES:** Hiking, National Park Service hikes and programs.

The 105-mile Skyline Drive is a slow but scenic two-lane road that wanders through the length of Shenandoah National Park. The road provides access to lodges, campgrounds, and overlooks from the north entrance at Front Royal to the south entrance near Waynesboro. The park brochure provided at entry stations identifies places of interest and park facilities according to mile markers alongside the west side of the road. The northern section of the park, nearest Washington, D.C., tends to be the most crowded.

# LEWIS MOUNTAIN CABINS

P.O. Box 727 • Luray, VA 22835 • (540) 999–2255

*Lewis Mountain Cabins*

Lewis Mountain Cabins is one of the smallest lodging units in all the national parks. The entire complex consists of one building with the registration desk and a small store, seven one-story cabins that provide a total of nine overnight rooms, and a tent cabin for hikers. Lewis Mountain Cabins has no lobby, dining room, swimming pool, or cocktail lounge. A small parking lot is beside the registration building, and all the cabins are a short walk away. The entire complex sits in a heavily forested area with no particularly good views but a lot of quiet and privacy. Lewis Mountain Cabins is at mile marker 57, in the central section of Shenandoah National Park. It is about 6 miles south of Big Meadows and the farthest south of any of the park's three lodging units.

All of the regular cabins at Lewis Mountain have electric heat and private baths but no air conditioning, telephone, or television. Two of the buildings are constructed as duplexes, with two cabin rooms per unit. These four cabin rooms each have one double bed and a private bath with a shower but no tub. Five of the buildings have two bedrooms, one on each side of a bathroom with a shower but no tub. One of these units is handicap accessible and has a bathroom with a combination shower-tub. The two-bedroom units, which cost about $25 per night more than the one-bedroom duplex cabins, have a double bed in each bedroom. The two-bedroom units also have a covered picnic table and grill (wood not supplied). Several picnic shelters with tables and grills are beside the row of cabins. The single tent cabin is actually hard-sided but has no bath or running water. A public bathroom is located in the nearby campground. Bunk beds have mattresses, but guests must supply their own linens.

Lewis Mountain Cabins is one of the least expensive lodging options in Shenandoah National Park. It is also one of the quietest, since you will have few neighbors. The wooden cabins are small and relatively old, with some dating to the late 1930s; however, the interiors are well maintained. Parking is directly in front of each cabin. This is a nice quiet place to stay overnight during a trip down Skyline Drive. It is not nearly as big as either Big Meadows or Skyland. However, remember to bring food to eat and wood to cook with. A small store in the registration building has limited groceries.

- **ROOMS:** Doubles, triples, and quads. Each cabin has a private bathroom.

- **RATES:** Single-bedroom cabins ($); two-bedroom cabins ($$); tent cabin ($). Slightly higher prices are charged on weekend nights and during all of October.

- **LOCATION:** Mile marker 57, near the midpoint of Skyline Drive. Lewis Mountain is about 6 miles south of Big Meadows.

- **SEASON:** First week in May to the last weekend in October.

- **FOOD:** No restaurant or other dining facilities are at Lewis Mountain. A small store with limited groceries is in the registration building.

- **FACILITIES:** Small store.

- **ACTIVITIES:** Hiking.

Shenandoah National Park contains more than 500 miles of hiking trails including a 95-mile stretch of the Appalachian Trail that runs the length of the park. Detailed trail maps are available at the park's contact stations.

# SKYLAND LODGE

P.O. Box 727 • Luray, VA 22835 • (540) 999–2211

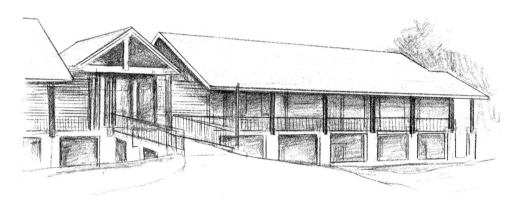

*Laurel Building at Skyland Lodge*

Skyland Lodge is a group of one- and two-story wooden buildings that sit on a hill over-looking a large valley. The main registration building has a medium-size lobby with a wall of windows toward the valley. No overnight rooms are in the one-story registration building, although a lodge building is immediately next door. An adjacent building contains a dining room, a gift shop, a taproom, and a small lounge area. Two lodge buildings (Whiteoak and Stony Man) are nearby, but many of the buildings and cabins are a substantial walk from the dining room. Nearly all the 177 rooms at Skyland Lodge, which sits at 3,680 feet, offer good views of the valley. Skyland Lodge is at mile marker 42, in the central section of Shenandoah National Park. It is 10 miles north of Big Meadows and the farthest north of any of the three lodging facilities in Shenandoah National Park.

The lodge offers four classes of accommodations. Most rooms are in a series of one- and two-story lodge units that overlook the valley. These buildings vary in size and age, but each room has two doubles or two queens and a private bath with a combination shower-tub. Rooms in the two-story units, including Canyon, Appledore, Craigin, Laurel, Raven's Nest, and Shenandoah, each have a balcony with a view. Rooms in all these buildings except Shenandoah also have a television. The newest buildings with the largest rooms are Laurel (view rooms) and Franklin (nonview rooms with television). The rooms at Laurel cost only a few dollars more than rooms in the older and nonview buildings, so you should try for one of these.

The lodge has six suites, two with views and four without. These units each have a bed-room with a double and a single, and a separate living room with a sofa bed. They rent for $35 to $60 per day more than regular rooms and are the only accommodations at Skyland other than one of the cabins to have a fireplace (wood provided).

The least expensive accommodations are twenty cabins that each have either one or two double beds and a private bathroom. Six cabins have a combination tub-shower, and the remainder have a shower only. Cabins are constructed two or four to a building. Only Byrd's Nest (cabin 68) has a fireplace. These units are scattered about Skyland, and none is particularly close to the registration building or dining room. One cabin (Peak View) has two bedrooms, one with two doubles and one with one double, and a bathroom.

Skyland Lodge is the largest lodging complex in Shenandoah National Park. That buildings tend to be widely scattered lends itself to quiet, but some rooms are fairly distant from the dining room, which means that you may have to either drive or walk a distance in order to eat. Most of the buildings are sited to take advantage of the views. If location and/or view are an important consideration, be certain this is stated when making a reservation. The large dining room is particularly nice and offers a pleasant place to eat.

The Skyland area was originally developed in the mid-1880s to mine copper. Surrounding timber was used to make charcoal for a copper smelter. It was not until the latter part of the century that the son of one of the original owners considered the possibility of developing the area as a resort. By the early 1900s Skyland had a dining hall, a recreation hall, bathhouses, and bungalows, all paid for by the sale of mineral rights, cabin sites, and loans. The developer ran Skyland as a concessionaire for the National Park Service until 1937.

- **ROOMS:** Doubles, triples, and quads. Suites will sleep up to five, and one double cabin will accommodate up to six adults. All rooms have a private bath with a shower or a combination tub-shower.

- **RATES:** Lodge units ($$$); cabins ($$); suites ($$$$/$$$$$). Slightly higher rates for weekends and daily in October. Rates are quoted for two adults. Additional adults pay an extra $5.00 per night. Children under seventeen are free.

- **LOCATION:** At milepost 42, about midway on Skyline Drive between the north and south entrances to Shenandoah National Park. Skyland is the northernmost lodging facility in the park.

- **SEASON:** End of March to the end of November.

- **FOOD:** A nice dining room ($$/$$$) serves breakfast, lunch, and dinner.

- **FACILITIES:** Restaurant, taproom, gift shop, conference rooms, stables, nature trail.

- **ACTIVITIES:** Hiking, horseback riding, nightly entertainment.

# WASHINGTON

## MOUNT RAINIER NATIONAL PARK

Tahoma Woods Star Route
Ashford, WA 98304
(360) 569–2211

M ount Rainier National Park contains 368 square miles, including the greatest single-peak glacial system in the contiguous United States. The ancient volcano is surrounded by snow, forests, and subalpine flowered meadows. The park is in southwestern Washington, approximately 80 miles south of Seattle. It is 64 miles west of the town of Yakima, Washington.

 ## Lodging in Mount Rainier National Park

Mount Rainier has two inns, which each offer very different lodging experiences. Recently remodeled National Park Inn is a relatively small lodge that sits in a heavily forested area but offers a view of Mount Rainier. The inn is cozy and quiet, with only twenty-five rooms. The much larger and busier Paradise Inn offers more of an alpine experience, at a higher altitude and with better mountain views. Despite the different environments, the two lodges are both in the southern end of the park and only about a dozen miles apart.

# MOUNT RAINIER NATIONAL PARK

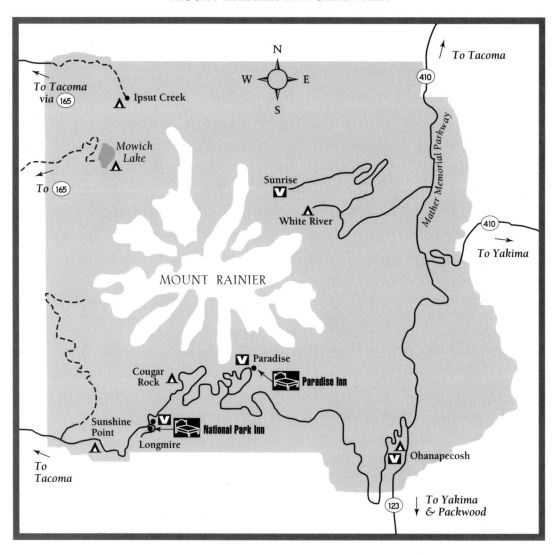

# NATIONAL PARK INN

Longmire, WA 98397 • (360) 569–2411

*National Park Inn*

National Park Inn is a small but nice two-story wooden lodge that offers a total of twenty-five overnight rooms, all but two of which are on the second floor. The inn is at an altitude of 2,700 feet, surrounded by old-growth forest of Douglas fir, western red cedar, and western hemlock. National Park Inn retains the character of an early 1900s lodge even though the building has been completely modernized. The inn is entered from the back, where a large parking lot is located. The lodge is on Highway 706, 6 miles from the southwest entrance to Mount Rainier National Park. It is 11 winding miles from the much larger inn at Paradise.

The twenty-five rooms at National Park Inn are all very different in terms of size, bedding, and bathroom facilities. In general, the rooms are comfortable but small. All of the rooms have heat but no air conditioning, telephone, or television. All but seven rooms have private baths, some of which contain a tub, a shower, or both. Rooms without a private bathroom have an in-room sink and access to community showers and baths on the second floor. Bedding varies from two twin beds, to a double bed and two twin beds, to two double beds. Although the rooms can be quite dissimilar, the cost for two adults depends only on whether or not a room has a private bath. Rooms with a bath cost approximately $25 per night more than rooms without a private bath. Rooms 3 and 7 each have baths and are much larger than average. Rooms along the front of the building, with the exception of room 18, have a view of Mount Rainier when the mountain isn't shrouded in clouds. All the rooms are entered from an inside corridor that is accessed via a stairway from the lobby area. No elevator is available. Two handicap-accessible rooms are on the first floor.

National Park Inn is much smaller and cozier than its sister lodge at Paradise. It is a comfortable place to rest overnight or to stay for several days. There aren't a lot of people here and activities in the immediate vicinity are minimal, but if you desire a comfortable and quiet place to read a book, get to know your spouse and kids, or just recharge your batteries, the National Park Inn can't be beat. A large covered porch with numerous chairs runs the length of the building. A small guest lounge just off the lobby has a large stone fireplace, sofas, tables, and chairs. Complimentary tea and cookies are served here each afternoon. An informal dining room on the opposite side of the lobby serves three meals a day. A tiny post office is located in a "closet" next to the registration desk. The general store next door sells gifts, limited groceries, beer, and wine. A National Park Service visitor center and a museum with exhibits on geology and wildlife are only a short walk from the inn. No pets are allowed, and no smoking is permitted anywhere in the building.

*The current National Park Inn was the annex of the original lodge, most of which burned in 1926. The inn was subsequently reopened and underwent a major remodeling in 1936. Another extensive renovation occurred in 1989, when the inn was essentially rebuilt from the ground up for reopening in May 1990. The adjacent building currently housing the gift shop was constructed in 1911 and is the only structure at this location that is still standing on its original site.*

- **ROOMS:** Doubles, triples, and quads. Eighteen of the twenty-five rooms have private baths. Community baths are on the second floor.

- **RESERVATIONS:** Mount Rainier Guest Services, P.O. Box 108, Ashford, WA 98304–0108. Phone (360) 569–2275; fax (360) 569–2770. First night's room charge required as a deposit. Cancellation requires seven days' notice plus a $5.00 handling fee.

- **RATES:** Rooms with baths ($$$); rooms without baths ($$). Rates are for two adults. Each extra person is $10. Children under two years are free with an adult. Special Winter Packages are available.

- **LOCATION:** Six miles from the southwest entrance to Mount Rainier National Park on Highway 706. The Inn is 11 miles from Paradise, the park's other lodge.

- **SEASON:** Open all year.

- **FOOD:** A pleasant dining room ($$) on the main floor is open for breakfast, lunch, and dinner. Snacks and drinks may be purchased at the gift shop/store next door.

- **TRANSPORTATION:** The nearest major airport is SeaTac, located between Seattle and Tacoma, Washington, where rental vehicles are available. Amtrak also serves these cities. Three ground shuttle services operate between Seattle and Mount Rainier National Park, including Grayline of Seattle (800–426–7232), Rainier Shuttle (360–569–2331), and Rainier Overland, Inc. (360–569–0851).

- **FACILITIES:** Dining room, post office, general store that sells gifts and some food items, museum, National Park Service visitor center, hiker information center.

- **ACTIVITIES:** Hiking, fishing, ranger-guided walks; board games can be checked out at the front desk to use in the guest lounge. Snowshoe walks and skiing in winter.

# PARADISE INN

Paradise Inn, WA 98398 • (360) 569–2413

*Main Lodge at Paradise Inn*

Paradise Inn is a large wooden two-story lodge building with an attached four-story annex that sit amid striking vistas of the park's snow-covered peaks, including Mount Rainier. The inn offers a total of 126 rooms, most of which are in the annex that is reached via an enclosed walkway from the lobby of the main building. The primary structure was completed in 1917, and the annex was added in the 1920s. The original lodge rooms received some renovation in 1990. Paradise Inn is located at the base of Mount Rainier in the southern end of Mount Rainier National Park, 17 miles from the park's southwest entrance station.

Paradise Inn is built on a hill, so that the outside entry to the lobby is on the third floor. A huge two-story lobby has a vaulted ceiling and runs most of the length of the building. Massive log ceiling beams frame a mezzanine that wraps around the inside of the second floor. The lobby is filled with tables, benches, sofas, and stuffed chairs. A large stone fireplace sits at each end of the room. The registration desk in the corner is beside the stairs to the rooms and the walkway to the annex. The parking lot just outside the front door is often crowded, so it may be necessary to temporarily park beside the entrance to unload luggage. Assistance with luggage is available at the registration desk.

Paradise Inn offers rooms of various size, bedding, and views, but all fall into four basic price categories. All of the rooms are nonsmoking and have heat but no air conditioning, telephone, or television. The thirty-one least expensive rooms without private bath are all in the main lodge building. These very small rooms have bedding that ranges from two twin beds, to one double bed, to one double bed and one single bed. Common bathrooms and shower rooms are at one end of a long hallway. The next classification includes eighty-eight rooms with bath that are located in the annex. Five handicap-accessible rooms are included in this category. Some bathrooms have a tub, some have a shower, and some have both.

Bedding in these rooms ranges from two twin beds to two double beds. The rooms with two doubles are larger. Rooms 113, 117, and 119 and the corresponding rooms on upper floors offer the most space. Rooms with a private bath rent for about $25 per night more than rooms without a bath.

One step above basic rooms with a private bath are a few rooms with two bedrooms and one bath. These rent for about $25 more than single rooms with a bath, so you might consider one of these if you are traveling with children or another couple. The most expensive rooms are two suites that each have a bedroom, sitting room, and bath. Rooms in both the main building and the annex offer varying views, so if what you see from outside your window is an important consideration, mention your interest when making reservations.

Paradise Inn is a pleasant but sometimes crowded place to stay. At an altitude of 5,400 feet, Paradise can be quite cool and foggy, even during summer. This is a heavily visited area of Mount Rainier National Park, and lots of people, both guests and visitors, seem to constantly browse through the lobby area. Tables and chairs on two sides of the mezzanine offer a more relaxing place to read, play cards, or just people-watch. Complimentary tea and cookies are offered here each afternoon from 3:00 to 5:00. An attractive 200-seat dining room with a beamed ceiling is just off the lobby on the main floor. A lounge, gift shop, snack bar, and post office are on the same floor. A large visitor center within walking distance of the lodge also has a snack bar and gift shop. The area around Paradise is noted for many varieties of subalpine flowers, which bloom in July and August as the snow is melting.

> Paradise Inn is constructed almost completely from Alaskan cedar taken just a few miles below the Paradise area. The logs were salvaged from an 1885 fire and hauled to the site by horse-drawn wagons. Most of the lobby's woodwork design was by a German carpenter who used only an adze in his work. He also built an unusual piano and a huge grandfather clock that remain in the lobby.

- **ROOMS:** Singles, doubles, triples, and quads. Not all rooms have private baths.

- **RESERVATIONS:** Mount Rainier Guest Services, P.O. Box 108, Ashford, WA 98304–0108. Phone (360) 569–2275; fax (360) 569–2770. The first night's rent is charged for the deposit at the time the reservations are made. A minimum of seven days' notice must be given for a full refund less a $5.00 handling fee.

- **RATES:** Rooms without a bath ($$); rooms with a bath ($$$); double rooms with a bath ($$$$); suites ($$$$$). Rates for double rooms and suites are quoted for three adults. All other rates are quoted for two adults. Each additional person is $10. Children under two years of age are free with an adult.

- **LOCATION:** Paradise Inn is on Highway 706, 17 miles from the southwest entrance to Mount Rainier National Park.

- **SEASON:** The lodge is open from mid-May through most of September, depending on weather.

- **FOOD:** A large dining room ($$$/$$$$) seats 200 and offers breakfast, lunch, and dinner. No reservations are taken. A snack bar ($$) near the gift shop offers sandwiches and beverages from 9:00 A.M. to 8:00 P.M. A snack bar ($$) with sandwiches, soups, and beverages is located in the visitor center and open from 10:00 A.M. to 7:00 P.M.

- **TRANSPORTATION:** The nearest major airport is SeaTac, located between Seattle and Tacoma, Washington, where rental vehicles are available. Amtrak also serves these cities. Three ground shuttle services operate between Seattle and Mount Rainier National Park, including Grayline of Seattle (800–426–7232), Rainier Shuttle (360–569–2331), and Rainier Overland, Inc. (360–569–0851).

- **FACILITIES:** Restaurant, gift shop, post office, lounge, snack bar, hiker information center, and nearby National Park Service visitor center.

- **ACTIVITIES:** Hiking, guided walks, evening programs in the lobby, fishing, and mountain climbing. Winter activities include snowshoeing, cross-country skiing, snowboarding, and tubing.

# OLYMPIC NATIONAL PARK

600 East Park Avenue
Port Angeles, WA 98362
(360) 452–0330

Olympic National Park comprises 1,442 square miles of mountain wilderness and includes active glaciers; 57 miles of wild, scenic ocean shore; and the finest remnant of Pacific Northwest rain forest. The strip of the park along the Pacific Ocean contains some of the most primitive coastline in the continental United States. Olympic National Park is composed of two sections, located in the northwest corner of Washington. Main access is via U.S. Highway 101, although roads penetrate only the perimeter of the park.

##  Lodging in Olympic National Park

The park contains four facilities with overnight accommodations that each provide a different visitor experience. Kalaloch Lodge sits directly on the Pacific Ocean and is perfect for beach walkers. Sol Duc Hot Springs Resort is great for those who want to spend time relaxing in a hot mineral bath. Lake Crescent Lodge and Log Cabin Resort are situated in heavily wooded areas on opposite sides of beautiful Lake Crescent. We have also included charming Lake Quinault Lodge, which sits across Lake Quinault from the park's southern boundary.

# OLYMPIC NATIONAL PARK

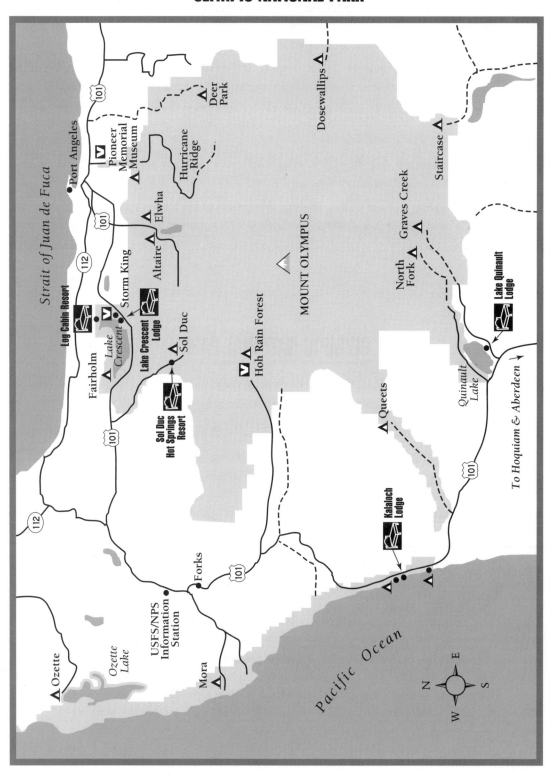

Strait of Juan de Fuca

Port Angeles

101

112

101

112

Pioneer Memorial Museum

Deer Park

Hurricane Ridge

Elwha

Altaire

Storm King

Log Cabin Resort

Lake Crescent

Lake Crescent Lodge

Fairholm

Sol Duc

Sol Duc Hot Springs Resort

Hoh Rain Forest

MOUNT OLYMPUS

Dosewallips

Staircase

Graves Creek

North Fork

Lake Quinault Lodge

Quinault Lake

Queets

To Hoquiam & Aberdeen

101

Kalaloch Lodge

Forks

101

USFS/NPS Information Station

Mora

Ozette

Ozette Lake

Pacific Ocean

N E S W

# LAKE CRESCENT LODGE

416 Lake Crescent Road • Port Angeles, WA 98363–8672 • (360) 928–3211

*Main Lodge Building at Lake Crescent*

Lake Crescent Lodge comprises a classic main lodge building surrounded at each end by several types of cabins and one- and two-story motel structures. The main wooden lodge, constructed in 1916 as the Lake Crescent Tavern, has only five overnight rooms, all upstairs and without a private bath. All other accommodations are separate but very near the main lodge. The entire complex sits on the south shore of Lake Crescent among giant hemlock and fir trees in the shadow of Mount Storm King. Registration for all lodging at Lake Crescent Lodge is just inside the door of the main building in the large lobby area highlighted by a huge stone fireplace. A gift shop, a restaurant, a lounge, and a beautiful sunroom are also on the main floor of the same building. Virtually all the accommodations, including the cabins, provide a view of beautiful Lake Crescent. Lake Crescent Lodge is located 21 miles west of Port Angeles, Washington, just off U.S. Highway 101.

The lodge offers several types of accommodations at a wide price range. All the rooms have heat but no air conditioning, television, or telephone. All rooms except those in the main lodge have a private bath. Pets are permitted in all units other than the main lodge and Pyramid Mountain Lodge. Parking is convenient to all the rooms. The least expensive accommodations are the five relatively small rooms on the second floor of the main lodge building. These rooms have paper-thin walls and are entered from an interior hallway via a lobby stairway. All have a double bed but no private bathroom. Two shower rooms and two small bathrooms are in the hallway. All five rooms are on the west side of the building and offer a terrific view of Lake Crescent and mountains that surround the opposite shore.

Sixteen one- and two-bedroom "Singer Tavern Cottages" are constructed two and three units to a building. Bedding in the one-bedroom units varies from one queen, to one king, to two doubles. The two-bedroom version has three double beds and a twin bed. These cottages sit back from the lake on a grassy area, although all have a lake view. Units 20 and 21 suffer from substantial foot traffic and should, if possible, be avoided. The Roosevelt Fireplace Cottages, with either one room or a living room plus dining room, were constructed in 1937. These units are quite a bit larger than the Tavern Cottages. The one-room cottages have two double beds, a sofa, and two chairs. The two-room version has three double beds, a sofa, and two chairs. Roosevelt Fireplace Cottages sit directly on the lake, and each unit includes a wood fireplace (wood is furnished), spacious rooms, and nice hardwood floors. They are surrounded at the back and sides by trees.

Three separate buildings house "motor lodge rooms." The Marymere Lodge is a one-story cement block building that sits back from the lake but still provides a lake view; trees surround the back and side of the building. All but one of the ten motel-type rooms at Marymere have two double beds, a desk, a chair, and a luggage bench. Each unit has a covered porch with chairs in the back. The two-story Storm King Motor Lodge sits in trees back from the lake but still provides a lake view. These ten rooms all have a double bed and a twin bed and are a little smaller and cost about $10 less than the rooms in Marymere. The Storm King units each have a balcony or patio with chairs. The two-story Pyramid Mountain Lodge was constructed in 1991 and is the newest lodging in the complex. This wooden structure sits back from the lake on a hill and has ten rooms, one of which is handicap accessible. The rooms in Pyramid Mountain each have two double beds and a private patio or balcony.

Lake Crescent is one of the cleanest and most scenic bodies of water in the United States. Surrounded by tree-covered mountains, the glacier-carved lake reaches a depth of 900 feet and varies in width from 0.5 mile to more than 2 miles along its 8.5-mile length. Approximately a dozen tributaries feed the 4,700-acre lake, which has only a single outlet. The steep slopes and cold water temperature cause the lake to be relatively free of algae and to take on a deep blue color.

If you don't mind using a common bathroom, the five second-floor rooms in the main lodge provide the best value and the best view. Open the front window in any of these rooms and you will enjoy a picture-postcard view. If a common bathroom is unacceptable and you plan to stay for a week or so, the Roosevelt Fireplace Cottages may be the best choice. These offer privacy and a view. They also cost about twice the price of the rooms in the main lodge.

Lake Crescent Lodge is in a picture-perfect setting. Lake Crescent is one of the country's most beautiful lakes, and the lodge takes full advantage of vistas the lake provides. This is a wonderful place to spend an active day or a restful week. Most of the activities are water-related. A wide grassy area with trees and chairs separates the main lodge from the lake. It is a perfect place to read a book, take a snooze, or watch guests use the swimming beach. Rowboats are available for rent at the lodge.

- **ROOMS:** Doubles, triples, and quads in most units. Some units will hold up to seven persons. All rooms outside the main lodge building have private bathrooms.

- **RESERVATIONS:** Lake Crescent Lodge, 416 Lake Crescent Road, Port Angeles, WA 98363–8672. Phone (360) 928–3211. Reservations require one night's deposit. Cancellation of forty-eight hours is required for a full refund.

- **RATES:** Main lodge rooms ($$); Singer Tavern Cottages ($$$$); Roosevelt Cottages ($$$$); motor lodge rooms ($$$/$$$$). Rates are quoted for two adults. Additional persons are $11.50 each. Pets are $10.00 each per night.

- **LOCATION:** Twenty-one miles west of Port Angeles, Washington, on U.S. Highway 101.

- **SEASON:** Late April through October. Four Roosevelt Fireplace Cottages are open on winter weekends, but no dining service is available.

- **FOOD:** A dining room ($$$) on the main floor serves three meals a day. Wine and beer are available in the lounge and dining room. A few snacks and beverages are available in the gift shop.

- **TRANSPORTATION:** Port Angeles offers scheduled airline service and rental vehicles. A city bus from Port Angeles to the lodge operates a daily schedule during summer.

- **FACILITIES:** Boat rental, boat dock, restaurant, lounge, swimming beach, and gift shop.

- **ACTIVITIES:** Swimming, hiking, boating, fishing.

# LAKE QUINAULT LODGE

P.O. Box 7 • Quinault, WA 98575–0007 • (360) 288–2900

*Lake Quinault Lodge*

Lake Quinault Lodge is a complex of six shake-covered buildings, including a two-story main lodge that encompasses the registration desk and lobby area. The main lodge has guest rooms on both floors, but the majority of rooms at this facility are in five buildings situated on either side of the main lodge building. The lodge sits in the middle of a rain forest, on a hill overlooking the south shore of Lake Quinault. The beautiful setting includes a large grass lawn that leads to the lake. Lake Quinault Lodge is on South Shore Road, 2 miles east of U.S. Highway 101. The turnoff from Highway 101 is 40 miles north of the town of Hoquiam. The lodge is in Olympic National Forest, across the lake from Olympic National Park. We have included this lodge because of its proximity to the park.

The lodge offers four basic types of rooms, all with heat but no air conditioning, telephone, or television. The main lodge building was constructed in 1926 with thirty-two rooms, including one suite. These rooms differ by size, bedding, bath, and view. In general, rooms in the main lodge are smaller than rooms in the other five buildings. Bedding varies from one queen bed to two double beds. Approximately half the rooms have a lake view and cost about $25 per night more than rooms that face the road and front drive.

At one end of the main lodge are two identical two-story buildings constructed in 1972, each with eight rooms that have a gas fireplace. These rooms contain one queen bed, a queen sofa bed, a table and chairs, and a full bath. Each room has a balcony or patio that overlooks the lake. Rooms in these two buildings are entered from outside walkways along the front of each floor. The Annex at the other end of the main lodge is the oldest building in the complex. A large covered porch wraps around the entire building. The nine rooms in the Annex vary by size and bedding that ranges from a double plus a twin to two doubles plus two twins. These rooms each have a private bath with a shower but no tub. A second-floor suite has a queen bed, a dining table, a sitting area, and a combination shower-tub.

Next to the Annex are two three-story Lakeside buildings, constructed in 1990. The two buildings contain a total of thirty-six rooms, including two suites. The rooms are nicely furnished and fairly spacious, with either two double beds or one king bed, a sofa bed, a table and chairs, and a small balcony that overlooks the lake. Two large fixed windows, and a sliding glass door, provide a wonderful view of trees and the lake. Suites are composed of two adjoining rooms. Lakeside rooms are entered from an outside walkway on each floor that is reached from either a stairway or a series of ramps. No elevator is in either building, and handicap-accessible rooms are on the first floor.

Lake Quinault Lodge offers plenty to do in a scenic outdoor setting. It is a wonderful place to spend several days or a week. The comfortable lobby, with a large brick fireplace, is a great place to read a book on a rainy day. When the weather clears, move out to a picnic table on the spacious back porch or down to one of the lawn chairs near the lake. Activities range from games such as badminton and volleyball, to swimming in the indoor pool, to canoeing on the beautiful lake. The main lodge dining room has a wall of large windows that provide a great view of the lake. A cozy pub on the main floor of the lodge offers beverages and food. Across the road from the lodge, a country store sells general merchandise, sandwiches, and groceries.

*The first log hotel to accommodate travelers to the Quinault area was built in the 1890s. The current lodge was constructed for only $90,000 during a ten-week period in 1926 despite the fact that all the materials and fixtures had to be hauled over 50 miles of dirt road. President Franklin Roosevelt visited the lodge in 1937. Guests to the lodge can still view original stenciled designs on the lobby's beamed ceiling.*

- **ROOMS:** Doubles, triples, and quads. A few rooms sleep more than four. Each room has a private bath, although some rooms have either a bathtub or a shower but not both.

- **RESERVATIONS:** Lake Quinault Lodge, P.O. Box 7, Quinault, WA 98575–0007. Phone (800) 562–6672 inside Washington or (360) 288–2900 outside Washington; fax (360) 288–2901. First night's payment is required. Three days' cancellation notice required for full refund less a $5.00 cancellation fee.

- **RATES:** Peak season, from June through October, main lodge rooms ($$$$$), suite ($$$$$); Fireplace units ($$$$$); Annex rooms ($$$$); Lakeside rooms ($$$$), suites ($$$$$). Rates reduced during most weekdays in off-peak season. Rates are for two; each additional person is $10. Children under five years are free. Pets are allowed in the Annex only at a rate of $10 per night per pet.

- **LOCATION:** On the south shore of Lake Quinault, 2 miles east of U.S. Highway 101 on South Shore Road.

- **SEASON:** The lodge is open year-round.

- **FOOD:** The dining room ($$$$) serves three meals a day. Reservations are required for dinner. Lunch and dinner from the same menu are also served in the pub during dining hours. A general store ($) across the street serves sandwiches and beverages and sells groceries, beer, and wine.

- **TRANSPORTATION:** The nearest scheduled air and rail service is in Seattle, where rental vehicles are available.

- **FACILITIES:** Heated indoor pool, sauna, game room, boat rentals, swimming beach, auditorium, playground equipment, pub, restaurant, gift shop, gas station, and general store. A large-screen TV is in the pub.

- **ACTIVITIES:** Guided walks, canoeing, boating, badminton, volleyball, horseshoes, and evening programs are popular during summer. Fishing, hiking, swimming, Ping-Pong, and board games are available year-round.

## LOG CABIN RESORT

3183 East Beach Road • Port Angeles, WA 98363 • (360) 928–3325

*Chalets at Log Cabin Resort*

Log Cabin Resort is a complex of freestanding cabins and linked A-frame chalets scattered in front of and beside a main lodge building that houses several motel-type rooms. The one-story wooden main lodge, constructed in the 1950s, contains the registration desk, a restaurant, a lobby, a small store, and lots of antiques. A parking lot immediately in front of the lodge can be used for registration; other parking is near the chalets and cabins. Virtually all of the cabins and rooms offer good views of beautiful Lake Crescent and the mountains surrounding the southern shore. Log Cabin Resort is located in the far northern section of Olympic National Park, on the north shore of Lake Crescent. It is 21 miles west of Port Angeles, Washington, 3.5 miles off U.S. Highway 101 on East Beach Road.

The resort offers four types of accommodations. All of the rooms have electric heat but no air conditioning, television, or telephone. The main lodge building has four attached motel-type rooms that each have two queen beds and a private bath with a shower but no tub. These rooms are paneled and have a large back window that provides a view of Lake Crescent. A table and two chairs are beside the window and a back door that opens to a private patio with table and chairs. The rooms are entered through an outside door directly beside the parking lot. All four rooms are nonsmoking accommodations.

Beside the lodge along the shoreline are two buildings that each contain six attached A-frame rooms with small lofts. These rooms have a double bed, a sofa bed, a sink, a refrigerator, and a private bathroom with a shower but no tub. A second double bed is in the loft reached via a stairway. Windows across the back allow good lake views from both the downstairs and the loft. A cement patio across the back of both buildings has a picnic table and grill for each room. These are all nonsmoking rooms.

Eight rustic cabins constructed in 1928, three with kitchens, are available in a variety of sizes, with several types of bedding that range upward from a double bed and a single bed. The cabins each have a private bath with either a shower or a tub. Each cabin has a covered front porch with chairs that allow guests a good view of the lake and mountains. The three cabins with kitchens that cost about $10 extra per night have a stove, oven, sink, and refrigerator. The least expensive accommodation is four relatively new camping log cabins with electricity but no plumbing. Each cabin has two double beds, but guests are required to provide their own bedding or it can be rented. Outside each cabin is a picnic table and a fire barrel. A common bathroom with showers is located just behind the cabins. These buildings are virtually identical to the camper cabins you will find in KOA campgrounds.

Log Cabin Resort is a fun place to spend several days in a magnificent mountain and lake setting inside Olympic National Park. Guests have plenty to do, with a roped lake swimming area just beside the lodge, boat rentals (canoes, paddleboats, and rowboats), and fishing. A 4-mile trail along an old railroad bed beside the lake passes by the resort. A nicely decorated restaurant has a wall of windows that looks out over the lake, and a patio area directly in back of the main lodge is available for outside dining.

- **ROOMS:** Singles, doubles, triples, and quads. The A-frame chalets and some of the cabins can hold up to six persons.

- **RESERVATIONS:** 3183 East Beach Road, Port Angeles, WA 98363. Phone (360) 928–3325; fax (360) 928–2088.

- **RATES:** Lodge rooms ($$$); A-frame chalet ($$$$); cabins ($$/$$$); camping log cabins ($). Rates are quoted for two adults. Each additional person is approximately $10.00 in all lodgings, with the exception of the camping cabins where each additional person is $5.00. Children six years old and under are free. There is an additional charge for pets, which are allowed only in the cabins.

- **LOCATION:** The resort is 18 miles west of Port Angeles, Washington, on U.S. Highway 101, and then 3.5 miles on East Beach Road on the north shore of Lake Crescent.

- **SEASON:** Valentines Day to Christmas.

- **FOOD:** An attractive dining room ($$/$$$) in the main lodge serves breakfast and dinner only. Sandwiches to go, including hamburgers and hot dogs, can be purchased in the gift shop ($) from 11:30 A.M. to 2:30 P.M.

- **TRANSPORTATION:** The nearest scheduled air service is at Port Angeles, where rental vehicles are available. A Port Angeles city bus stops at the resort twice a day, at 1:00 and 6:00 P.M.

- **FACILITIES:** Swimming beach, boat rental, boat launch, gift shop, limited groceries, Laundromat, and fishing supplies.

- **ACTIVITIES:** Fishing, hiking, boating, swimming.

# KALALOCH LODGE

157151 Highway 101 • Forks, WA 98331–9396 • (360) 962–2271

*Main Lodge Building at Kalaloch*

Kalaloch Lodge is a complex of wooden buildings that include a main lodge, many free-standing cabins, a motel-style unit, and a gas station, all sitting on a bluff overlooking the Pacific Ocean. Only a few overnight rooms are in the main lodge building. The registration desk for all rooms is on the first floor of the main lodge, which sits beside Highway 101. This building also contains the restaurant, coffee shop, cocktail lounge, and gift shop. All of the cabins and other lodging units are adjacent to and within easy walking distance of the main lodge. Kalaloch Lodge is located on U.S. Highway 101, 35 miles south of Forks, Washington. The lodge is 95 miles southwest of Port Angeles, Washington.

The lodge offers a total of sixty guest rooms in four categories, all of which have electric heat and a private bath but no air conditioning, telephone, or television (except the suite in the main lodge). The main lodge building contains ten overnight rooms, including two suites. All but one of the rooms are on the second floor and are accessed from a central hallway that is reached from a stairway behind the registration desk. These rooms each have a bath with a shower but no tub. Room size and bedding vary, with five rooms having one queen bed and other rooms having up to two queen beds and a sofa bed. The suite has an L-shaped combination living room–bedroom with one king bed and a sofa bed. This is the only room in the entire complex with a television set. Rooms 1 (on the first floor), 6, 7, and 8 and the suite provide an ocean view. Rooms 5 and 9, with two double beds and a sofa bed, are quite large.

The Sea Crest House has six regular rooms, plus four suites divided between two floors. This building sits behind two bluff cabins. The six regular motel-style rooms each have two queen beds and a private bath with a shower but no tub. Each room has its own patio or balcony. The suites have a sitting room with a fireplace (wood provided) and a separate bedroom with one or two queen beds plus a sofa bed.

Eighteen bluff cabins sit in a semi-circular pattern directly on the Pacific Ocean and provide a great view of the sea. About half of these cabins have either a fireplace or a wood stove (wood provided). All but four have one bedroom, with bedding that varies from one queen bed to two double beds. The other four have two bedrooms, with two double beds, a single bed, and two sofa beds. Most of the bluff cabins have carports and kitchens that include a sink, stove, oven, and refrigerator. Three of these buildings are modern duplexes with vaulted ceilings. The six cabins in these three buildings do not have kitchens or carports. Twenty-two freestanding log cabins each have two bedrooms, with bedding that varies from two queen beds to two double beds and a sofa bed. They have a wood stove and a kitchen area with a stove, sink, and refrigerator. These cabins have nice roomy interiors with paneled walls, tile floors, and a ceiling fan. Most of the log cabins sit fairly close together behind the bluff cabins and do not have a direct ocean view but are nonetheless very close to the bluff overlooking the ocean. These rent for slightly less than the bluff cabins.

Kalaloch Lodge is a great place to stay if you want to experience the Pacific Ocean. The lodge sits directly on the ocean, and the roar of the sea can be heard from your room. A wide sandy beach just below the bluff can be reached via an easy trail beside one of the cabins. The ocean water is relatively cold so you probably won't want to swim, but walks along the beach are one of the pleasures of staying here. National Park Service rangers lead daily walks along the beach and to various points in the park. The main lodge building has a restaurant, coffee shop, and second-floor cocktail lounge, while most of the cabins have kitchens for guests who want to prepare their own meals. The restaurant and lounge each have big windows that overlook the ocean. Keep in mind that this coastal area is often breezy and can get quite foggy, so be prepared for the possibility of chilly weather. Of course, the wind, fog, and cool air are all part of the experience of a visit to the Pacific Northwest.

- ■ **ROOMS:** Doubles, triples, and quads. A few cabins can hold more than four persons. All rooms have a private bath, although many have a shower but no bathtub.

- ■ **RESERVATIONS:** Kalaloch Lodge, 17151 Highway 101, Forks, WA 98331–9396. Phone (360) 962–2271; fax (360) 962–3391.

- ■ **RATES:** Main lodge ($$/$$$); Sea Crest House ($$$$); bluff cabins ($$$$$); log cabins ($$$$/$$$$$).

- **LOCATION:** Directly on the Pacific Ocean, 35 miles south of Forks, Washington, on U.S. Highway 101.

- **SEASON:** Kalaloch Lodge is open year-round.

- **FOOD:** A restaurant ($$$) serves breakfast, lunch, and dinner. The same menu, plus several additional items, is available in the adjacent coffee shop ($$/$$$), which is open from 7:00 A.M. to 10:00 P.M. Limited groceries can be purchased at the store/gas station beside the main lodge building.

- **TRANSPORTATION:** The nearest major city with scheduled air and train service is Olympia, Washington, where rental vehicles are available.

- **FACILITIES:** Restaurant, coffee shop, lounge, gift shop, gas station, and small store.

- **ACTIVITIES:** Walking, beachcombing, whale watching, kite flying, and surf fishing. Ranger-guided walks are offered each day during summer months.

## SOL DUC HOT SPRINGS RESORT

P.O. 2169 • Port Angeles, WA 98362 • (360) 327–3583

*Cabin at Sol Duc Hot Springs Resort*

Sol Duc (a Native American term meaning "sparkling water") Hot Springs Resort is a complex consisting of a single two-story wooden lodge building constructed in the 1980s and twenty-nine modern wooden buildings that provide thirty-two rooms. The cabins are clustered in a grassy area in front of the main lodge. The resort is known primarily for more than twenty hot mineral springs that feed pools located behind the lodge. A regular swimming pool is in the same complex. The resort is situated in the Sol Duc River Valley, surrounded by the heavily treed mountains of Olympic National Park. Sol Duc Hot Springs Resort is 42 miles west of Port Angeles, Washington, in the northwest corner of Olympic National Park. It is on a paved road 12 miles southeast of U.S. Highway 101.

The only accommodations at Sol Duc Hot Springs Resort are twenty-nine cabins constructed in the early 1980s. Three cabins are duplex units, so that a total of thirty-two rooms are available. No overnight accommodations are in the main lodge building. The lodge lobby houses a gift shop, convenience grocery store, restaurant, and registration desk. The twenty-nine freestanding cabins are virtually identical in size and outside appearance but have various bedding combinations that range from two double beds to two queen beds and a sofa bed. Each cabin has a front porch with bench and heat but no air conditioning, telephone, or television. All the cabins have a private bath with a combination tub-shower. Three duplex units have cabins with two double beds and a kitchen furnished with a sink, refrigerator, stove, and oven. These units are near the main lodge and rent for about $10 more per night than cabins without a kitchen.

Most people are drawn to Sol Duc Hot Springs Resort to take advantage of the natural hot springs. The resort has three circular pools of hot mineral water and a regular swimming pool, all located behind the main lodge building. The largest hot-water pool and a small shallow pool for children each contain mineral water at a temperature of 99 to 101 degrees Farenheit. Another small pool contains mineral water at a temperature of 105 degrees Farenheit. These pools are relatively shallow and designed for sitting and walking, not swimming. A larger swimming pool in the same complex has regular water that is heated. Both the larger mineral water pool and the swimming pool have ramps for handicap access. The mineral water pools and the swimming pool are available without charge to resort cabin guests; other visitors can use the facilities for a fee.

The first hotel at Sol Duc Springs was opened in 1912. The elaborate hotel, constructed by a man who claimed the mineral springs had cured him of a fatal illness, included tennis courts, bowling alleys, golf links, a theater, and a three-story sanatorium with beds for one hundred patients. Unfortunately, sparks from the fireplace ignited the shingle roof and burned down the hotel only four years after its completion. According to legend, the fire short-circuited the hotel's wiring, causing the organ to begin playing Beethoven's "Funeral March" while the building was burning.

Sol Duc Hot Springs Resort is a good place to get away from the hustle and bustle of the workaday world. You can hike in the morning, soak in the mineral water pool after lunch, get a professional massage in the late afternoon, take a nap in your cabin, and walk to the lodge for supper. After that, it's time for a good night's sleep so you can start all over again the next morning. A restaurant in the main lodge serves breakfast and dinner, while lunch is available at a snack bar beside the pool. Plenty of hiking trails near the resort lead into the rain forest and to the beautiful Sol Duc Falls. Evening programs on natural history are usually offered nightly at the nearby campground by National Park Service rangers.

■ **ROOMS:** Doubles, triples, and quads. A few rooms with a sofa bed can handle up to six individuals (four adults and two children, maximum). All rooms have a full bath.

- **RESERVATIONS:** Sol Duc Hot Springs Resort, P.O. Box 2169, Port Angeles, WA 98362. Phone (360) 327–3583; fax (360) 327–3593. First night's deposit is required. Cancellation requires forty-eight hours' notice plus a $5.00 fee.

- **RATES:** Cabin with or without kitchen ($$$). Cabins with kitchen are about $10 extra. Rates are quoted for two persons. Extra persons are charged $12.50. Children under four years stay free.

- **LOCATION:** Twelve miles southeast of U.S. Highway 101. The resort is in the northern part of Olympic National Park, 42 miles from Port Angeles, Washington.

- **SEASON:** The lodge is open to overnight guests from mid-May to the third week of September. The pools open earlier and remain open later in the year than the lodge.

- **FOOD:** A restaurant ($$/$$$) in the main lodge building serves breakfast and dinner. Sandwiches and beverages are available at the poolside snack bar ($) from 11:00 A.M. to 4:00 P.M. A few groceries, beer, and wine are sold near the registration desk.

- **TRANSPORTATION:** No public transportation is available to the lodge. Port Angeles, Washington, is the nearest city with scheduled air service and rental vehicles.

- **FACILITIES:** Swimming pool, heated mineral pools, restaurant, snack bar, store with gifts and snacks, and licensed massage practitioners.

- **ACTIVITIES:** Swimming, hiking, fishing, and soaking in mineral baths. Evening National Park Service campfire programs.

# WYOMING

## GRAND TETON NATIONAL PARK/
## JOHN D. ROCKEFELLER, JR. MEMORIAL PARKWAY

P.O. Drawer 170

Moose, WY 83012

(307) 739–3300

Grand Teton National Park comprises 310,000 acres of some of America's most spectacular landscape, including the Teton Range, which many people consider the most beautiful mountain range in the United States. The 24,000-acre John D. Rockefeller, Jr. Memorial Parkway provides a scenic link between Grand Teton National Park and Yellowstone National Park. These two areas are located in northwestern Wyoming, directly south of Yellowstone National Park. The entrance fee at Grand Teton is good for entrance to Yellowstone, and vice versa.

###  Lodging in Grand Teton National Park

Grand Teton National Park and the John D. Rockefeller, Jr. Memorial Parkway together provide a total of seven lodging facilities. Flagg Ranch Village is the only one of the seven that is located in the parkway, which lies between Grand Teton and Yellowstone. Triangle X Ranch, the only working dude ranch in a national park, is the most unusual lodging facility in the park, and maybe in any park. The least expensive facilities are at Colter Bay. The view rooms at Jackson Lake Lodge are probably the most upscale accommodations. Jenny Lake Lodge, with a four-star rating, is a very nice and quaint facility but is relatively expensive, even considering that horseback riding, bicycles, and two meals a day are included in the price.

# GRAND TETON NATIONAL PARK/
# JOHN D. ROCKEFELLER, JR. MEMORIAL PARKWAY

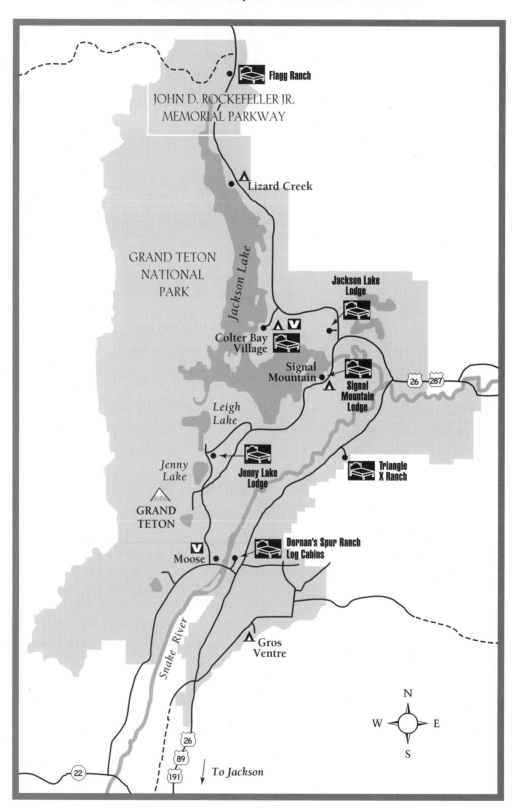

Flagg Ranch

JOHN D. ROCKEFELLER JR.
MEMORIAL PARKWAY

Lizard Creek

GRAND TETON
NATIONAL
PARK

Jackson Lake

Jackson Lake
Lodge

Colter Bay
Village

Signal
Mountain

Signal
Mountain
Lodge

26  287

Leigh
Lake

Jenny
Lake

Jenny Lake
Lodge

Triangle
X Ranch

GRAND
TETON

Moose

Dornan's Spur Ranch
Log Cabins

Snake River

Gros
Ventre

N
W        E
S

26
89
191

22

To Jackson

# COLTER BAY VILLAGE

P.O. Box 240 • Moran, WY 83013 • (307) 543–3100

*Cabins at Colter Bay Village*

Colter Bay Village is a major recreation center for Grand Teton National Park. The lodging facility at Colter Bay consists of 208 rooms in log cabins and sixty-six tent cabins. RV sites and a campground are also available. Colter Bay has no hotel, motel, or main lodge building. A small cabin rental office handles registration for the log cabins, while a separate office farther down the road takes care of registration for the tent cabins. The two types of accommodations are in separate areas, but both are close to the restaurants and other facilities of Colter Bay Village. The lodging facilities here are the least expensive in Grand Teton National Park. Colter Bay Village is located on the shore of Jackson Lake, about 15 miles south of the north entrance to Grand Teton National Park.

Colter Bay has two very different types of accommodations. The least expensive lodging is in sixty-six tent cabins. This lodging is about as basic as you will find outside your own tent. The tent cabins are constructed of two canvas walls and a canvas roof connected to two log walls. The cabins each contain a wood stove (wood is not provided but can be purchased), electric light, and two sets of bunk beds with thin vinyl-covered mattresses. A picnic table is on a canvas-covered porch just outside the front door. Guests are responsible for everything else, including sheets, blankets, pillows, and utensils. Sleeping bags, cots, blankets, and pillows can be rented at the registration office. Two restroom facilities without showers are in the immediate area. The tent cabins sit on a hill, with some units offering a view of the Tetons. Showers (fee) are available at a nearby launderette.

Colter Bay also has 208 log cabins. Most of the cabins are constructed two, three, or four to a building. All except the dormitory units have a private bath with a shower. These are nice, roomy units, both inside and out. Parking is immediately in front of each unit. Bedding ranges from one double to two doubles and a single in the one-bedroom units. Forty-two cabins have two bedrooms, one on each side of a common bathroom. These units are arranged with several types of bedding that range up to two double beds in each of the two bedrooms. Two log buildings in the cabin area house a total of nine rooms without private bath. These inexpensive rooms are nice, but occupants must use a community bathroom. The log cabins are clustered in an area of pine trees.

Colter Bay Village is a pleasant place to spend several days in Grand Teton National Park. Although the main village area, with restaurants, gift shops, and the National Park Service visitor center, is generally bustling with people and vehicles, the lodging is far enough away to escape most of the noise and congestion. At the same time, it is close enough that guests can avail themselves of the facilities. If you don't mind a room without a private bath, the semiprivate dorm rooms are the best value, at about half the price you will pay for the smallest cabin and only a few dollars more than you will pay for a tent cabin, where you have to supply your own bedding. Colter Bay Village offers a variety of activities, including horseback riding, raft trips, fishing, lake cruises, and boating. A pool at Jackson Lake Lodge is available to Colter Bay guests.

- **ROOMS:** Doubles, triples, and quads. A few two-bedroom units can handle up to eight persons. Most of the cabins have a private bath. None of the tent cabins have a private bath.

- **RESERVATIONS:** Grand Teton Lodge Company, P.O. Box 240, Moran, WY 83013. Phone (307) 543–3100. A one-night deposit is required, and it must be paid by either check or money order.

- **RATES:** Tent cabins ($); semiprivate dorm cabins ($); one-bedroom cabins ($$/$$$); two-bedroom cabins ($$$/$$$$). Quoted rates are for two adults. Additional adults in tent cabins are $3.00 each and in log cabins are $8.00 each. Children eleven and under are free with an adult.

The Snake River begins near the south boundary of Yellowstone National Park and flows into Jackson Lake. After leaving the lake, the Snake winds for 27 miles through Grand Teton National Park. Many visitors to Grand Teton choose to explore the river on a guided float trip. Both morning and afternoon trips are available. Children must be at least six years old to participate.

- **LOCATION:** North section of Grand Teton National Park, 40 miles north of Jackson, Wyoming.

- **SEASON:** Mid-May to late September for log cabins. Early June to early September for tent cabins.

- **FOOD:** A restaurant ($$) and food court ($) each serve breakfast, lunch, and dinner. A snack bar ($) is also available. Groceries can be purchased.

- **TRANSPORTATION:** The nearest scheduled air service is at Jackson, Wyoming, where rental vehicles are available. With advance notice, a van from Jackson Lake Lodge will meet flights. A shuttle operates between Colter Bay and Jackson Lake Lodge.

- **FACILITIES:** Restaurant, food court, snack bar, grocery store, gift shop, tackle shop, stables, marina, boat rental, service station, launderette, post office, National Park Service visitor center.

- **ACTIVITIES:** Hiking, fishing, boating, boat cruises, horseback riding, float trips, ranger/naturalist talks and walks during the day, evening campfire programs.

# DORNAN'S SPUR RANCH LOG CABINS

P.O. Box 39 • Moose, WY 83012 • (307) 733–2522

*Dornan's Spur Ranch Cabins*

Dornan's Spur Ranch is a lodging complex of twelve modern log cabins clustered in a courtyard behind a log registration building. The cabins are down a small hill from Dornan's, a small commercial center, which includes a grocery and outdoor restaurant. The entire complex sits in a basin next to the Snake River. The cabins are on privately owned land within the boundaries of Grand Teton National Park. Dornan's is located near the south end of the park, at Moose Junction.

The twelve log cabins at Dornan's are constructed two units to a building. All the cabins have a combination living room/kitchen area, a full bathroom, and either one or two bedrooms. The kitchen is fully equipped with refrigerator, stove, oven, and all utensils. Each bedroom has one queen bed, and the living room has a sofa bed. Furniture in all the cabins is handcrafted lodgepole pine. The cabins, built in 1992, have hardwood floors except in the bedrooms and are quite roomy. Each cabin has a covered porch off the living room. One cabin is handicap accessible.

Dornan's log cabins are among the nicest accommodations in Grand Teton National Park. The cabins are a short walk from Dornan's small commercial area, which offers a gas station, a gift shop, a sporting goods store, a chuck wagon restaurant, and a grocery with many specialty gourmet items. A bar adjacent to a liquor store, with a sizable variety of wines, has large picture windows that offer spectacular views of the Teton Mountain Range. Dornan's sells and rents various sports equipment and offers both scenic and whitewater float trips. That the cabins are open during the winter enables guests to take advantage of the area's many winter sports offerings.

- ◼ **ROOMS:** One-bedroom cabins can hold up to four persons. Two-bedroom units hold up to six. All cabins have a full bath and full kitchen.

- **RESERVATIONS:** Dornan's Spur Ranch Log Cabins, P.O. Box 39, Moose, WY 83012. Phone (307) 733–2522; fax (307) 733–3544. First night's deposit required, and a $25 fee is imposed for cancellations of two weeks or more. No refund on cancellations within two weeks.

- **RATES:** One-bedroom cabins ($$$$/$$$$$); two-bedroom cabins ($$$$$). Rates are reduced from October through May.

- **LOCATION:** South end of Grand Teton National Park, at Moose Junction. The cabins are 12 miles north of Jackson, Wyoming.

- **SEASON:** Open year-round.

- **FOOD:** A chuck wagon outdoor restaurant serves breakfast, lunch, and dinner ($$) during summer months. A bar serves lunch and Friday and Saturday dinners ($$) when the outdoor restaurant is closed. Groceries are available at the store.

- **TRANSPORTATION:** Air service is available to Jackson, Wyoming, where vehicles can be rented.

- **FACILITIES:** Grocery, bar, liquor store, outdoor restaurant, gift shop, sports shop, gas station.

- **ACTIVITIES:** Hiking, fishing, float trips on the Snake River, canoeing. Winter activities include cross-country skiing and snowmobiling.

*Dornan's is probably most famous for the gourmet grocery and large wine selection. The grocery has a deli, a bakery, and a selection of gourmet specialty foods that would do some big-city groceries proud. Next door the liquor store advertises that it offers 1,500 choices of wine. The chuck wagon dinner offers all you can eat of ribs, roast beef, and stew, beginning nightly at 5:00 P.M.*

# FLAGG RANCH RESORT

P.O. Box 187 • Moran, WY 83013 • (307) 543–2861

*Cabin at Flagg Ranch Resort*

Flagg Ranch Resort consists of a new lodge building, three two-story motel units with fifty-four rooms, and one hundred new cabins. Registration for all accommodations is in the main lodge building, which contains no overnight rooms. The main lodge building is quite attractive and has a lobby area in front of a large stone fireplace. The lodge also contains a restaurant, gift shop, grocery, and cocktail lounge. The lodge is quite close to the cabins, but the three motel units are more of a walk. Flagg Ranch is located at the north end of the John D. Rockefeller, Jr. Memorial Parkway, south of the south entrance to Yellowstone National Park and north of the north entrance to Grand Teton National Park. It is just off the parkway.

The ranch offers two basic categories of lodging: cabins and motel units. The new and spacious cabins are constructed either two to a building or four to a building. Each of the cabins has heat, a telephone, and a full bath with a combination tub-shower. None of the units have television. The most expensive cabins are duplex units that each have one king bed, a lounge chair, and a covered porch with two rocking chairs. Most of these cabins offer a nice view of the distant mountains. Cabins with two queen beds are the same size but rent for about $10 less per night. These cabins do not have a back porch, and they sit in a wooded setting. Plentiful parking is near the cabins. Three cabins with two queen beds are handicap accessible.

The three two-story wooden motel buildings are clustered on the bank of the Snake River near the highway. They are about a ten-minute walk from the lodge. These buildings offer a total of fifty-four rooms, including four suites. The regular rooms are large, and each has two double beds and a full bath but no telephone or television. The rooms each have a sliding glass door, and units on the second floor have a back balcony. Four suites each have a bedroom with a double bed plus a single bed, as well as a separate sitting room with a sofa bed, refrigerator, microwave, wet bar, and television. The suites rent for about $15 per night more than the regular motel rooms.

Flagg Ranch offers nice new lodging at a convenient location between Yellowstone National Park and Grand Teton National Park. The lodging units are all relatively large, and the main lodge building is very attractive. Several activities are available for guests, including horseback riding, river rafting, and fishing. Winter activities include snowmobiling, snow-coach rides, cross-country skiing, and snowshoeing. Rentals are available, and an activities information desk is just inside the lodge's front door.

■ **ROOMS:** Doubles, triples, and quads. All rooms have a private bath with a combination tub-shower.

■ **RESERVATIONS:** Flagg Ranch Resort, P.O. Box 187, Moran, WY 83013. Phone (800) 443–2311; fax (307) 543–2356.

■ **RATES:** Motel units ($$$); suites ($$$$); king cabins and queen cabins ($$$$). Rates are quoted for two adults. Children seventeen and under are free. Pets are charged an additional $5.00 per night. Rates vary through the year, with summer being most expensive. Several packages are available during fall and winter.

> *Flagg Ranch was established between 1910 and 1916 at its present location by an early guide and pioneer in this area, which is believed to have been a favorite camping spot for both Indians and fur trappers. The ranch is the oldest continually operating resort in the upper Jackson Hole area. It has served as both a dude ranch and a lodging facility, offering overnight accommodations to early trappers and present-day travelers. The ranch name is derived from the flag that flew from the Snake River Military Station, once located here.*

■ **LOCATION:** North end of John D. Rockefeller, Jr. Memorial Parkway, 2 miles south of the south entrance to Yellowstone National Park. The ranch is just off the highway.

■ **SEASON:** Mid-May through mid-October and mid-December through mid-March.

■ **FOOD:** A nice restaurant ($$$) offers breakfast, lunch, and supper. Groceries are available at a small store in the main lodge building.

■ **TRANSPORTATION:** The nearest scheduled air service is at Jackson, Wyoming. Flagg Ranch provides round-trip transportation from Jackson/Teton Village (fee charged).

■ **FACILITIES:** Restaurant, cocktail lounge, gift shop, grocery store, gas station, stables, Laundromat.

■ **ACTIVITIES:** Hiking, fishing, river rafting, horseback riding. Winter activities include snow-coach tours, cross-country skiing, snowshoeing, and snowmobiling.

# JACKSON LAKE LODGE

Grand Teton Lodge Company • P.O. Box 250 • Moran, WY 83013 • (307) 543–3100

*Main Lodge Building at Jackson Lake*

Jackson Lake Lodge is a very large central lodge building flanked on both sides by numerous multiple-unit wooden buildings that house cottage units. These cottages are hidden from view by surrounding trees. Overnight rooms are also on the third floor of the lodge. The three-story cement lodge sits on a bluff overlooking a large meadow and Jackson Lake, both of which sit in front of the spectacular mountain range. Registration is just inside the main entrance. The lodge building has a large second-floor lobby with two unique corner fireplaces, many comfortable chairs and sofas, and a two-story wall of windows with a picture-perfect view of the Tetons. The lodge also has a dining room, grill, cocktail lounge, gift shop, and apparel shop, all on the second floor. A large parking lot is just behind the lodge and plentiful parking is near each of the cottage units. Arriving guests can use the entrance drive to register and, for guests who will be staying in the lodge, drop off luggage. An elevator is in the lodge. Jackson Lake Lodge is located on the eastern shore of Jackson Lake, 5 miles northwest of Moran Junction, about 35 miles north of the town of Jackson.

The lodge offers three basic types of rooms: view rooms, lodge rooms, and cottages. All the rooms have heat, a telephone, and a private bath but no air conditioning or television. Cottages comprise the vast majority of the 385 rooms at the Jackson Lake complex. Rooms in the main lodge, all on the third floor, are mostly alike except for the view. Rooms on the west side of the building, with large windows that provide great views of the Tetons, cost about $75 more per night than similar rooms on the east side of the building. Nearly all the rooms have two double beds with a full bathroom. The more costly "view rooms" also have a refrigerator, a wet bar, and down comforters on the beds. All the rooms in the lodge are quite large and attractively decorated. The lodge has one suite about twice the size of a regular room that has a sitting area with a sofa and chairs, one king bed, a wet bar, and a refrigerator. The suite provides a view of the mountains.

Motel-type cottages furnish 348 rooms. Most of the cottages have two double beds, comfortable furniture, beamed ceilings, and a full bath. The cottages are quite roomy and mostly one-story, constructed six or eight to a building. Those with a back patio rent for about $12 extra per night. Three two-story buildings house cottages with view rooms that rent for the same as the lodge view rooms, or about $62 per night more than regular cottage units. A fourth two-story building has patio cottages. Several handicap-accessible cottage rooms are available. We believe the best value is a non–view room in the lodge. These are the cheapest rooms available (although not by much), and it is nice being in the same building where all of the facilities are located. If you want a view, walk (or take the elevator) down one flight of stairs to the second-floor lobby.

Jackson Lake Lodge is a pleasant place to stay, especially if you enjoy spectacular scenery. The location offers unsurpassed views, and all of the rooms in the complex are relatively large and comfortable. Several choices are available for dining, and the main dining room on the second floor has large windows with views that rival those of the lobby. The chef will even cook fish that you catch and clean. The lodge also offers more stores than are usually found in a national park lodge building. A variety of activities are available, including swimming in the heated pool, horseback riding, float trips, and park bus tours.

- **ROOMS:** Doubles, triples, and quads. All rooms have a private bath.

- **RESERVATIONS:** Grand Teton Lodge Company, P.O. Box 240, Moran, WY 83013. Phone (307) 543–3100. If staying two or more nights, a two-night deposit by check or money order is required. Forty-eight hour cancellation is required for deposit refund.

- **RATES:** Main lodge rooms with no view ($$$), main lodge room with a view ($$$$$); lodge suite ($$$$$); cottages with no view ($$$$); cottages with a view ($$$$$). Rates are for two adults. Additional persons are $8.50 each per night. Children eleven and under are free.

- **LOCATION:** Jackson Lake Lodge is located on the eastern shore of Jackson Lake, 6 miles northwest of Moran Junction, about 24 miles north of the town of Moose.

- **SEASON:** Mid-May through mid-October.

- **FOOD:** The dining room ($$$$) and an adjacent grill ($/$$) serve three meals daily. The grill uses the same menu for lunch and dinner. A pool grill ($/$$) is open during July and August.

- **TRANSPORTATION:** The nearest airport is in Jackson, Wyoming, where rental cars are available. A shuttle service (fee charged) operates several times per day between Jackson and the Jackson Lake Lodge.

Colter Bay Village, Jackson Lake Lodge, and Jenny Lake Lodge are all operated by Grand Teton Lodge Company. The same firm also operates Jackson Hole Golf & Tennis Club, which is 8 miles north of Jackson, outside the park boundaries. The club has six tennis courts and an eighteen-hole championship course golf course designed by Robert Trent Jones, Jr.

- **FACILITIES:** Restaurant, coffee shop, cocktail lounge, gift shops, apparel shop, newsstand, outdoor heated swimming pool, service station, stable, medical clinic.

- **ACTIVITIES:** Horseback riding, swimming, float trips, hiking, evening ranger/naturalist programs.

# JENNY LAKE LODGE

P.O. Box 240 • Moran, WY 83013 • (307) 733–4647

*Cabin at Jenny Lake Lodge*

Jenny Lake Lodge consists of a main log lodge building that sits in a grassy area in front of thirty-seven log cabins. The complex is located at the base of the Tetons, across the road from beautiful Jenny Lake. The main lodge building, with hardwood floors and vaulted ceilings, houses the registration desk, the dining room, and a cozy lobby with stuffed furniture and a large stone fireplace. Lobby and dining room windows provide good mountain views. A wooden front deck has chairs and benches that face the mountains. A few of the cabins are freestanding, but most are duplex units. The cabins are nicely spaced in an area of pine trees. The facility is quaint, quiet, well maintained, and fairly expensive. Unlike cabin rates at most other national park facilities, the rates here include each day's breakfast, a seven-course dinner, and horseback riding. Lunch is also served at an extra charge. Jenny Lake Lodge is located in the middle of Grand Teton National Park, approximately 20 miles north of Jackson, Wyoming.

Two types of cabin accommodations are available at the lodge. All the cabins have heat and a private bath with a shower-tub combination but no air conditioning, telephone, or television. Thirty-two one-room cabins are similar from the outside but vary somewhat in decor, view, and bedding, which ranges from one queen bed, to one king bed, to two double beds. Each cabin has a covered front porch with two rocking chairs. Some of the cabins face the mountain range and provide great views from the front porch. Six suites each have one large room with a wood stove (wood provided) and sofa bed in the sitting area. Bedding in these units varies from two doubles, to two queens, to a king. All the cabins at Jenny Lake Lodge are quite nice, but try to get one with a front porch view of the mountains.

Jenny Lake Lodge is a wonderful place where you can relax, hike, and sightsee without worrying about much of anything. The rustic nature of the lodge and cabins provides a taste of the West but with style. Two meals a day and horseback riding are included, the chef will cook any fish you catch, and the staff will even take care of your laundry. If you choose to enjoy an extended stay and want to eat somewhere different, you can obtain vouchers for dinner at Jackson Lake Lodge or the restaurant at Jackson Hole Golf & Tennis Club. Fly into Jackson and the staff will, with prior notice, pick you up. The only downside to Jenny Lake Lodge is the expense, which is approximately double what you are likely to pay at Jackson Lake Lodge. On the other hand, if cost isn't a factor, this is your place to enjoy the Tetons.

*Jenny Lake Lodge is the descendant of a small 1920s dude ranch called Danny Ranch on the same site. Five cabins and a portion of the original main lodge building remain as part of the existing complex, which gained its current name in 1952. The original log building now houses the lodge dining room. Cabins have been modernized and added to over the years. A major restoration was undertaken in the late 1980s, and four new cabins were added in 1993.*

- **ROOMS:** Singles, doubles, triples, and quads. All the cabins have a full bathroom.

- **RESERVATIONS:** Grand Teton Lodge Company, P.O. Box 240, Moran, WY 83013. Phone (307) 733–4647. Up to a three-day deposit is required for stays of three days or more. Three-week cancellation is required for full refund.

- **RATES:** All cabins ($$$$$). Additional persons are $105 extra per day. Children two years and under are free with an adult. Breakfast, dinner, and horseback riding are included in the price.

- **LOCATION:** Midsection of Grand Teton National Park, approximately 20 miles north of Jackson, Wyoming.

- **SEASON:** First part of June to the first of October.

- **FOOD:** A cozy dining room serves breakfast, lunch, and a seven-course dinner. Breakfast and dinner are included in the price of a room. Sunday dinner is a buffet.

- **TRANSPORTATION:** Daily air service is available from Denver, Colorado, and Salt Lake City, Utah, to Jackson, Wyoming, where rental vehicles are available. The lodge operates a free pickup service at the airport, with prior notice.

- **FACILITIES:** Restaurant, stables, bicycles, gift shop, tour desk. Guests have free use of the Jackson Lake Lodge heated swimming pool. A National Park Service visitor center is 3 miles away.

- **ACTIVITIES:** Hiking, fishing, horseback riding, and bicycling. Guided walks and evening campfire programs originate at the National Park Service visitor center.

# SIGNAL MOUNTAIN LODGE

P.O. Box 50 • Moran, WY 83103 • (307) 543–2831

*Rustic Log Cabins at Signal Mountain Lodge*

Signal Mountain Lodge is a complex consisting of a two-story registration building, a separate building with a restaurant and coffee shop, a convenience store, and seventy-eight cabins that sit to the side and up a hill from the registration building. Only the cabins provide rooms for overnight lodging. The lodge complex is in an attractive setting on the east shore of Jackson Lake, with views of the Tetons in the distance. The registration building has a small but nice lobby area, with windows that provide an excellent view of the mountains. The lodge is located approximately 7 miles west of the Moran Entrance Station and about 4 miles south of Jackson Lake Lodge.

Five classifications of cabins are offered at Signal Mountain Lodge. The cabins are constructed two, three, or four to a building. All of the cabins have electric heat, a telephone, and a full bath with a combination tub-shower but no air conditioning or television. The least expensive accommodation is the Rustic Log Cabin, available in both one- and two-bedroom versions. One-bedroom units come in different sizes, with bedding that ranges from one double bed to two double beds and a sofa bed. The two-bedroom units have a bedroom on each side of a bathroom. Bedding in these units varies from two double beds to three double beds. Five of the one-bedroom units have fireplaces and rent for about $20 per night extra; firewood is provided. Most of the Rustic Log Cabins have a porch with chairs. Cabins 137 and 143 sit on the lake, while cabins 139, 146, and 147 sit on a hill above the lake and have lake views. Most of the Rustic Cabins have views that are obscured by other lodging units.

Twelve larger Country Rooms scattered about the complex each have bedding that ranges from two queen beds to one king bed. These units are more modern motel-style rooms, and each has a refrigerator. They rent for about $20 more per night than the one-bedroom Rustic Log Cabins. Three Deluxe Country Rooms, all in the same building, each have two connecting rooms with a king bed and a sofa bed. They each have a small refrigerator and stone fireplace and rent for about $50 per night more than the regular Country Rooms.

Twenty-eight Lakefront Retreats are constructed four units to a building, with two units up and two units down. These large one-room units sit directly on Lake Jackson and offer great views of the mountains. The units have a living room/kitchen with a sofa bed, microwave, stove top, and refrigerator. The bedroom area, with either two queens or a king bed, can be closed off. Utensils and dishes are not included. These rent for about $15 more than the Deluxe Country Rooms.

One Family Bungalow has two units that can be rented as a whole or separately. One unit comprises a bedroom with two queens and a sofa bed, as well as a separate kitchen with a microwave, stove top, and full-size refrigerator. The attached unit has one room with a queen bed, sofa bed, and small refrigerator. The building has a large deck with picnic tables and an outdoor barbecue.

Signal Mountain Lodge is a relatively quiet facility in a beautiful setting. Everything is on a small scale, from the registration building, to the dining room, to the individual cabin units. It lacks the large lobby area that makes Jackson Lake Lodge so attractive, but the same views are available with fewer crowds by getting out of your cabin and walking down the road.

H ole *is a term that was used by fur trappers to describe a high valley surrounded by mountains. The valley of Jackson Hole is named for trapper David Jackson, who reportedly spent the winter months in 1829 along the shore of Jackson Lake. Jackson Hole is 40 miles in length and varies from 8 to 15 miles in width.*

- **ROOMS:** Doubles, triples, and quads. Several rooms with a sofabed can handle up to six persons. All rooms have a private bath.

- **RESERVATIONS:** Signal Mountain Lodge, P.O. Box 50, Moran, WY 83013. Phone (307) 543–2831, Monday through Friday, from 8:00 A.M. to 5:00 P.M. Mountain Standard Time; open twenty-four hours May through early October.

- **RATES:** Rustic Log Cabins ($$$); Country Rooms ($$$); Deluxe Country Rooms ($$$$$); Lakefront Retreats ($$$$$); Family Bungalow—one room ($$$$) and two rooms ($$$$$). Rates are by the room and not the number of persons.

- **LOCATION:** On Jackson Lake, 7 miles west of Moran Junction.

- **SEASON:** Mid-May to the first week in October.

- **FOOD:** A dining room ($$$/$$$$) and cafe ($) offer breakfast, lunch, and dinner. Windows in the dining room provide a view of the lake and mountains. Limited groceries are in a convenience store.

- **TRANSPORTATION:** The nearest scheduled air service is in Jackson, Wyoming, where rental vehicles are available.

- **FACILITIES:** Marina with boat rentals, restaurant, cafe, gift shop, convenience store, gas station.

- **ACTIVITIES:** Boating, fishing, hiking, guided fishing trips, evening naturalist programs, raft trips. Bicycles are available without charge.

# TRIANGLE X RANCH

Moose, WY 83012 • (307) 733–2183

*One-Bedroom and Two-Bedroom Cabins at Triangle X Ranch*

Triangle X Ranch is the only operating dude ranch in a national park. It has also been used as location for several movies, including John Wayne's first picture and the classic western *Shane*. The ranch has all of the buildings you would expect in a working ranch, as well as nineteen freestanding log cabins that provide overnight accommodations. The ranch sits on a hill overlooking Jackson Hole and the Teton Mountain Range. One of the many buildings in the ranch complex contains the dining room and a separate lobby with chairs and tables. All of the cabins are within a short walking distance of the dining room. Triangle X requires a minimum stay of one week (June through August) that begins and ends on Sunday. The ranch is particularly appealing to people who enjoy horseback riding, since this is the main activity for guests. Triangle X Ranch is on the eastern side of Grand Teton National Park, 25 miles north of Jackson, Wyoming, just off U.S. Highways 26, 89, and 191. It is 6 miles south of Moran Junction.

A total of nineteen log cabins are available for guests. All of the cabins have electricity, heat, and a private bathroom with a combination tub-shower but no telephone or television. Cabins are available with one, two, and three bedrooms. The two-bedroom and three-bedroom units each have two full bathrooms. Most of the cabins have two single beds in each bedroom. While all the cabins have a very rustic outside appearance, the interiors are quite nice, with wood walls and heavy pine furniture. The ceilings are slightly vaulted. Each cabin has a covered front porch with chairs that provide great views.

Triangle X Ranch is a wonderful place to stay if you enjoy mountain scenery, horseback riding, and an overall western experience. With each guest spending an entire week at the ranch, it is a certainty you will make some friends during your stay here. Three meals a day, served family-style, and horseback riding (except Sunday) are included as part of the package. Meals are announced by the ring of the dinner bell. Each guest is assigned his or her own horse at the beginning of the week's stay. The evenings each have a different scheduled activity, including square dancing, moonlight horseback rides, ranger talks, cookouts, and campfire gatherings. Triangle X offers float trips and pack trips at extra cost.

- **ROOMS:** One to three persons in a one-bedroom unit; three to five persons in a two-bedroom unit; five to six persons in a three-bedroom cabin. All cabins have a private bath with a combination tub-shower.

- **RESERVATIONS:** Triangle X Ranch, Moose, WY 83012. Phone (307) 733–2183; fax (307) 733–8685. Minimum stay of one week during June, July, and August. Four days at other times. Required deposit of 30 percent of total cost. Credit cards are not accepted.

- **RATES:** Including all meals and horseback riding ($$$$$). A 15 percent charge for gratuities is added to all bills.

- **LOCATION:** East side of Grand Teton National Park, 25 miles north of Jackson, Wyoming. The ranch is 6 miles south of Moran Junction, on U.S. Highways 26, 89, and 191.

- **SEASON:** Late May to the first week in November.

- **FOOD:** Three meals a day are served family-style in the ranch dining room. Meals are included in the quoted rates.

- **TRANSPORTATION:** Scheduled airlines serve Jackson, Wyoming, where rental vehicles are available. The ranch will pick up at the airport for a fee.

- **FACILITIES:** Stables, dining room, Laundromat, gift shop.

- **ACTIVITIES:** Horseback riding, breakfast and dinner cookouts, square dancing, fishing, hiking, float trips.

*Triangle X Ranch has served as home to four generations of the same family. The ranch was purchased by John S. Turner in the summer of 1926. Turner started construction of his home and welcomed guests the same summer. The ranch was self-sufficient, with refrigeration provided by ice cut from nearby ponds and stored in piles of sawdust. In the late 1920s Turner sold the property to a land company owned by John D. Rockefeller, who eventually donated the land to the federal government. Today the grandson of John Turner operates the ranch as a concessionaire of the National Park Service.*

# YELLOWSTONE NATIONAL PARK

P.O. Box 168
Yellowstone National Park, WY 82190
(307) 344–7381

Yellowstone National Park, America's first and probably best-known national park, comprises nearly 3,400 square miles of lakes, waterfalls, mountains, and some 10,000 geysers and hot springs. The park contains almost 300 miles of roads. Most of the major attractions are near Grand Loop Road, which makes a figure eight in the park's central area. The road's east side provides access to canyons, mountains, and waterfalls, while the west side leads to areas of thermal activity. Most of the park is in the northwestern corner of Wyoming, with overlapping strips in Montana and Idaho.

##  Lodging in Yellowstone National Park

Yellowstone has nine lodging facilities, the best known of which is Old Faithful Inn. Two other lodges are in the Old Faithful area. Other lodges are at Grant Village, Mammoth Hot Springs, Roosevelt, Canyon Village, and Lake Village. Accommodations range from very rustic cabins, to a wonderful one-hundred-year-old hotel, to relatively new motel-type accommodations. All nine of the lodging facilities are operated by the same firm, so the registration desk at any of the lodges can determine whether vacancies exist at any of the other lodges. Yellowstone is very busy, so it is important to make reservations as early as possible. You may be able to obtain a room as a walk-in, although you aren't likely to have much choice regarding the facility or cost.

- **RESERVATIONS FOR ALL ACCOMMODATIONS INSIDE THE PARK:** AmFac Parks & Resorts, Reservations Office, P.O. Box 165, Yellowstone National Park, WY 82190. Phone (307) 344–7311. Deposit is required for first night's lodging at each location where you will be staying. Cancellation notice of forty-eight hours during the summer season required for refund of deposit. Fourteen days advance notice required for cancellation of winter reservations.

- **TRANSPORTATION:** Scheduled airlines serve Bozeman, Montana, on the north side; West Yellowstone, Montana, on the west side; Cody, Wyoming, on the east side, and Jackson, Wyoming, south of Grand Teton National Park. Rental vehicles are available at all four locations. Scheduled bus service is available to Bozeman and Livingston, Montana. Bus service also operates between Cody and the park. No public transportation system operates within Yellowstone National Park, although scenic bus tours along the upper and lower loop roads are scheduled from various lodging locations in the park. Heavy traffic, poor road conditions, and seemingly continual repairs can make driving in Yellowstone an aggravating affair.

# YELLOWSTONE NATIONAL PARK

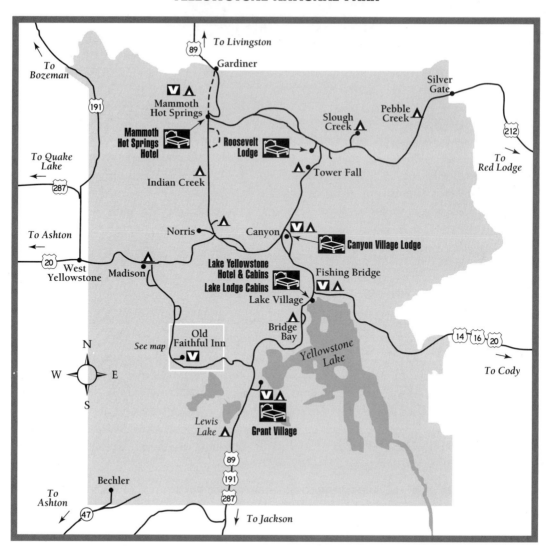

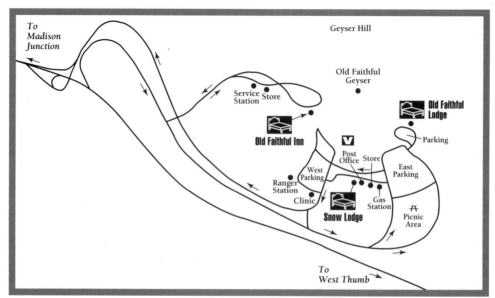

# CANYON LODGE AND CABINS

Yellowstone National Park, WY 82190 • (307) 344–7901

*Frontier Cabins at Canyon Lodge and Cabins*

anyon Lodge is a large commercial complex that includes hundreds of cabins and one newer three-story lodge building. The vast majority of the 609 rooms at Canyon Lodge are one-story cabins constructed four or eight to a building. The village also has a large general store/coffee shop, restaurant, snack bar, lounge, and gift shop. This is a busy commercial center of the park, but most of the overnight rooms are far enough away that you will be able to enjoy a relatively quiet stay. It is also large enough that you may have a hike to the restaurant, depending upon the location of your cabin. The registration desk is in a separate building near the cafeteria and restaurant. After registering you will need to drive to your room. The village derives its name from the Grand Canyon of the Yellowstone River that is a half-mile away. Canyon Village is near the center of the park, approximately 42 miles from the east entrance and 40 miles from the west entrance at West Yellowstone.

Canyon Lodge and Cabins has three types of accommodations. All of the rooms have heat and private baths but no telephone, television, or air conditioning. None of the rooms have balconies. Adequate parking is available near all the rooms. The least expensive and most plentiful lodging is the 472 Frontier Cabins built in the 1950s and 1960s; these are concentrated in two large sections behind the main lodge building. These cabins are all constructed eight to a building. The bathroom has a shower but no bathtub. Cabin size varies according to bedding, which ranges from two twin beds to two double beds and a single. All of these cabins rent for the same rate even though room size varies, so it is best to ask for a room with two double beds. We believe that these cabins offer the best lodging value (but not the nicest accommodations) at Canyon Village.

One hundred Western Cabins are constructed four or six units to a building. These units are larger, are newer (1970s and 1980s), and rent for about twice as much as the Frontier units. Each Western Cabin has two double beds, a table with two chairs, and a bathroom with a tub-shower combination. Like most of the Frontier Cabins, the Western units are fairly widely spaced among pine trees which allows for some privacy. Some of the units are constructed with windows on two sides of each room.

Cascade Lodge, the newest facility at Canyon Lodge (it opened in 1993), is a single three-story building with thirty-seven virtually identical rooms. This lodge probably has the nicest rooms in Yellowstone. Each of the large rooms has two double beds, comfortable furniture, and a bath with a tub-shower combination. Rooms on the second and third floors seem somewhat larger and provide better views because of dormer windows. If you don't mind climbing stairs (there is no elevator), a room on the third floor is best. Cascade Lodge has two handicap-accessible rooms on the first floor.

Canyon Lodge and Cabins is the most centrally located of all the lodging facilities at Yellowstone National Park, so it is a perfect place to settle in and explore this large park. Canyon Village offers just about anything you desire when you return from a long day of touring. The location, number of lodging places, and variety of facilities make this a very busy place. A restaurant, cafeteria, coffee shop, and snack bar offer an array of meals and prices. You will also find a large general store with books, supplies, gifts, and groceries. A cocktail lounge and post office are also in the village. A National Park Service visitor center contains a geology display. Stables are available for horseback riding.

*Canyon Lodge sits within walking distance of the North Rim of the Grand Canyon of the Yellowstone. A half-mile trail leads from cabin P26 to the North Rim's Grandview Point. From here North Rim Trail leads either 1 mile northeast to Inspiration Point or about 1 mile southwest to the Lower Falls. The entire North Rim Trail, which begins at South Rim Drive Bridge and ends at Inspiration Point, is slightly less than 3 miles, and a portion of it is paved. A variety of trails are also on the south side of the canyon.*

- **ROOMS:** Doubles, triples, and quads. All rooms have a private bath.

- **RATES:** Frontier Cabins ($); Western Cabins ($$$); Cascade Lodge ($$$).

- **LOCATION:** Near the middle of Yellowstone National Park, 40 miles from the west entrance at West Yellowstone.

- **SEASON:** June through the first week in September.

- **FOOD:** Restaurant ($$/$$$); cafeteria ($); coffee shop ($); snack bar ($).

- **FACILITIES:** Restaurant, cafeteria, snack bar, coffee shop, gift shop, Laundromat, general store with groceries, nature store, post office, gas station, stables, National Park Service visitor center.

- **ACTIVITIES:** Horseback riding, hiking, evening ranger program.

# GRANT VILLAGE

Yellowstone National Park, WY 82190 • (307) 344–7901

*Grant Village*

Grant Village consists of a registration building plus six modern two-story lodge buildings that each contain about fifty rooms. The wooden lodge buildings, constructed from 1982 to 1984, sit staggered across a hillside above the south shore of the West Thumb of Yellowstone Lake. Rooms on each side of the building are entered from a central corridor on each floor. Half the rooms in each of the six lodge buildings face the lake, and the other half face parking areas and a pine forest. Each building has a small first-floor lobby with chairs, while the newer buildings also have a small second-floor lobby with tables and chairs. Adequate parking is directly beside each building. There are no elevators in the buildings, but bell service is available at the registration building. Grant Village is located in the south end of Yellowstone, in the West Thumb area. It is the southernmost lodging facility in the park, 20 miles north of the south entrance to Yellowstone.

Two types of rooms are offered at Grant Village. All rooms have heat, a telephone, and a private bath. Most bathrooms have a shower, but some offer a combination tub-shower. None of the rooms have air conditioning, television, or a balcony. All of the rooms are of good size, but approximately 200 in four newer buildings are a little larger and cost about $15 extra per night. The two classes of rooms are so similar that the small price difference probably isn't worth paying. Rooms facing the lake and rooms facing the parking area rent for the same price, so it is best to request a lake-view room. Second-floor lakeside rooms in Lodge A and Lodge F, which sit closest to the lake, have the best window views. The eight corner rooms in the four newer buildings have an extra side window. A total of twelve handicap-accessible rooms are available.

Grant Village is a good place to spend a restful night at Yellowstone, especially if you are arriving late or will be leaving from the park's south entrance. The village is away from most of the heavily visited tourist areas and free from the congestion they attract. Another advantage is that the village sits only 17 miles from the park's main attraction, Old Faithful. In addition to lodging, Grant Village also has two restaurants, a grill, a post office, a gift shop, a service station, a Laundromat, a boat launch, and a National Park Service visitor center. Three eating establishments with varying menus and prices are separate but only a short walk from the lodges. The Grant Village Restaurant near Lodge A is an unusual building with a high vaulted wooden ceiling and windows that provide a view of Yellowstone Lake. A cozy cocktail lounge is just off the entrance area. A less expensive restaurant, Lake House, sits directly on the lake and serves breakfast and dinner. Windows on three sides of the building provide good views of the lake. A general store near the registration building houses a grill that serves breakfast, sandwiches, ice cream, and beverages. A salad bar is also available.

- **ROOMS:** Doubles, triples, and quads. All rooms have a private bath with shower or combination tub-shower.

- **RATES:** Newer rooms ($$$); older rooms ($$).

- **LOCATION:** At the south end of the park, 22 miles north of the south entrance.

- **SEASON:** The end of May through the third week of September.

- **FOOD:** Grant Village Restaurant ($$/$$$) serves three meals daily in an unusual and attractive building. Lake House ($$) serves breakfast and dinner only. A grill ($) in the general store serves breakfast, sandwiches, and beverages. The store also has a good offering of groceries.

- **FACILITIES:** Two restaurants, cocktail lounge, grill, general store, gift shop, service station, boat ramp, picnic area, post office, Laundromat, National Park Service visitor center.

- **ACTIVITIES:** Hiking, fishing, evening ranger programs at the amphitheater.

# LAKE LODGE CABINS

Yellowstone National Park, WY 82190 • (307) 344–7901

*Frontier Cabins at Lake Lodge and Cabins*

Lake Lodge Cabins is a complex consisting of a large log lodge building with a registration desk and support services, plus 186 wood cabins that sit on a hill overlooking the lodge. No guest rooms are in the main registration building, which contains a cafeteria, a gift shop, a cocktail lounge, and a large lobby area with two fireplaces. The lodge building has a large covered front porch that contains chairs and overlooks Yellowstone Lake. The entire complex sits back from the lake, and the cabins offer no good views. Parking is adjacent to each cabin unit. The lodge is located at Lake Village, in the eastern section of Yellowstone National Park. It is 30 miles from the east entrance station to the park.

Lake Lodge Cabins offers two types of cabin accommodations. All of the cabins have heat and private bath, most with shower but no tub. There is no air conditioning, telephone, or television in any of the cabins. Most of the cabins are constructed four to a building, although a few buildings have two units and others have six. The least expensive alternative is the eighty-six Frontier Cabins, with size and bedding that vary from unit to unit. The smallest Frontier units have one double bed; larger units have two double beds and a rollaway. These cabins look very rustic on the outside but the inside is fairly nice. The cabins sit near the lodge in an area devoid of trees.

One hundred Western Cabins are identical to those at Canyon Lodge and Cabins. All are the same size, with bedding that ranges from two double beds to two double beds and a rollaway. These cabins are bigger than the Frontier units and cost about twice as much. All these cabins have private bathrooms, most with a combination tub-shower. The layouts differ from building to building so that a few Western Cabins have sliding glass doors with a small porch in the back, while others do not. Other units are laid out so that each cabin has windows on two walls. Western Cabins toward the rear of the complex (units F, G, H, and J) are spaced farther apart and are surrounded by trees.

Lake Lodge Cabins provides modestly priced accommodations. In fact, the Frontier Cabins are among the park's cheapest rooms with private bath. The Lake Village area is very scenic and relatively quiet, at least compared with the Old Faithful area. These are also the closest accommodations to Fishing Bridge and Bridge Bay Marina. The less expensive Frontier Cabins are a good value but offer little more than basic lodging.

- **ROOMS:** Doubles, triples, and quads. A few rooms can handle a rollaway for a fifth person. All cabins have private baths.

- **RATES:** Frontier Cabins ($); Western Cabins ($$$). Rates quoted for two adults. Additional adults are $8.00 extra per night. Children eleven and under are free with an adult.

- **LOCATION:** On the north shore of Yellowstone Lake, in the east-central section of Yellowstone National Park. The lodge is approximately 30 miles from the east park entrance and 43 miles from the south entrance.

- **SEASON:** Mid-June to mid-September.

- **FOOD:** Cafeteria ($). A nearby general store has a coffee shop ($) and limited groceries. Nearby Lake Yellowstone Hotel has a lovely dining room and a small deli.

- **FACILITIES:** Gift shop, Laundromat, cafeteria, cocktail lounge. A general store is a short walk from the lodge. Nearby Lake Yellowstone Hotel offers additional facilities.

- **ACTIVITIES:** Hiking, fishing.

> Yellowstone Lake, at 20 miles long, 14 miles wide, and an average depth of 139 feet, is North America's largest mountain lake. The Yellowstone River serves as the lake's outlet and provides one of the summer's best wild trout spawning shows at Fishing Bridge. The lake drains into the Atlantic Ocean via the Gulf of Mexico.

# LAKE YELLOWSTONE HOTEL AND CABINS

Yellowstone National Park, WY 82190 • (307) 344–7901

*Lake Yellowstone Hotel*

Lake Yellowstone Hotel and Cabins, also called Lake Hotel, consists of a three- and four-story hotel building, an adjacent two-story Annex, and 110 closely clustered cabin units that sit behind the hotel. The hotel, Annex, and cabins offer a total of 296 rooms. The large hotel is the oldest hotel in the park today. An extensive renovation to return the hotel to its 1920s appearance was completed in 1991. The first floor houses the registration desk, lobby, and dining room. The wonderful lobby and sunroom, with some of the hotel's original wicker furniture, has large windows that overlook Yellowstone Lake. The 1920s-era dining room has windows with a similar view. A drive to the front of the hotel provides access for registration and dropping off luggage. The parking area is on the back side of the hotel. Lake Yellowstone Hotel and Cabins is located in the east-central portion of Yellowstone National Park, on the north shore of Yellowstone Lake. It is 30 miles from the east entrance to the park.

Lake Yellowstone Hotel and Cabins offers three basic types of lodging: hotel rooms, Annex rooms, and cabins. The hotel has 158 rooms, including one suite. Hotel rooms all have full baths, heat, and telephone but no air conditioning or television. Room size varies, with the largest rooms being located in the West Wing. Bedding ranges from one queen bed to three queen beds. A few rooms have two double beds. Rooms with a lake view are priced about $10 per night higher than rooms facing the parking lot. One suite has two bedrooms, each with a queen bed, and a sitting room with a refrigerator. These are attractively decorated and comfortable rooms.

The Annex has thirty-six rooms, which vary in size and bedding. All of the rooms have heat, private bath with shower, and telephone but no air conditioning or television. Annex rooms are of a nice size and cost about $30 per night less than nonview rooms in the hotel. Some Annex rooms have one double bed, while others have two double beds. None of the rooms in the Annex offer particularly good views, although those on the east side look out at pine trees, while those on the west side overlook the parking area. The Annex also has five handicap-accessible rooms. The first floor has a very small lobby area, with several stuffed chairs and couches.

Frontier Cabin units are mostly constructed as duplexes, with rooms that back up to one another. The cabins are closely clustered in an area devoid of trees behind the hotel and away from the lake. Parking is available beside each cabin unit. The cabins vary in size, and bedding can be either two double beds or two double beds plus a single bed. All the cabins have a private bath with shower only (one unit has a tub only). The cabins are plain but of adequate size. Cabin units rent for about half the price of a room at the hotel.

Lake Yellowstone Hotel is a quiet place to spend your vacation in Yellowstone National Park. The hotel captures the ambience of an earlier period and is reminiscent of Yosemite's even older Wawona Hotel. The airy and bright lobby area is a great place to read a book, with occasional glances out the windows at the lake. Chamber music is frequently played here in the evenings. The equally delightful dining room, just off the lobby, offers three meals a day. A small deli, just down the hall, serves sandwiches, ice cream, and beverages. The hotel and cabins are a short walk from a general store and Lake Lodge Cabins, which offers a cafeteria and a Laundromat. If you desire an inexpensive place to stay, choose the cabins. If you want to experience Yellowstone in a grand old hotel, opt for a room in the main hotel. The Annex kind of splits the difference.

*Construction on Lake Yellowstone Hotel began in 1889 in an area once populated by Indians, fur trappers, and mountain men. The first guests arrived two years later. Additions engineered by the architect of Old Faithful Inn in the early 1900s nearly tripled the number of rooms at the hotel to 210. The East Wing, with 113 additional rooms, was completed in the early 1920s. The hotel had fallen into disrepair by the 1980s, when a decade-long renovation was initiated to return the building to its glory years of the 1920s.*

- **ROOMS:** Doubles, triples, and quads. A few rooms sleep up to six. All rooms, including cabins, have private bathrooms.

- **RATES:** Cabins ($$); Annex ($$$); hotel ($$$$); suite ($$$$$).

- **LOCATION:** East-central section of the park, on the north shore of Yellowstone Lake. The hotel is 30 miles from the park's east entrance.

- **SEASON:** From mid-May to late September.

- **FOOD:** A 1920s-era hotel dining room ($$$) serves three meals a day. A breakfast buffet is available. A deli ($) on the first floor opens late each morning for sandwiches, beverages, and ice cream. A cafeteria ($) at Lake Lodge Cabins, a short walk from the hotel, serves three meals a day.

- **FACILITIES:** Hospital, restaurant, small deli, gift shop, ATM, post office. Nearby is a general store. Lake Lodge Cabins has a cafeteria.

- **ACTIVITIES:** Hiking, fishing, evening music in the hotel lobby.

# MAMMOTH HOT SPRINGS HOTEL AND CABINS

Yellowstone National Park, WY 82190 • (307) 344–7901

*Mammoth Hot Springs Hotel*

I f you have ever desired to stay at an old Army fort, then Mammoth Hot Springs is your place. The hotel and some of the surrounding buildings were once part of a small military post that served as headquarters for the U.S. Army when it was in charge of this park. Some of the original Army buildings continue in use as administrative offices for personnel of the National Park Service. The current lodging complex at Mammoth comprises a four-story hotel plus 126 cabin units that together provide a total of 222 rooms. A separate and smaller lodge building adjacent to the hotel is open in winter months for guests but is utilized in summer for employee housing.

Registration for all lodging is on the first-floor lobby of the hotel. A covered porch runs across the front of the hotel. Bell service is available at the front desk. The cabin units are clustered in grassy areas behind the hotel. Each cabin has its own parking area, and adequate parking is available for the hotel. Mammoth Hot Springs Hotel and Cabins is located near the north entrance to Yellowstone National Park, 5 miles south of Gardiner, Montana.

The lodging complex offers various types of rooms, both in the hotel and in the cabins. No rooms available in summer are specifically designated handicap accessible. Ninety-six hotel rooms, all on the first, second, third, and fourth floors, each have steam heat and telephone but no air conditioning or television. An elevator is near the registration desk. The hotel has sixty-nine rooms with private bath that rent for about $20 per night more than twenty-seven rooms without private bath. Community bath and shower rooms are on each floor. Rooms without a bath have either one double bed and one single bed or two double beds. Regular hotel rooms with bath have a double and a single bed, two double beds, or two doubles and a single bed. Some bathrooms have a tub, some have a shower, and some have both. Corner rooms are a little larger and have two windows. The hotel also has two suites that each have two queen beds and a sitting room with television.

The cabins are either freestanding or two to a building while sharing one wall. The least expensive lodging facilities at Mammoth are forty-six Budget Cabins without private bath.

These cabins each have a sink, and bedding is either two double beds or two double beds plus a single. Eighty Frontier Cabins have a private bath with a shower but no bathtub and rent for about $30 more per night than the Budget Cabins without bath. Cabins in both these groups are virtually identical in size. Frontier Cabins have either two double beds or two doubles and a single. Four of the Frontier Cabins have a hot tub on a private porch and rent for about $40 nightly more than the other Frontier Cabins.

Staying in Mammoth seems a world apart from most of Yellowstone's other lodging facilities. The geography in this section of the park is unique, and the buildings are not what one usually expects in a national park. It is fun to spend a half-day or so just walking around the area and viewing the buildings. An interesting dining room across the street, decorated in a kind of Art Deco style, serves three meals a day. Windows overlook the old military parade ground, which sits in front of the hotel. A grill offering breakfast and sandwiches is next door to the dining room in the same building. A general store next door sells supplies and limited groceries, and a nearby stable offers horseback riding.

*The hotel and cabins currently operating at Mammoth are only the latest chapter in a long history of lodging in this area. The first crude hotel in the park was built at Mammoth in 1871. The much larger and more elaborate National Hotel was constructed here in 1883. An annex that was added to the National Hotel in 1911 serves as the main lodging section of today's Mammoth Hot Springs Hotel. The remainder of the old National Hotel was torn down. The current hotel's front section containing the lobby, a map room, and a gift shop, was added in 1936–37, one year before the first ninety-six cabins were completed behind the hotel.*

A National Park Service visitor center in one of the old military buildings has exhibits on the park's early history. On the downside, Mammoth is at the extreme north end of the park, some distance away from Old Faithful and many of Yellowstone's other popular sites. This means that a stay at Mammoth is likely to result in additional driving.

- **ROOMS:** Doubles, triples, and quads. A few rooms can handle five adults. Some hotel rooms and cabins have private baths.

- **RATES:** Budget Cabins ($); Frontier Cabins ($$); hotel rooms without bath ($); hotel rooms with bath ($$); suites ($$$$$). Rates are quoted for two adults except suites that are for up to four adults. Additional adults pay $8.00 each per night. Children eleven and under are free. Special packages are offered during the winter season.

- **LOCATION:** North end of Yellowstone National Park, 5 miles south of Gardiner, Montana.

- **SEASON:** Summer season is from mid-May to the first week of October. Winter season is from mid-December to early March. During winter months, only the hotel and Aspen Lodge are open.

- **FOOD:** A large dining room ($$$) across the street from the hotel offers three meals a day. A grill ($) next to the dining room sells sandwiches and breakfast. A general store sells limited groceries.

- **FACILITIES:** Stables, restaurant, cocktail lounge, grill, gift shop, general store, post office, nature store, National Park Service visitor center. Winter season: ski shop, ice-skating rink, and skate rental.

- **ACTIVITIES:** Walking on the boardwalk that winds through the hot springs area, hiking, horseback riding, evening programs. Winter activities include ice skating, cross-country skiing, snowmobiling, snowcoach rides.

## OLD FAITHFUL INN

Yellowstone National Park, WY 82190 • (307) 344–7901

*Old Faithful Inn*

Old Faithful Inn is the most famous of all the national park lodges. The structure's unique appearance is so familiar that the Disney Company constructed a replica of the inn for its Disney World theme park. The older midsection of the inn, constructed in 1903–04, contains the scenic lobby, a registration desk, a restaurant, a gift shop, and a number of lodging rooms. The East Wing was added a decade later, and the West Wing fifteen years after that. The hotel is well maintained, and all of the facilities, including the rooms, are clean and comfortable. The large lobby, with log beams and a vaulted ceiling that soars 85 feet above the first floor, has multiple overhanging balconies. A mezzanine with chairs, tables, and sofas wraps around the entire second floor. Oddly shaped logs are used as decoration and for support of the railings and log beams. A huge clock ticks away on the front of a massive four-sided stone fireplace that highlights the lobby.

The inn doesn't directly face Old Faithful, but arriving guests are likely to discover that the famous geyser is the first thing they see. Good views of Old Faithful are obtained from several locations in the hotel, including the large second-floor porch and some of the lodging rooms. All of the lodging rooms at the facility are in the older main section and the two attached wings. No cabins or separate buildings are part of the hotel, although two other lodging facilities with cabins are nearby. The registration desk for Old Faithful Inn sits on the left as you enter the lobby. The drive that leads to the front entrance can be used for registration and dropping off luggage. Bell service is available to assist with luggage. A large parking area is in front of the hotel, a relatively short walk from the entrance. Lodging rooms are on three floors, so some climbing of stairs may be required, especially in the older section. Each of the wings has an elevator. Old Faithful Inn is in the southwest portion of Yellowstone National Park, 30 miles from the entrance station at West Yellowstone.

The inn offers 325 rooms that vary by size, bedding, bath, views, and how recently they were remodeled. Accommodations range from "Old House" rooms without private bath in the original central log building to relatively large, recently remodeled rooms with private bath in each of the wings. Room rates vary accordingly. All of the rooms have heat, but none have air conditioning, telephone, or television.

The largest rooms are in the East Wing, which was renovated in 1993–94. These are very nice rooms, with modern bathrooms. Some of these rooms offer a view of Old Faithful. One section of the West Wing was renovated a year later, while another section of the same wing has older rooms. Bedding ranges from two twin beds, to two double beds, to suites that have two queen beds with a separate sitting room. Although the range of accommodations is wide, the rooms are generally nice enough that you will probably be satisfied, especially if you are accustomed to staying in old hotels. Our choice would be "Old House" rooms in the original lodge. A limited number of these have private baths. Those without private baths offer the lowest rates. Although these rooms tend to be dark, and can also be noisy if they are close to the lobby, the log walls provide the ambience of an old lodge. Renovated rooms in the East Wing are especially nice and bright but are also more costly.

Old Faithful Inn is the classic national park lodge. If you plan to visit Yellowstone, stay at least one night here. It is convenient to the geysers and a good base for exploring this section of the park. Staying at Old Faithful Inn is likely to satisfy your desire to capture the ambience of a national park vacation. Be forewarned that the inn is a busy place and the Old Faithful area is congested. Both guests and visitors constantly roam through the lobby, the mezzanine, and the second-floor porch, so if you are seeking quiet, this isn't the place. On the other hand, you've got to see Old Faithful, so you might as well do it from where you are staying.

- **ROOMS:** Doubles, triples, and quads. A few rooms in the Old House can sleep up to six persons. Most but not all of the rooms have a private bath.

> **O**ld Faithful geyser's eruption intervals range from 30 to 120 minutes and average about 75 minutes. Estimates for the next eruption are posted inside Old Faithful Inn. This famous geyser, like other geysers, is caused when surface water seeps down porous rock to be heated under pressure to very high temperatures. As the superheated water rises and nears the surface, it converts to the steam you see when an eruption occurs.

- **RATES:** Old House rooms without private bath ($); rooms with private bath ($$ to $$$$), depending on size, location, and view; suites ($$$$$). The inn's rooms are fairly evenly distributed among the various rate categories. Rates are quoted for two adults. Additional persons are $8.00 each per night. Children eleven and under are free when staying with an adult.

- **LOCATION:** Southwest section of Yellowstone National Park, 30 miles from the entrance station at West Yellowstone.

- **SEASON:** Beginning of May through the third week of October.

- **FOOD:** Restaurant ($$$/$$$$) on main floor serves breakfast, lunch, and dinner; snack bar ($) offers sandwiches and ice cream; coffee shop ($) in adjacent general store serves breakfast, lunch, and dinner. Other eating facilities are nearby.

- **FACILITIES:** Restaurant, snack bar, tour desk, gift shop, ATM. Many additional facilities, including a gas station, gift shops, stores, and restaurants, are in the immediate area.

- **ACTIVITIES:** Walking through nearby geyser area, tours of the inn, hiking.

## OLD FAITHFUL LODGE CABINS

Yellowstone National Park, WY 82190 • (307) 344–7901

*Frontier Cabins at Old Faithful Lodge and Cabins*

Old Faithful Lodge Cabins consists of a main lodge building and 132 cabins, constructed two to four to a building. The main lodge was constructed in the late 1920s and contains no overnight accommodations. The cabins sit behind and to one side of the main lodge, which houses the registration desk. The impressive lobby area has large windows that provide an excellent view of Old Faithful. A big stone fireplace is surrounded with chairs and sofas for reading, visiting, and relaxing. The main building also has a cafeteria, ice cream shop, bake shop, and gift shop. Old Faithful Lodge Cabins is in the southwest section of Yellowstone National Park, 30 miles from the west entrance at West Yellowstone. It is a short walk from the better-known Old Faithful Inn.

The lodge offers three cabin classifications, although all of the units are virtually identical except for bathroom facilities. All of the cabins are relatively small. They are paneled and carpeted. Cabins directly behind the main lodge are clustered closely together in an area with few trees. Cabins to the side are more widely spaced but sit in a field of gravel. Adequate parking is available beside each cabin.

The least expensive forty-seven Budget Cabins have a sink but no bathroom facilities. A centrally located bathhouse has toilets and showers. Bedding in these units is either one double bed or one double plus a single bed. Most of these cabins, which have connecting doors to adjoining units, sit behind the lodge. Two Economy Cabins, which sit directly behind the lodge, have a sink and toilet but no shower or tub. These units have one double bed and a single bed. Eighty-three Frontier Cabins each have a private bath with a toilet, sink, and shower. Bedding in these units ranges from one double, to a double and a single, to two double beds. Frontier Cabins cost approximately $15 extra per night compared with the price of Budget Cabins without bath.

Old Faithful Lodge Cabins offers basic but inexpensive accommodations in the geyser area of Old Faithful. In fact, the Budget Cabins are the least expensive lodging facilities in all of Yellowstone National Park. The main lodge has a large cafeteria divided into sections that specialize in various food categories, such as salads, pasta, and Southwestern. Even though you won't want to do much other than sleep in your cabin, the lodge offers an attractive atmosphere for reading, talking, and relaxing. Staying at the lodge also allows you to enjoy nearby Old Faithful Inn.

- **ROOMS:** Doubles, triples, and a few quads. More than half the cabins have a private bath.

- **RATES:** All cabins ($). Rates are quoted for two adults. Additional adults are charged $8.00 extra per night. Children eleven and under are free with an adult.

- **LOCATION:** Southwest section of Yellowstone National Park, 30 miles from the entrance station at West Yellowstone.

- **SEASON:** Mid-May to mid-September.

- **FOOD:** A large cafeteria ($) offers breakfast, lunch, and dinner. Two snack shops ($) serve bakery goods, ice cream, and yogurt.

- **FACILITIES:** Cafeteria, snack shops, tour desk, gift shop. Many stores and restaurants are in the immediate vicinity.

- **ACTIVITIES:** Walking through the geyser area, hiking.

Boardwalks and unpaved paths meander through Upper Geyser Basin, near Old Faithful Lodge Cabins. A boardwalk that begins near the lodge leads around Old Faithful Geyser and through a large area of pools, geysers, and springs. One path is designated for both people and bicycles. One 3-mile loop leads to Morning Glory Pool and returns to the lodge. Both shorter and longer trails are in the basin area.

# OLD FAITHFUL SNOW LODGE AND CABINS

Yellowstone National Park, WY 82190 • (307) 344–7901

*Old Faithful Snow Lodge*

Snow Lodge consists of a two-story main lodge building with thirty-one overnight rooms plus thirty-four cabins that sit some distance away. All the cabins are clustered in a gravel area behind a gas station. The cement block lodge building once served as an employee dorm and is currently the only facility in the Old Faithful area that is open during winter. The first floor of the lodge has a restaurant, a cocktail lounge, a gift shop, and a small lobby area with chairs surrounding a wood-burning stove. All the overnight rooms in the lodge are on the second floor. Registration for all lodge rooms and the cabins is in the main lodge building. Parking is more convenient for guests who stay in the cabins than for those who stay in the main lodge. No bell service is available here. Old Faithful Snow Lodge is in the southwestern area of Yellowstone National Park, 30 miles from the west entrance at West Yellowstone. The lodge sits across a large parking area from Old Faithful Inn.

The lodge offers three types of accommodations. All of the rooms have heat but no air conditioning, telephone, or television. The least expensive rooms are the thirty lodge rooms without a private bathroom. These rooms are very small, but each contains a desk, a chair, and one double bed and a single bed. Little room is left over. One lodge room has a bath and costs about $5.00 extra per night. Community bathrooms are in the hall. The least expensive cabins are the ten Frontier units with bath; these cost about $15.00 per night more than lodge rooms. These cabins are fairly small, with bedding of one double bed or two double beds. The private bathroom has a shower but no tub. Twenty-four Western Cabins are much larger and nicer, and each has a full bath and two double beds. These units rent for about $20.00 more per night than Frontier Cabins. One Western Cabin is handicap accessible.

During winter months Snow Lodge opens two-story Snowshoe Lodge, with a total of thirty-seven rooms. The lodge is accessible only by over-the-snow vehicles in winter. Twenty-five units on the first floor have one double and one single bed, as well as a private bath with a shower but no tub. Twelve two-room units on the second floor each have one double bed plus one single bed in each room; the two rooms share a private bath in between, with a shower but no tub. Snowshoe Lodge is located between the main lodge building and the cabins.

Snow Lodge is at the center of activity in the Old Faithful area. Rooms here generally cost more than those at Old Faithful Lodge but less than those at Old Faithful Inn. The Western Cabins at Snow Lodge are definitely nicer than any of the less expensive cabins at Old Faithful Lodge. Snow Lodge also offers a dining room, a gift shop, and a cocktail lounge. Many more facilities are offered in the immediate vicinity.

- **ROOMS:** Doubles, triples, and quads. All the cabins have a private bath. Only one of the lodge rooms has a private bath.

- **RATES:** Lodge rooms without bath ($); lodge room with bath ($$); Frontier Cabins ($$); Western Cabins ($$$).

- **LOCATION:** Southwest section of Yellowstone, 30 miles southeast of the west entrance, at West Yellowstone.

- **SEASON:** Mid-May to the first week in October and mid-December to the first week in March.

- **FOOD:** A dining room in the main lodge building serves breakfast, lunch, and dinner. A fast-food outlet is across the street. Additional eating facilities are nearby.

- **FACILITIES:** Restaurant, cocktail lounge, gift shop. Other facilities nearby include a post office, service station, gift shops, and stores selling groceries and merchandise.

- **ACTIVITIES:** Hiking, walking through the nearby geyser area. Winter activities include snowcoach tours, guided ski tours, snowmobiling.

O*ld Faithful Snow Lodge and Mammoth Hot Springs Hotel are the only two facilities that offer winter accommodations. Reservations should be made well in advance of your planned arrival. Only Mammoth is accessible by car. Old Faithful Snow Lodge is accessible only by over-the-snow vehicles. Skiing, snowshoeing, and ice skating (Mammoth) are popular activities. Ski rentals, waxes, trail maps, and other equipment are available at both locations.*

# ROOSEVELT LODGE CABINS

Yellowstone National Park, WY 82190 • (307) 344–7901

*Frontier Cabins at Roosevelt Lodge Cabins*

Named for an area that served as a favorite campsite for President Theodore Roosevelt, Roosevelt Lodge Cabins consists of a log registration and dining building and an adjacent small store. These two structures are surrounded on three sides by eighty rustic wood cabins that were constructed mostly in the 1920s. The main building has a registration desk flanked on one side by a lobby and a large stone fireplace and on the other side by a family-style dining room. Chairs fill a covered front porch that runs the length of the building. The lodging complex sits on a hill surrounded by pine trees and overlooking a valley with a background of mountains. The relatively isolated location places the lodge away from the congestion that plagues other such facilities in the park. Roosevelt Lodge Cabins is in the northeast corner of Yellowstone National Park, 23 miles southeast of the north entrance near Mammoth.

The lodge has four categories of cabins. The cabins are closely clustered and provide basic lodging at economy prices. The least expensive options are the forty-five Rough Rider Cabins and eighteen Rustic Shelters that have a wood stove for heat and no private bathroom. Community bathrooms and shower houses are available for guests who stay in either of these units. The cabins in each classification rent for an identical amount even though size and bedding can vary. Rates are for up to two adults. Rough Rider bedding varies from one double bed to three double beds. Rustic Shelters, which rent for a few dollars less than Rough Rider units, have bedding that ranges from two single beds to two double beds. Guests must supply their own sheets, blankets, and pillows; towels are provided.

Nine Economy Cabins have electric heat, a half-bath, and two double beds. These cabins are larger and rent for about $15 more per night than either of the above-mentioned units. Eight Frontier Cabins have electric heat, a full bath with a shower but no tub, and either one or two double beds. These are slightly larger than the Economy units.

Roosevelt Lodge Cabins offers relatively inexpensive accommodations for a stay at Yellowstone National Park. The lodging facilities are basic, and support facilities are limited in comparison to those at most of the other lodging complexes in the park. A nice dining room on one side of the main lodge building serves three meals a day. A small store next door has limited supplies and groceries. A small lobby in the main registration building has wicker chairs and benches surrounding a large stone fireplace. Horseback riding and stagecoach rides are available at the nearby stables.

- **ROOMS:** Doubles, triples, and quads. A few cabins hold up to six adults. Most of the cabins do not have a private bath.

- **RATES:** Frontier Cabins ($$); all others ($).

- **LOCATION:** Northeast section of Yellowstone, 23 miles southeast of the north entrance.

- **SEASON:** June through August.

- **FOOD:** A dining room serves three meals a day. An Old West Cookout via horseback or covered wagon is offered each evening. Limited groceries are sold at a small store.

- **FACILITIES:** Store, dining room, gift counter, stables.

- **ACTIVITIES:** Hiking, horseback riding, stagecoach rides.

The northeast corner of Yellowstone National Park is known as Roosevelt Country. This area of fir-, aspen-, and pine-covered rolling hills has 132-foot Tower Fall as its main attraction. The fall is a short drive south of the lodge. This area of the park offers some of the nation's best fly-fishing.

# Association Of Partners for Public Lands Member List

Since 1920, national park cooperating associations have been serving the interests of visitors to America's national parks and other public lands by providing high-quality publications and theme-related merchandise. The non-profit, Congressionally authorized associations use revenues generated from bookstores and other activities to support the educational and interpretive missions of the parks. The Association Of Partners for Public Lands (APPL) assists these organizations by providing training programs, a communications network, and representation intended to foster professional management practices and their missions of public service. For information, contact the Association Of Partners for Public Lands at 8375 Jumpers Hole Rd., Suite 104, Millersville, MD 21108 (phone 410–647–9001; fax 410–647–9003). The APPL welcomes contributions to support its education programs and the Partnership Fund, a joint National Park Service–APPL grant program that aids park interpretive programs.

Alaska Natural History Association
Frankie Barker, Executive Director
401 W. First Avenue
Anchorage, AK 99501-2251
Fax: (907) 274-8343
e-mail: np-anch-anha

Anza-Borrego Desert National History
  Association
Betsy Knaak, Executive Director
P.O. Box 310
Borrego Springs, CA 92004-0310
Fax: (760) 767-3099

Appalachian Mountain Club
Chris Thayer, Regional Facilities
  Manager
P.O. Box 298
Gorham, NH 03581
Phone: (603) 466-2721
Fax: (603) 466-2720

Arizona Memorial Museum
  Association
Gary Beito, Executive Director
1 Arizona Memorial Place
Honolulu, HI 96818
Phone: (808) 422-5664
Fax: (808) 541-3168
Web site: members.aol.com/azmemph
  /index.htm

Arizona Strip Interpretive Association
Joyce H. Wright, Business Manager
  (ext. 275)
345 East Riverside Drive
St. George, UT 84790-9000
Phone: (801) 688-3275
Fax: (801) 673-5729

Badlands Natural History Association
Midge Johnson, Executive Director
P.O. Box 47
Badlands National Park
Interior, SD 57750-0047
Phone: (605) 433-5489
Fax: (605) 433-5404
e-mail: Marianne Mills@nps.gov

Bent's Old Fort Historical Association
Pamela Martinez, Executive Director
35110 Highway 194 East
LaJunta, CO 81050
Phone: (719) 384-2800
Fax: (719) 384-2800

Big Bend National History Association
Mike Boren, Executive Director
P.O. Box 196
Big Bend National Park, TX 79834
Phone: (915) 477-2236
Fax: (915) 477-2357

Blacks Hills Forests and Parks
  Association
Steve Baldwin, Executive Director
Route 1, Box 190
Hot Springs, SD 57747-9430
Phone: (605) 745-7020
Fax: (605) 745-7021
e-mail: 211-0888@mcimail.com

Bryce Canyon Natural History
  Association
Gayle Pollock, Executive Director
Bryce Canyon National Park
Bryce Canyon, UT 84717-0002
Phone: (801) 834-4600
Fax: (801) 834-4102
e-mail:brca_cooperatingassociation
@nps.gov

Cabrillo National Monument
  Foundation
Karen Eccles, General Manager
1800 Cabrillo Memorial Drive
San Diego, CA 92106-3601
Phone: (619) 222-4747
Fax: (619) 222-4796
e-mail: cabrillo@pacbell.com

Canyonlands Natural History
  Association
Brad Wallis, Executive Director
3031 S. Highway 191
Moab, UT 84532
Phone: (801) 259-6003
Fax: (801) 259-8263
e-mail: CNHA@nps.gov
Web site: www.moabutah/com/cnha/

Capitol Reef Natural History
  Association
Shirley Torgerson, Executive Director
Capitol Reef National Park
HC 70, Box 15
Torrey, UT 84775-9602
Phone: (801) 425-3791, ext. 115
Fax: (801) 425-3026

Carlsbad Caverns Guadalupe
  Mountains Association
Rick LoBello, Executive Director
T.K. Kajiki, Management Assistant
P.O. Box 1417
Carlsbad, NM 88221-1417
Phone: (505) 785-2322, ext. 481
Fax: (505) 785-2318
e-mail: caca_ccgma@nps.gov
Web site: www.caverns.com/~ccgma

Colorado National Monument
  Association
Dustin "Dusty" Dunbar, Executive
  Director
Colorado National Monument
Fruita, CO 81521-9530
Phone: (970) 858-3617
Fax: (970) 858-0372
e-mail: colm_cooperatingassocia-
tion@nps.gov

Cradle of Forestry in America
  Interpretive Association
Harry R. Hafer, Executive Director
100 S. Broad Street
Brevard, NC 28712-3730
Phone: (704) 884-5713
Fax: (704) 884-4671
e-mail: cfaia@citcom.net
Web site: www.cradleofforestry.com

Crater Lake Natural History
  Association
Laurie Pohll, Business Manager
P.O. Box 147
Crater Lake, OR 97604
Phone: (541) 594-2211, ext. 498
Fax: (541) 594-2299

Craters of the Moon Natural History
Association
Judy Rindfleisch, Executive Director
P.O. Box 29
Arco, ID 83213
Phone: (208) 527-3257
Fax: (208) 527-3073
e-mail: crmo_nha@nps.gov

Death Valley Natural History
Association
Janice Newton, Executive Director
Donald Rust, Business Manager
P.O. Box 188
Death Valley, CA 92328
Phone: (760) 786-3285 or 2331
Fax: (760) 786-2236
e-mail: DEVA_natural_history_associa-
tion@nps.gov

Devils Tower Natural History
Association
Lynn Conzelman, Business Manager
P.O. Box 37
Devils Tower, WY 82714-0037
Phone: (307) 467-5283, ext. 110
Fax: (307) 467-5350
e-mail: detocooperatingassociation
@nps.gov

Dinosaur Nature Association
Richard C. Millett, Executive Director
1291 East Highway 40
Vernal, UT 84078-2830
Phone: (801) 789-8807
Fax: (801) 781-1304
e-mail: DNA@easilink.com
Web site: www.eaze.com/dna

Eastern National
Chesley A. Moroz, President
Rich Jamochian, Director of Finance
Barbara Bell, Human Resource
   Manager
Richard Creighton, Operations
   Manager
446 North Lane
Conshohocken, PA 19428-2203
Phone: (610) 832-0555
Fax: (610) 832-0242
e-mail:
   EasternNational@ix.netcom.com
Web site: www.EasternNational.org

Eastern Sierra Interpretive Association
Martha Miklaucic, Executive Director
308 W. Line Street, Suite D
Bishop, CA 93514
Phone: (760) 872-3070
Fax: (760) 872-3069

Flaming Gorge Natural History
Association
Carol Chavers, Executive Director
P.O. Box 188
Dutch John, UT 84023
Phone: (801) 885-3305
Fax: (801) 781-5251

Florida National Parks and
Monuments Association
Caulion Singletary, President
Beryl Given, Director, Bookstore
   Operations
10 Parachute Key #51
Homestead, FL 33034-6735
Phone: (305) 247-1216
Fax: (305) 247-1225
e-mail: fnpma@np-ever
Web site: www.nps.gov/ever/fnpma.
   htm

Fort Clatsop Historical Association
Sandra S. Reinebach, Business
   Manager
Route 3, Box 604-FC
Astoria, OR 97103
Phone: (503) 861-2471
Fax: (503) 861-2585

Fort Frederica Association
Bill Burdell, Association Manager
Fort Frederica National Monument
Route 9, Box 286-C
St. Simons Island, GA 31522
Phone: (912) 638-3639
Fax: (912) 638-3639
e-mail: FOFR_cooperating_assoc@
   nps.gov

Fort Laramie Historical Association
Patricia Fullmer, Business Manager
Fort Laramie National Historic Site
HC 72, Box 389
Fort Laramie, WY 82212
Phone: (800) 321-5456
   (307) 837-2662
Fax: (307) 837-2120
e-mail: fola_flha@nps.gov

Fort Union Association
Marvin L. Kaiser
RR 3, Box 71
Williston, ND 58801-9455
Phone: (701) 572-9083
Fax: (701) 572-7321
e-mail: fous_administration@nps.gov

George Washington Birthplace
National Monument Association
Jeanne B. Straughan, Store Manager
Route 1, Box 718
Washington's Birthplace, VA 22443
Phone: (804) 224-7895

George Washington Carver Birthplace
District Association, Inc.
Dena Matteson, Association
   Coordinator
5646 Carver Road
Diamond, MO 64840-8314
Phone: (417) 325-4151
Fax: (417) 325-4231

Glacier Natural History Association
LeAnn Simpson, Executive Director
P.O. Box 428
West Glacier, MT 59936-0428
Phone: (406) 888-5756
Fax: (406) 888-5271
e-mail: glac_cooperating_associa-
   tion@nps.gov
Web site: www.nps.gov/glac/gnha1.
   htm

Glen Canyon Natural History
Association
Mary L. Frederickson, Executive
   Director
Tami Corn, Operations Manager
32 N. 10th Avenue, Suite 9
P.O. Box 581
Page, AZ 86040
Phone: (520) 645-3532
Fax: (520) 645-5409
e-mail: vistas@page.az.net
Web site: www.pagelakepowell.com

Golden Gate National Parks
Association
Greg Moore, Executive Director
Charles Money, Director of
   Operations
Fort Mason, Building 201
San Francisco, CA 94123
Phone: (415) 561-3000
Fax: (415) 561-3003
e-mail: goga_npa@nps.gov

Grand Canyon Association
Robert Koons, Executive Director
P.O. Box 399
Grand Canyon, AZ 86023-0399
Phone: (520) 638-2481
Fax: (520) 638-2484
e-mail: rkgca@thecanyon.com
Web site: www.thecanyon.com/gca/

Grand Teton Natural History
Association
Sharlene Milligan, Executive Director
Grand Teton National Park
P.O. Box 170
Moose, WY 83012-0170
Phone: (307) 739-3606
Fax: (307) 739-3438
e-mail: GTNHA@sisna.com

Great Basin Natural History
Association
Janille Baker, Manager
Great Basin National Park
Baker, NV 89311-9700
Phone: (702) 234-7270
Fax: (702) 234-7269

Great Smoky Mountains Natural
History Association
Terry L. Maddox, Executive Director
115 Park Headquarters Road
Gatlinburg, TN 37738-4102
Phone: (423) 436-7318
Fax: (423) 436-6884
e-mail: Terry@smokiesnha.org
Web site: www.nps.gov/grsm/

Harpers Ferry Historical Association
Deborah Piscitelli, Executive Director
P.O. Box 197
Harpers Ferry, WV 25425-0197
Phone: (304) 535-6881
Fax: (304) 535-6749
e-mail: hfha@intrepid.net
Web site: www.nps.gov/hafe.htm

Hawaii Natural History Association
Kathleen English. Executive Director
P.O. Box 74
Hawaii National Park, HI 96718
Phone: (808) 967-7604
Fax: (808) 967-8186
e-mail: havo_ superintendent@nps.gov

Historic Hampton, Inc.
Rosa Sands, Executive Administrator
Hampton National Historic Site
535 Hamton Lane
Towson, MD 2126-1397
Phone: (410) 828-9480
Fax: (410) 823-8394

Isle Royal Natural History Association
Jill Burkland, Executive Director
800 E. Lakeshore Drive
Houghton, MI 49931-1869
Phone: (906) 482-7860
Fax: (906) 487-7170
e-mail: IRNHA@portup.com

Jefferson National Expansion
Historical Association
David A. Grove, Executve Director
10 South Broadway, Suite 1540
St. Louis, MO 63102-1728
Phone: (314) 436-1473
Fax: (314) 231-8765
e-mail: JNEHA_cooperating_associa-
tion@nps.gov
Web site:
www.st~louis.mo.us.st~louis/arch/

Joshua Tree National Park Association
Ken Tinquist, Executive Director
74485 National Park Drive
Twentynine Palms, CA 92277
Phone: (760) 367-1488
Fax: (760) 367-5583

Kennesaw Mountain Historical
Association, Inc.
David Layman, Business Manager
900 Kennesaw Mountain Drive
Kennesaw, GA 30152
Phone: (770) 422-3696
Fax: (770) 528-8398
e-mail: kemo_administration@np-ser

Lake States Interpretive Association
Suzzett Promersberger, General
Manager
3131 Highway 53
International Falls, MN 56649-8904
Phone: (218) 283-2103
Fax: (218) 285-7407

Land Between the Lakes Association
Gaye Luber, Executive Director
100 Van Morgan Drive
Golden Pond, KY 42211-9001
Phone: (502) 924-2088
Fax: (502) 924-2093

Lassen Loomis Museum Association
Anne Dobson, Business Manager
Lassen Volcanic National Park
P.O. Box 100
Mineral, CA 96063-0100
Phone: (916) 595-3399
Fax: (916) 595-3262

Lava Beds Natural History Association
P.O. Box 865
Tulelake, CA 96134
Phone: (916) 667-2282
Fax: (916) 667-2737

Mesa Verde Museum Association, Inc.
Rovilla R. Ellis, Executive Director
Tracey Hobson, Business Manager
P.O. Box 38
Mesa Verde National Park, CO 81330-
0038
Phone: (970) 529-4445
Fax: (970) 529-4498
e-mail: np-meve cooperatingassocia-
tion@nps.gov
Web site: mesaverde.org

Mount Rushmore History Association
Brenda Hill, Business Manager
P.O. Box 208
Keystone, SD 57751-0208
Phone: (605) 574-2523, ext. 128
Fax: (605) 574-2307
e-mail: aoru_cooperatingassocia-
tion@nps.gov

National Park Trust
Paul Pritchard, President
1776 Massachusetts Avenue, NW
Suite 110
Washington, DC 20036
Phone: (202) 659-0996
Fax: (202) 861-0576
e-mail: NPTrust@aol.com

Natural Areas Association
Therese Feinauer
P.O. Box 645
145 Zion Park Boulevard
Springdale, UT 84767-0645
Phone: (801) 772-2445
Fax: (801) 772-2447

Northwest Interpretive Association
Mary Quackenbush, Executive
Director
909 First Avenue, Suite 630
Seattle, WA 98104-1060
Phone: (206) 220-4140
Fax: (206) 220-4143
e-mail: mary_quakenbush@nps.gov

Ocmulgee National Monument
Association
Patty Ellis, Business Manager
1207 Emery Highway
Macon, GA 31201
Phone: (912) 752-8257
Fax: (912) 752-8259

Oregon Trail Museum Association
Jolene Kaufman, Business Manager
Scotts Bluff National Monument
Box 27
Gering, NE 69341-0027
Phone: (308) 436-2975

Ozark Interpretive Association
Betty Kerschensteiner
P.O. Box 1279
Mountain View, AR 72560
Phone: (501) 757-2211
Fax: (501) 269-3000

Parks and History Association
Michael Metallo, Executive Director
126 Raleigh Street, S.E.
Washington, DC 20032
Phone: (202) 472-3083
Fax: (202) 755-0469
e-mail: parks_and_history@np-ncr
Web site: www.nps.gov/pha

Petrified Forest Museum Association
Paul DoBell, Acting Executive
Director
P.O. Box 2277, Park Road 1
Petrified Forest NP, AZ 86028
Phone: (520) 524-6228, ext. 239/261
Fax: (520) 524-3567

Pipestone Indian Shrine Association
Maddie Redwing, Business Manager
Pipestone National Monument
P.O. Box 727
Pipestone, MN 56164
Phone: (507) 825-5463
Fax: (507) 825-2903

Point Reyes National Seashore
  Association
Dino Williams, Business Manager
Point Reyes National Seashore
Point Reyes, CA 94956
Phone: (415) 663-1155
Fax: (415) 663-8132

Red Rock Canyon Interpretive
  Association
Denise Wiegand, Executive Director
HCR 33, Box 5500
Las Vegas, NV 89124-9808
Phone: (702) 363-1921
Fax: (702) 363-6779

Redwood Natural History Association
Linda Appanaitis, Executive Director
1111 Second Street
Crescent City, CA 95531-4123
Phone: (707) 464-9150
Fax: (707) 464-1812

Rocky Mountain Nature Association
Curt Buchholtz, Executive Director
Rocky Mountain National Park
Estes Park, CO 80517
Phone: (970) 586-1294
Fax: (970) 586-1310
e-mail: curtbuchholtz@np_roma
Web site: www.rmna.org/bookstore/

Roosevelt-Vanderbilt Historical
  Association
Anne Meisner
P.O. Box 235
Hyde Park, NY 12538
Phone: (914) 229-9300
Fax: (914) 229-7718

Sequoia Natural History Association,
  Inc.
Mark Tilchen, Executive Director
HCR 89-Box 10
Three Rivers, CA 93271-9792
Phone: (209) 565-3756
Fax: (209) 565-3728
e-mail: snha_sequoianp@nps.gov
Web site: www.nps.gov/seki/snha.htm

Shenandoah Natural History
  Association
Greta Miller, Executive Director
3655 US Highway 211 E
Luray, VA 22835-9036
Phone: (540) 999-3581
Fax: (540) 999-3583
e-mail: gretamiller np_shen@nps.gov
Web site: nps.gov/shen/snha/
  snhahome.htm

Southwest Natural and Cultural
  Heritage Association
Lisa D. Madsen, Executive Director
6501 Fourth Street NW, Suite 1
Albuquerque, NM 87107-5800
Phone: (505) 345-9498
Fax: (505) 344-1543

Southwest Parks and Monuments
  Association
T.J. "Tim" Priehs, Executive Director
John Pearson, Director of Operations
221 N. Court Avenue
Tucson, AZ 85701-1045
Phone: (520) 622-1999
Fax: (520) 623-9519
e-mail: spma@nps.gov

Steamtown Volunteer Association, Inc.
Loriann Zelinski, Executive Director
150 S. Washington Avenue
Scranton, PA 18503-2079
Phone: (717) 346-7275 or 0660
Fax: (717) 346-7093

Theodore Roosevelt Nature and
  History Association
Jane Muggli Paulson, Executive
  Director
P.O. Box 167
Medora, ND 58645-0167
Phone: (701) 623-4884
e-mail: paulson_jane@nps.gov

Valley Forge Park Interpretive
  Association
Michael J. Fitzgerald, Business
  Manager
Valley Forge National Historic Park
Valley Forge, PA 19482-0953
Phone: (610) 783-1074
Fax: (610) 783-1074

Weir Farm Heritage Trust
Constance Evans, Executive Director
735 Nod Hill Road
Wilton, CT 06897
Phone: (203) 761-9945
Fax: (203) 761-9116

Yellowstone Association
Patricia Cole, Executive Director
P.O. Box 117
Yellowstone NP, WY 82190-0117
Phone: (307) 344-2293
Fax: (307) 344-2486
e-mail: yacole@aol.com
Web site: www.nps.gov/yellassn.htm

Yosemite Association
Steven P. Medley, President
Patricia Wight, Sales Manager
P.O. Box 230
El Portal, CA 95318
Phone: (209) 379-2646
Fax: (209) 379-2486
Internet: yose_yosemite_association@
  nps.gov
Web site: http://yosemite.org

Zion Natural History Association
Jamie Gentry, Executive Director
Joann Hinman, Business Manager
Zion National Park
Springdale, UT 84767
Phone: (801) 772-3265 or 3264
Fax: (801) 772-3908